Higher Education and Capacity Building in Africa

Higher education has recently been recogi ___.ver for societal growth in the Global South and capacity building ...rican universities is now widely included in donor policies. The question is: how do capacity-building projects affect African universities, researchers and students? Universities and their scientific knowledges are often seen to have universal qualities; therefore, capacity building may appear straightforward.

Higher Education and Capacity Building in Africa contests such universalistic notions. Inspired by ideas about the 'geography of scientific knowledge' it explores what role specific places and relationships have in knowledge production, and analyses how cultural experiences are included and excluded in teaching and research. Thus, the different chapters show how what constitutes legitimate scientific knowledge is negotiated and contested. In doing so, the chapters draw on discussions about the hegemony of Western thought in education and knowledge production. The authors' own experiences with higher education capacity building and knowledge production are discussed and used to contribute to the reflexive turn and rise of auto-ethnography.

This book is a valuable resource for researchers and postgraduate students in education, development studies, African studies and human geography, as well as anthropology and history.

Hanne Kirstine Adriansen is Associate Professor at the Department of Education, Aarhus University, Denmark.

Lene Møller Madsen is Associate Professor at the Department of Science Education, University of Copenhagen, Denmark.

Stig Jensen is Associate Professor and former director at the Centre of African Studies, University of Copenhagen, Denmark.

Routledge Studies in African Development

Self-Determination and Secession in Africa
The post-colonial state
Edited by Redie Bereketeab

Economic Growth and Development in Africa
Understanding global trends and prospects
Horman Chitonge

African Youth and the Persistence of Marginalization
Employment, politics and prospects for change
Edited by Danielle Resnick and James Thurlow

HIV and East Africa
Thirty Years in the Shadow of an Epidemic
Janet Seeley

Development Discourse and Global History
From colonialism to the sustainable development goals
Aram Ziai

Higher Education and Capacity Building in Africa
The geography and power of knowledge
Edited by Hanne Kirstine Adriansen, Lene Møller Madsen and Stig Jensen

Higher Education and Capacity Building in Africa

The geography and power of knowledge under changing conditions

Edited by Hanne Kirstine Adriansen, Lene Møller Madsen and Stig Jensen

Routledge
Taylor & Francis Group

LONDON AND NEW YORK

First published 2016 by Routledge

2 Park Square, Milton Park, Abingdon, Oxfordshire OX14 4RN
711 Third Avenue, New York, NY 10017

Routledge is an imprint of the Taylor & Francis Group, an informa business

First issued in paperback 2017

British Library Cataloguing-in-Publication Data
A catalogue record for this book is available from the British Library

Library of Congress Cataloging-in-Publication Data
Higher education and capacity building in Africa : the geography and power of knowledge / edited by Hanne Kirstine Adriansen, Lene Møller Madsen and Stig Jensen.
pages cm. -- (Routledge studies in African development)
1. Universities and colleges--Africa. 2. Education, Higher--Africa.
3. Economic development--Effect of education on--Africa. I. Adriansen, Hanne Kirstine. II. Madsen, Lene Møller. III. Jensen, Stig. IV. Series: Routledge studies in African development.
LA1503.H51 2016
378.6--dc23
2015022249

ISBN: 978-1-138-83815-4 (hbk)
ISBN: 978-0-8153-9405-1 (pbk)

Typeset in Goudy
by Saxon Graphics Ltd, Derby

Contents

Conclusion 237

List of illustrations

Acknowledgements

It is impossible to thank all those who have helped us shape and sharpen our ideas about higher education and capacity building in Africa. We would, however, like to extend a special thanks to the contributors of this volume for their energy, active participation and positive approach. We would also like to express our gratitude to our external reviewers: Karen Valentin, Lone Lindholt, Anne Sørensen, Jürgen Enders and Holger Bernt Hansen. The Centre of African Studies (CAS) at the University of Copenhagen has been our 'base' for the project and we are grateful for the immeasurable administrative and secretarial support from Sarah Wolf, Ida Folden Brink and Iben Wirth Carlsen. We would also like to extend our gratitude to William Frost and Language Services at Aarhus University.

This book is the outcome of the efforts of many people who have been engaged in issues related to higher education and capacity building in Africa over a number of years. The intellectual starting point of the book was a seminar series held at CAS in the autumn of 2013. We are grateful for contributions from Bevlyne Sithole, Michael Whyte and Peter Kragelund, who turned their presentations into chapters for the book, and for the contribution from Tove Degnbol, Head of Department, Technical Advisory Services, DANIDA, and Lasse Møller, Chief Technical Advisor, DANIDA, who gave us insights in the new Danish strategy in support of development research with a special focus on Africa. Our appreciation also goes to all the participants who made these seminars possible and contributed to the lively discussions that made us believe in the importance of this book.

Another important event for the development of the book was the workshop for the authors held at CAS in October 2014. During this, we shared our draft chapters and discussed issues related to the geography and power of knowledge in higher education in Africa, which not only made this book more coherent but which also resulted in a more pleasant journey. The book has also been strengthened through support and valuable comments from our editors Khanam Virjee, Bethany Wright and Margaret Farrelly from Routledge–Earthscan, and from four anonymous reviewers.

Finally, a special thanks to our families, friends, colleagues and students. We hope this book will inspire and provoke students, scholars and practitioners, in Africa and beyond.

Acknowledgments

Contributors

Hanne Kirstine Adriansen is Associate Professor at the Department of Education, Aarhus University, Denmark, where she is also the international coordinator. Originally trained as a human geographer, her research interests include spatial aspects of education and knowledge production as well as internationalisation of higher education. She has extensive fieldwork experience from West and North Africa where she has worked in close collaboration with local universities and other research institutions. She has also participated in a number of research capacity-building projects in Africa and Asia. Her current research projects concern geographies of knowledge and place-making through student mobilities.

Thilde Bech Bruun is Assistant Professor at the Department of Plant and Environmental Sciences, University of Copenhagen, Denmark. She holds a MSc and a PhD in geography. Since 2009 she has been the coordinator of the SLUSE program and responsible for the associated field course in 'Interdisciplinary Land Use and Natural Resource Management'. She is also teaching interdisciplinary field methodology courses in collaboration with Makerere University in Uganda, Sokoine University in Tanzania and Egerton University in Kenya. She has extensive field work experience from South East Asia, West Africa and the Solomon Islands, where she has conducted research in collaboration with local universities as well as been engaged in capacity-building projects. Her current research projects concern climate change mitigation, causes and effects of land use changes and sustainable intensification of small scale farming systems.

Torben Birch-Thomsen is Associate Professor at the Department of Geosciences and Natural Resource Management, Section of Geography, University of Copenhagen, Denmark. He is trained as a human geographer, and his research interests are within the fields of environmental and socioeconomic effects of land use change and intensification. Particular interests are within the relations between livelihood strategies of rural communities, farming systems, land use changes and rural-urban linkages with special reference to East-, West- and Southern African conditions. From 1999 to 2007 he was a board member, representing the University of Copenhagen, in the Danish University

Consortia on Environment and Development (DUCED) with specific focus on Sustainable Land Use and Natural Resource Management (SLUSE). He is still an active participant in the collaboration with partner countries in Africa and Asia. During 2002–2005 he was a member of the Project Steering Committee of the SACUDE SLUSE (Southern African Consortium of Universities for Development and Environment – Sustainable Land use Project), representing DUCED SLUSE.

Marie Ladekjær Gravesen is PhD Fellow at the Department of Cultural and Social Anthropology, University of Cologne, Germany, where she is part of the interdisciplinary Marie Curie project 'Resilience in East African Landscapes'. With a background in English History, Anthropology and African Studies her interests includes the dynamics of climate change adaptation, conflicts between customary and statutory knowledge systems, as well as (post)colonial power relations and their implications over time. During long stays in Sierra Leone, Ghana and Kenya she has worked for different development agencies and consultancies. Her current project concerns the land conflicts that emerge when agriculturalists' private property discourses meet the open-access and mobility ideologies of pastoralists in the former White Highlands of Kenya.

Godfrey Hampwaye is Senior Lecturer in the Department of Geography and Environmental Studies at the University of Zambia in Lusaka and has worked at this university for over 20 years. He obtained his PhD in Geography at the University of Witwatersrand in South Africa. His field of specialisation is Economic Geography, with research interests in local economic development, urban agriculture, firm strategies and Asian investments in Africa. Over the years, he has published scholarly articles in several peer reviewed journals. In the recent past, he was head of the Department of Geography and Environmental Studies and an Assistant Dean in charge of postgraduate studies in the School of Natural Sciences at the University of Zambia. Currently, he is also Senior Research Affiliate to the School of Tourism and Hospitality at the University of Johannesburg, South Africa.

Trevor Hill is Associate Professor and Academic Leader of the Discipline of Geography, University of KwaZulu-Natal, South Africa, where he teaches courses in biogeography, natural resource management, GIS and palaeo-ecology. He has been involved with SACUDE SLUSE (Southern African Consortium of Universities for Development and Environment – Sustainable Land Use Project) since its inception and still offers courses developed during the project. He is a strong believer in the trans-disciplinary approach. Trevor prefers getting his 'hands dirty' and spending as much time as possible in the field with students! He considers the most important take home message from the Consortium's work to be: it's about personalities and working with people you enjoy the company of and with whom you share a common environmental and educational vision. Once you have this in place, everything else will follow.

Stig Jensen is Associate Professor and former director at the Centre of African Studies, University of Copenhagen, Denmark. He holds a MA in political science and a PhD in geography. Stig is or has been affiliated to several national and international educational and research networks such as African Studies in Europe and the Programme and Research Council at the Nordic Africa Institute. He is a board member of Copenhagen University Ghana initiative cooperating with University of Ghana – Legon, a steering committee member of Sustainable Science Centre, Developing Countries Initiative and Summer University Initiative all at Copenhagen University. He has acted as a member of the evaluation team of DANIDA's bilateral Programme for Enhancement of Research Capacity in Developing Countries (ENRECA).

Fergus Kerrigan is Senior Legal Adviser in international programmes at the Danish Institute for Human Rights where he advised a three-year international research partnership programme on human rights and informal justice. He is a member of the executive committee of the Commission on Legal Pluralism He is the main author of a study on Informal Justice Systems for the UN and of the Zambian Justice System for the Zambian Ministry of Justice. He authored a study on the rights of sexual and gender minorities in Africa. His main professional focus is on analysis and methodologies to further access to justice. He is commencing a research project on access to justice, legal pluralism and conflict management with a focus on African countries.

Peter Kragelund is Head of Department at the Department of Society and Globalisation, Roskilde University, Denmark. Peter holds a MSc in Human Geography from the University of Copenhagen and a PhD in International Development Studies from Roskilde University. He has been involved in capacity-building programmes in Ghana and Zambia and is currently involved in a large-scale research programme in Kenya, Tanzania and Zambia, involving capacity building at MA and PhD levels. His main interests concern changes in the global economy and how it affects developing countries. In particular, his research has examined the relationship between foreign actors, development cooperation and local politics in sub-Saharan Africa.

Lene Møller Madsen is Associate Professor at the Department of Science Education, University of Copenhagen, Denmark. She is trained as a human geographer and has worked within education for the past ten years. Her research areas include students' academic integration into higher education and students' engagement in the geosciences. She has been involved in a number of Danish research capacity-building projects in both West and East Africa mainly concerning PhD supervision and PhD education in general. She is currently involved in an EU founded project on enhancing three Bachelor programmes in Eastern Africa focusing on inquiry approaches. She serves as a member of the Science Development Council at the Faculty of Science, University of Copenhagen.

Cheikh Mbow is serving as a Senior Scientist on Climate Change and Development at World Agroforestry Centre (ICRAF) Nairobi, Kenya and Adjunct Professor at Michigan State University's Department of Forestry in the US. He holds a PhD and wrote his Habilitation Thesis (*Doctorat d'Etat*) on land use dynamics and climate change mitigation. He is lead author of the Agriculture, Forestry and Other Land Use (AFOLU) in the IPCC's Fifth Assessment Report, and a member of the Scientific Committee of Future Earth. He is a regional expert on disturbances of savanna vegetative systems and above-ground carbon stock assessments. He coordinated the GOFC-GOLD Regional Network for West Africa. Cheikh is currently investigating land management influence agroforestry practices for improved food security under severe climate change.

Muhammad Mehmood-Ul-Hassan is Head of Capacity Development at the World Agroforestry Center, (ICRAF) Nairobi, Kenya. He also coordinates capacity development across CGIAR Research Program on Forests, Trees and Agroforestry. Originally trained as an agricultural scientist, his research interests include trans-disciplinarity in research, science policy and practice, and the role capacity development plays in management of natural resources. He has extensive fieldwork experience from South, Central and South East Asia as well as from West and East Africa where he has worked in close collaboration with policy makers, natural resource managers, academics and national agricultural research institutions. He has also participated in a number of research capacity development projects in Africa, Asia and Europe.

Ole Mertz is Professor in Geography at the Department of Geosciences and Natural Resource Management, Section of Geography, University of Copenhagen, Denmark. He is trained as an agronomist and human geographer and has worked within research and education for the last 20 years. His research focuses on land systems science and he has a specific interest in livelihood and environmental consequences of change in smallholder agriculture in developing countries. He has led numerous research projects including the EU-funded I-REDD+ project. He worked for the SLUSE programme during its 5 initial years in 1998–2004 and was leading the initial design of the SLUSE field course described in Chapter 4 in this volume.

Rajani Naidoo is Professor of Higher Education and Director of the International Centre for Higher Education Management at the University of Bath, United Kingdom. Her research focuses on transformations in global political economy, trans-national higher education partnerships and the contribution of universities to the global public good. She has delivered keynotes at numerous international conferences in a wide range of countries including Finland, Mexico, the UK, Ireland, South Africa and Trinidad and Tobago. Funded research has included a study of the changing nature of the academic profession; student engagement; and trans-national higher education partnerships. She has been appointed as expert advisor to a range of international bodies and has recently been an international reviewer for the Finnish Academy of Science. She sits on the Executive Editorial Board of the *British Journal of Sociology of Education* and the *International Journal of Sociology of Education*.

Jonas Østergaard Nielsen is a Junior Professor and Research Group Leader in IRI THESys and the Department of Geography, Humboldt University of Berlin, Germany. He studied social anthropology at Auckland University, New Zealand, and the University of Copenhagen, Denmark, and obtained his doctorate in human geography in 2010 at the University of Copenhagen. From 2010 to 2013, he worked as a Postdoctoral Fellow in the European Research Council-funded project Waterworlds, Department of Anthropology, University of Copenhagen. His research is concerned with the human dimensions of global climate change, human-environmental relations, issues of global–local interactions and urbanisation in sub-Saharan Africa. A central theme throughout his work has been causality and how to understand the impact of different drivers of change on local lives. Since 2007, he has conducted extensive ethnographic fieldwork in Burkina Faso.

Thomas Theis Nielsen is Associate Professor in Geography at the Department of Environmental, Social and Spatial Change at Roskilde University, Denmark. He obtained his PhD in Geography from the Faculty of Science, University of Copenhagen in 2000 based on his thesis on the use of satellite images in monitoring bush fires in sub-Saharan Africa. Since then he has maintained studies of environmental issues and satellite remote sensing, but is today engaged in very varied research and teaching activities, ranging from geographical didactics to political geography. He has been involved in a number of international research and capacity-building projects, mostly in sub-Saharan Africa. His current research activities are concerned with maps and how maps are used in communication of a range of topics all imbued with high political potency.

Bevlyne Sithole is Adjunct Senior Research Fellow at the Research Institute for Environment and livelihoods at Charles Darwin University, Australia, and Trustee at Shanduko, Center for Agrarian Research in Zimbabwe. She has worked in a variety roles in different kinds of research organisations including government research department (Department of Natural Resources, Government of Zimbabwe); interdisciplinary university centres (Center for Applied Social Sciences in Zimbabwe; the Tropical Ecosystems Research Center at Commonwealth Scientific Industrial and Technical Research Organisation, Australia; Research Institute for Environment and Livelihoods, Charles Darwin University; Center for African Studies at University of Copenhagen) and in international research organisations (starting at the Stockholm Environment Institute and Center for International Forestry Research). She has also taught on several regional interdisciplinary courses including the EU funded Master's in Tropical Resource Ecology (MTRE) at the University of Zimbabwe and interdisciplinary research methods at Wondo Genet College of forestry and Agriculture, University of Hawassa, Ethiopia. Her current work includes developing participatory research tools for community based indigenous researches in Northern Australia while leading the Aboriginal Research Practitioners Network.

Thuita Thenya is Lecturer at the Department of Geography and Environmental Studies, University of Nairobi, Kenya, where he lectures in biogeography and natural resources management. Initially trained in botany and geography and later specialising in biogeography for his MSc and PhD, since 2000 he has been working at the Department of Geography and Environmental Studies. He has worked extensively (research and outreach) on participatory forest management and wetland ecology for the last 15 years. He is the departmental coordinator for Horn of Africa Environmental Network, a network of institutions of higher learning and civil societies in Eastern Africa with its headquarter in Ethiopia. Thenya has been affiliated to Wangari Maathai Institute (WMI) at the University of Nairobi since 2010, starting with its setup, formulation of academic programmes, and now teaching and coordinating the WMI PhD training programme. He has also been involved in coordinating SLUSE-Kenya since its initiation in Kenya in 2012, and a PhD experiential course involving WMI and Swedish University of Agricultural Sciences. At the WMI he is the Kenya coordinator of a collaborative project on forestry research involving University of Nairobi-WMI, University of Copenhagen, Green Belt Movement and Kenya Forest Research Institute. His current research projects are in natural resources management with particular focus on resource utilisation and associated impacts.

Michael Whyte is emeritus Associate Professor with the Department of Anthropology at the University of Copenhagen, Demark. He has carried out research in Uganda since 1969 and also in Western Kenya and Lesotho. His research covers topics in kinship and social organisation, agricultural development, food security and food issues, HIV/AIDS and, most recently, land and land conflict in a post-conflict context. He is co-editor of *Beyond Territory and Scarcity: Exploring Conflicts over Natural Resource Management* (2005). He has been part of the research capacity development collaboration with Makerere University since 1989 and with Gulu University since 2008.

Susan Reynolds Whyte is Professor at the Department of Anthropology, University of Copenhagen, Denmark. She carries out research in East Africa on social efforts to secure well-being in the face of poverty, disease, conflict and rapid change. She uses concepts of pragmatism, uncertainty and temporality to examine relationships between people, institutions, ideas and things. For two decades she has worked with African colleagues on Enhancement of Research Capacity projects. One result of that collaboration is *Second Chances* (Duke University Press, 2014), which is a 'polygraph' (not a monograph) by four Danish and four Ugandan scholars on the first generation of AIDS survivors.

1 Why study higher education and capacity building in Africa?

An introduction

Hanne Kirstine Adriansen, Lene Møller Madsen and Stig Jensen

Introduction

This book takes an innovative approach to understanding higher education and capacity building in Africa; inspired by ideas about the 'geography of scientific knowledge' (Livingstone, 2003; Meusburger, 2015a; Meusburger et al., 2010), it addresses capacity building of African universities. While education has been high on the development agenda for years, universities have been recognised only recently as key drivers for societal growth in the Global South. Capacity building of the African higher education sector is now widely included in donor policies in the Global North. The question is how capacity-building projects of universities in Africa affect their knowledge production. Universities and the scientific knowledges they hold are often seen to have ubiquitous qualities; therefore, capacity building may appear straightforward. However, the type of institutions and knowledges promoted worldwide are the outcome of development in learned institutions in Western Europe and North America over the past 200–300 years. From a universalistic perspective, the promotion of higher education is seen as a key to modernising Africa, whereas from a post-colonial perspective, the promotion of higher education is perceived as just another imperialist approach to Africa. In this book, we have another starting point as we want to explore what role specific places and relationships have in research, and analyse how cultural experiences are included and excluded in teaching and research. Thus, the different chapters show how what constitutes legitimate scientific knowledge is negotiated and contested at African universities. In doing so, we draw on discussions about the hegemony of Western thought in education and knowledge production. Methodologically, the chapters in the book adopt a reflexive approach, using the authors' own experiences with higher education capacity building and knowledge production, through which we aim to contribute to the reflexive turn and rise of auto-ethnography (e.g. Archer, 2010; Foley, 2002; Venkatesh, 2013). Our objectives are twofold:

- to analyse how different places and cultural contexts influence and transform knowledges in African higher education;
- to explore – through a reflexive approach – how capacity building affects scientific knowledge production in African universities.

These objectives are achieved through case-based studies from a number of different countries from West, East and Southern Africa. Thus, the book is not a country-based overview over capacity-building efforts in higher education and it does not provide a comprehensive introduction to knowledge production in Africa. However, in order to provide a background and common frame for the individual chapters in the book, Chapter 2 presents a brief introduction to the history of universities in Africa, trends in capacity-building efforts in higher education, and analytical ideas about education, curriculum and knowledge production.

Why write a book on higher education in Africa?

The twenty-first century has seen a renewed interest in Africa from the rest of the world, as well as a new self-understanding on the African continent. The turn of the millennium was marked with optimism, and the World Bank argued that Africa could claim the twenty-first century (World Bank, 2000). Fifteen years into the twenty-first century, newspapers in the Global North frequently carry articles both about the high growth rates in Africa and about the people risking their lives crossing the Sahara and the Mediterranean in the hope of a brighter future. Meanwhile, African writers, such as Dayo Olopade in her *The Bright Continent* (2014), reveal the sense of renewed optimism detectable among African youth: a spirit of entrepreneurship and a belief in the possibilities of technology for creating their own future. This optimism is in some ways similar to the African renaissance dating back to the founders of Pan-Africanist[1] thought in the late nineteenth century (Zeleza, 2009) and later articulated by Cheikh Anta Diop in his series of essays starting in 1946 (Diop, 1996). However, it was its resurgence during the 1990s in post-apartheid South Africa that re-initiated the call for an Africanisation of universities on the continent (e.g., Makgoba, 1999; Nkoane, 2006). Charles Manga Fombad explains:

> Advocates of this approach to education have been driven by the desire for an emancipatory Afrocentric system that frees African education from the continuous and dominant influence of Euro- and American-centric cultural values in favour of reclaiming African indigenous cultural values.
>
> (Fombad, 2014: 383)

This Africanisation can be seen as a counter discourse to the widespread call for internationalisation of African universities. These opposing trends and the role of capacity building call for a book on higher education in Africa. Moreover, during the past 20 years, universities have been recognised as a key driver for societal growth in the Global South and therefore international interest in universities and scientific knowledge has intensified in recent years. Aid agencies in the Nordic countries are among those currently working on new policies to strengthen research capacity in the Global South, and therefore increasing assistance is given to this sector. The expectations and pressures on higher education in Africa are multi-faceted and growing. There is increasing demand for higher education from African youth, civil society and both the private and public sectors; however, several African countries also have to address accusations of low teaching quality and limited relevance of research for burning societal problems. Therefore, projects focusing on qualitative reforms in teaching and learning processes based on frameworks from the Global North are mushrooming; however, there is little focus on how these projects affect the different modes of knowledge inherent in African universities. More knowledge is needed on how to understand the interrelationship between capacity building and knowledge production, and there is need for critical reflections on the exogenous-driven initiatives to higher education development in Africa. However, to talk about Africa as an entity is both contentious and problematic, potentially giving rise to an invalid generalisation, or homogenisation, of the continent that disregards 'the diverse subcultural and ethnic groups and their many languages and different religious beliefs' (Shizha, 2014: 1871). We want to oppose essentialist claims about Africa, but still find it valid to write this book about higher education in countries of sub-Saharan Africa due to their commonalities: a colonial past and relatively underdeveloped present.[2] By using a case-based approach that recognises geographical differences, it is both possible and fruitful to focus on sub-Saharan Africa and some of the recent trends in higher education and capacity building seen here.

Without essentialising Africa, we wish to contribute to a better understanding of the multi-faceted and dynamic development evident in Africa at this point in time. By using a spatial approach for exploring the current and future development of knowledge production in Africa, we want to explore how scientific knowledge is negotiated and contested in parallel to societal changes in general and capacity building in particular, and thus how scientific knowledge becomes local.

Geographies of science and spaces of education

This book is a contribution to the bourgeoning field of spatial research on education and knowledge production (e.g. Brooks et al., 2012; Fenwick et al., 2011; Gulson and Symes, 2007; Livingstone, 2003; Meusburger, 2015a, 2015b; Meusburger et al., 2010). Building on the geographical or spatial turn in the humanities and social sciences, new interdisciplinary fields have emerged (Warf and Arias, 2008). We are primarily inspired by 'geographies of science' and 'spaces of education'.

Geographies of science is an interdisciplinary field which began as a conversation between geography and science studies (Jöns et al., 2010). It pays attention to the ways scientific knowledge is produced and consumed with a special focus on space:

> Instead of marveling at the apparent universality and 'placelessness' of scientific knowledge, scholars interested in the geographies of science have focused on the specific circumstances of scientific practices and on the ways

in which the travels of scientists, resources, and ideas shape the production and circulation of scientific knowledge.

(Jöns et al., 2010: ix)

In his seminal book *Putting Science in Its Place*, the geographer David Livingstone (2003) argues that space matters in the production of science even though this goes against the common understanding of scientific knowledge as universal, neutral and objective.

Recent years have also seen a number of studies from both education and geography concerning the spatial dimensions of education (e.g. Fenwick et al., 2011; Gulson and Symes, 2007; Hanson Thiem, 2009). Some of these studies use the spatial approach to focus on the uneven geographies of e.g. ranking and student mobilities (Waters and Brooks, 2012). Proponents of spatial approaches in education argue that spatial analysis can help question those assumptions about education that are taken for granted: for instance, that the dominance of neo-liberal ideas leads to homogeneity – a spatial analysis can show how neo-liberal policies are played out differently in various national contexts, leading to national differences and not only homogeneity (Brooks et al., 2012).

In this book, we want to understand what role specific locations have in the making of research, how scientific knowledge is related to place, and to analyse how local experience is addressed and adopted into teaching and research. In innovative ways we bring together geographies of scientific knowledge and capacity building by exploring local aspects of global knowledge.

Positioning the book and its authors

Before we begin this exploration of how scientific knowledge is negotiated and contested in capacity building, it is necessary to provide clarification about the nature of the book, and both who the authors are and what position they are writing from.

The book is a research monograph which means it is an edited volume presenting new material that has not previously been published elsewhere, with a team of contributors writing different chapters, and editors leading the project and contributing to the volume too. All chapters are based on new empirical research produced especially for this book. We are entering an emerging field combining higher education and capacity building in the Global South. The book is rooted in the discipline of geography, both due to the spatial perspective and because the majority of the authors have a background in geography. However, some of the authors have a background in anthropology, development studies or environmental studies; thus, the book is also transdisciplinary in its approach. It is written by 20 researchers (7 women and 13 men), both established and younger researchers, from 9 different countries from both the Global North and the Global South – Denmark, Ireland, Kenya, Pakistan, Senegal, South Africa, USA, Zambia and Zimbabwe – even though many do not live in these countries anymore. They have all conducted research in Africa. This illustrates the difficulties in determining what it means to be e.g. African or Scandinavian and who has the right to speak about a certain place. That being said, there is no doubt the book is situated in a Scandinavian or, more precisely, Danish context; the majority of authors are from Denmark or somehow affiliated with Denmark through capacity-building projects. Hence, the book is written from the periphery of the dominant Anglo-American knowledge production, although mainly based on literature written in English.

The dominance of authors from the Global North may lead some readers to question how these authors can write about Africa, as Patrick Chabal argues:

> Westerners are singularly ill suited to understanding Africa. This has partly to do with the colonial legacy [...] But it also has to do with a pervasive and powerful post-colonial argument: it is the very legacy of the Enlightenment that has brought about imperialism and a social theory that devalues the, particularly African, non-Western 'other'.
>
> (Chabal, 2009: 18)

While Chabal can be criticised for essentialising 'the African', we agree that there is a need to decolonise knowledge about Africa. There are various ways to do that; in this book, the focus is on focus on reflexivity[3] and positionality.[4] Moreover, all chapters except one (Chapter 6) are in various ways experience-based, which means the authors are writing based on their experiences. The African[5] authors write about their experiences in African and Northern universities, the non-African authors write about their experiences with the capacity-building projects they have been involved in. While all chapters (except Chapter 6) can be seen as written by insiders, some have been co-authored by an outsider who has strengthened the analytical distance to the material.[6] We do not argue that African scholars can decolonise the field from Western domination, as they have themselves been taught in an education system that is largely based on Western epistemologies; we do argue, however, that by using a reflexive approach, we can highlight some of the power relations inherent in our knowledge production. This is, however, also a very difficult, time-consuming and personal way of conducting research; it can be difficult for a researcher to maintain an analytical gaze when his/her own work and life are under scrutiny.

Structure and themes of the book

This book has grown out of an engagement with and interest in higher education and capacity building in Africa. In various ways, the editors have all been involved in Danish capacity-building projects in African universities. Inspired by teaching PhD courses within the Danish Building Stronger Universities programme (Danske Universiteter, 2011), we started reflecting on our role and involvement in capacity building (see Adriansen and Madsen, 2013). The idea of writing a book together was initiated with a seminar series at the Centre of African Studies, University of Copenhagen, where we invited researchers from both the Global

North and Global South to discuss higher education and capacity building in Africa. Based on the seminar contributions and a successful book proposal where we invited additional authors, we held a workshop during which themes and links between the different emerging chapters were found and discussed.

In the following, the structure of the book is presented together with a short presentation of the individual chapters, organised in three parts, and the concluding chapter. The three parts are: Part I – Capacity building of African universities – asymmetrical power relations?; Part II – Researching and teaching climate change in Africa – whose reality counts?; and Part III – Creating and using academic knowledge in Africa – decolonising research?

Capacity building of African universities – asymmetrical power relations?

By studying at the institutional level, the chapters in Part I all have a macro-perspective on capacity building of African universities. In Chapter 3, Michael and Susan Whyte represent a perspective from the Global North, reflecting on dilemmas of knowledge production in Ugandan universities. Based on their long-term involvement with Makerere University and the recently established Gulu University, they study how we can respect what is unique to African universities, while still providing useful resources based on Danish university culture. They critically engage in discussions of capacity building that focus on how African universities can 'catch up' with universities in the Global North rather than trying to understand the realities in the specific local settings. In Chapter 4, focus is turned towards collaboration on teaching. In a joint perspective from the Global North and the Global South, Bevlyne Sithole, Torben Birch-Thomsen, Ole Mertz, Trevor Hill, Thilde Bech Bruun and Thuita Thenya analyse a long-term capacity-building project regarding an inter-disciplinary course for Danish, Kenyan and South African students in the areas of development, environment and natural resource management. The authors analyse how to build long-term partnerships and give insights into how teachers and students view the course and its interaction with rural communities. Finally, Chapter 5 by Peter Kragelund and Godfrey Hampwaye analyses a South–South relationship: China's engagement in establishing a Confucius Institute at the University of Zambia. This is compared to French, German and British cultural institutions. They study if the Confucius Institute in Zambia as an example of South–South collaboration is different from North–South collaboration and if the Chinese initiative could be termed soft power. In doing so they engage in reflections on new ways forward in African university partnerships and new directions in the internationalisation of African higher education.

All three chapters in Part I address the interrelations between African universities and capacity building. Hence, in this part of the book, the reader is introduced to institutional aspects of knowledge production within African universities. In different ways, all three chapters address the relations between external actors providing funding and the power relations in the collaboration. The Zambian case provides a clear example of this, where South–South collaboration may not lead to less asymmetrical partnerships than 'traditional' North–South collaboration. The chapters also touch upon the spatio-temporal aspects of collaboration: e.g. the importance of time for establishing the necessary trust between partners or the importance of location – whether a university in located in the capital, like Makerere University, or the periphery, like the newly established Gulu University.

Researching and teaching climate change in Africa – whose reality counts?

The chapters in Part II investigate how knowledge is negotiated and produced at village level, individual level and project level, respectively. In Chapter 6 by Jonas Østergaard Nielsen, Marie Ladekjær Gravesen and Stig Jensen, the focus is on village level and local knowledge in a rural community in Burkina Faso. It analyses how changing conditions such as climate change affect local knowledge and power structures, highlighting the importance of education in this context. They study what happens to local knowledge when surrounding conditions change. This involves a critical reflection on adaptations to change. In their analysis of power and knowledge, they highlight the fluid and negotiated nature of local knowledge. Chapter 7 by Hanne Kirstine Adriansen, Muhammad Mehmood-Ul-Hassan and Cheikh Mbow zooms in on the individual level – the life of an African climate change researcher. By using an auto-ethnographic approach, the authors analyse the conditions for producing scientific knowledge in Africa today. They point to three intertwined issues of importance for scientific knowledge production: an inherited, colonial curriculum; the apparent universality of theories and methods; and the cultural production of African researchers. In Chapter 8, Lene Møller Madsen and Thomas Theis Nielsen explore the production of scientific knowledge at project level by focusing on how academics in a Danish-West African capacity-building project negotiate and legitimate the knowledge production. The concept of capacity building can be argued to be encapsulated in a Western hegemonic discourse of how and where knowledge is legitimately produced and consumed. Reflecting on this, the authors study in what ways the negotiation and production of scientific knowledge in the project are embedded in this hegemonic discourse.

In Part II, climate change and climate change research are used as a lens for studying the geography and power of knowledge and education. The chapters address four intertwined issues: local experience-based knowledge; tensions between different modes of knowledge; production of scientific knowledge; and research capacity building. Indirectly, all three chapters ask whose reality counts. Is it the reality of the old, illiterate but knowledgeable man or the young, educated man in the rural village of Burkina Faso? Is it the West African climate change researcher's local experience-based knowledge or is it the French curriculum presented to him in school? Is it the Danish researchers in charge of a capacity-building programme or the African researchers who are the target of the programme? In illustrating the negotiations of whose reality counts, this part of the book highlights the geography and power of knowledge.

Creating and using academic knowledge in Africa – decolonising research?

The chapters in Part III provide critical reflections on the power and politics of knowledge. In Chapter 9, Bevlyne Sithole reflects on what it means to be African within a higher education setting. Based on her own experience of being a researcher from Zimbabwe living outside Africa, she discusses knowledge and empowerment as a black scholar moving around in the diaspora: sometimes melting in, sometimes standing out and sometimes in the in-between places where her own thoughts, positions and locations become blurred. She addresses what it means to be African and who has the right to speak about African issues. In doing so, she challenges ideas about ownership of knowledge. Chapter 10 by Rajani Naidoo, Hanne Kirstine Adriansen and Lene Møller Madsen is an analysis of Khanya College, a tertiary access programme for students designated as 'black' established during societal transformation in apartheid South Africa. Based on a life-history interview with the first author, who was a lecturer at Khanya College, the authors specify and discuss the ways in which Khanya College engaged with (South) African history and identity, while at the same time preparing students for the apartheid (white, racial, Euro-centric) South African university system. This balance between empowering students through pride in their African culture and providing them with access to powerful knowledge is discussed in terms of epistemic access to university and society at large. Finally, in Chapter 11 Fergus Kerrigan provides a tour d'horizon, drawing on his extensive experience of co-operating with individuals and organisations to improve access to justice in African countries. He addresses the challenges of contemporary African legal scholarship and the intersections of global, national and local value assumptions and sources of knowledge. He studies how African universities can equip law graduates to provide African societies with legal tools suited to their needs and contexts, and at the same time navigate the demands of international human rights standards on their own terms. This is done by tracing the history of law studies in the European university tradition, looking into African social structures, values and the protection of human rights, and finally by addressing legal pluralism.

All the chapters in Part III address issues of universality and particularity of knowledge, and thus what is particular to Africa. It is argued that universality and particularity are two sides of the same coin; within law, for example, a common language and framework of legal principles serves as an instrument for the assertion and legitimation of distinct and particular identities. In different ways, the chapters illustrate the struggles over the right to define what constitutes an African, an African curriculum and African (human) rights. And in doing so, the chapters also ask how to decolonise research.

Chapter 12 concludes by relating the previous chapters to the themes of Africanisation, the power of knowledge, internationalisation, universal and particular knowledge, the geographies of science and the role of universities for societal development.

Notes

1 Pan-Africanism is both an ideology and a movement. It encourages solidarity of Africans worldwide, believing that the fate of all African peoples and countries are intertwined (Legum, 1965). Linked to Pan-Africanism is Afro-centrism, which while not a new concept (Asante, 1998, 2007) has been revitalised on the continent in recent years due to factors such as indigenisation and growing self-consciousness. The Afrocentric approach is revolutionary-oriented as far as the questioning of the white hegemonic Eurocentric orientation to knowledge is concerned. Its purpose is the reconceptualisation of the social and historical reality of African people by asserting the central role of the African subject based on the context of African history (Ferreira, 2010).

2 As Paul Tiyambe Zeleza argues: 'Contemporary Africa is simply incomprehensible if one does not understand the complex, complimentary, and combative histories of colonialism and nationalism' (Zeleza, 2009: 160). To mention a few common results of this history: African indigenous cultures have been marginalised and neglected in education (Breidlid, 2013), an inherited colonial educational system after independences (Teferra and Altbach, 2004) and as a result a 'colonization of the African mind' (Wa Thiong'o, 1994).

3 Reflexivity refers to: 'self-reflection at all stages of research [...] The term reflexivity is often closely tied to attempts to situate knowledge, to recognize the positionality of researcher and the subjects of research, and to seek to overcome power imbalances in the research encounter' (Ogborn et al., 2014: 95).

4 Positionality is the notion that: 'personal values, views, and location in time and space influence how one understands the world [...] Consequently, knowledge is the product of a specific position that reflects particular places and spaces' (Warf, 2006: 2257).

5 By African author, we refer to those authors born and raised on the African continent. Likewise, the non-African authors are those born and raised outside the African continent. Chapter 9 illustrates how the right to represent the African experience can be contested.

6 The distinction between being an insider and an outsider is not an easy one. Sikes and Potts (2008) have noticed that being an insider is common within educational research. They define an insider as somebody who is attached to or involved in the organisation or its social groups prior to commencing the study. While we agree with this position, it does not capture the dynamic aspect of the insider position. Therefore, we prefer to adopt Narayan's (1993) stance that we all belong to a number of communities simultaneously. To us, an insider is somebody who is considered an insider by the other members of a given community and/or who participates on par with the other members of that community. As pointed out by Kitchin and Tate, being an insider may make research more difficult: 'You may fail to notice pertinent questions or issues because of the inability to step back from a situation and fully assess the circumstances' (Kitchin and Tate, 2000: 29). On the other hand, the insider position also provides advantages such as easy access to the field and close knowledge of the context, culture and language (Adriansen and Madsen, 2009).

References

Adriansen, H.K. and Madsen, L.M. (2009) 'Studying the making of geographical knowledge: the implications of insider interviews', *Norwegian Journal of Geography*, 63 (3), 145–153.

Adriansen, H.K. and Madsen, L.M. (2013) *Quality Assurance or Neo-imperialism: Developing Universities in the Third World*, abstract for SRHE Annual Research Conference: Experiencing Higher Education: Global Trends and Transformations, Newport 11–13 December 2013.

Archer, M.S. (2010) *Conversations About Reflexivity*. London and New York: Routledge.

Asante, M.K. (1998) *The Afrocentric Idea–Revised and Expanded Edition*. Philadelphia: Temple University.

Asante, M.K. (2007) *An Afrocentric Manifesto: Toward an African Renaissance*. New Jersey: Wiley.

Breidlid, A. (2013) *Education, Indigenous Knowledges, and Development in the Global South: Contesting Knowledges for a Sustainable Future*. New York: Routledge.

Brooks, R., Fuller, A. and Waters, J.L. (eds) (2012) *Changing Spaces of Education: New Perspectives on the Nature of Learning*. New York: Routledge, pp. 21–38.

Chabal, P. (2009) *Africa – The Politics of Suffering and Smiling*. London: Zed Books and University of KwaZulu-NatalPress.

Danske Universiteter (2011) *Building Stronger Universities in Developing Countries First Phase, August 2011 – July 2013 Inception Report November 2011*. Available at: http://dkuni.dk/English/OurWork/~/media/Files/Internationalt/BSU/Inception%20report%20introduction.ashx (accessed 27 January 2015).

Diop, C.A. (1996) *Towards the African Renaissance: Essays in African Culture and Development 1946–1960*. London: Kamak House.

Fenwick, T., Edwards, R. and Sawchuk, P. (2011) *Emerging Approaches to Educational Research: Tracing the Socio-material*. New York: Routledge.

Ferreira, A.M. (2010) 'Book review: Asante, M.K. (2007). An Afrocentric Manifesto. Oxford, UK: Polity', *Journal of Black Studies*, 40 (6), 1275–1277.

Foley, D.E. (2002) 'Critical ethnography: the reflexive turn', *International Journal of Qualitative Studies in Education*, 15 (4), 469–490.

Fombad, C.M. (2014) 'Africanisation of legal education programmes: the need for comparative African legal studies', *Journal of Asian and African Studies*, 49 (4), 383–398.

Gulson, K.N. and Symes, C. (eds) (2007) *Spatial Theories of Education: Policy and Geography Matters*. New York: Routledge.

Hanson Thiem, C. (2009) 'Thinking through education: the geographies of contemporary educational restructuring', *Progress in Human Geography*, 33 (2), 154–173.

Jöns, H., Livingstone, D.N. and Meusburger, P. (2010) 'Interdisciplinary geographies of science'. In: Meusburger, P. et al. (eds) *Geographies of Science*. Dordrecht: Springer, pp. ix–xvii.

Livingstone, D. (2003) *Putting Science in its Place: Geographies of Scientific Knowledge*. Chicago: University of Chicago Press.

Kitchin, R. and Tate, N.J. (2000) *Conducting Research in Human Geography: Theory, Methodology and Practice*. London: Prentice Hall.

Legum, C. (1965) *Pan-Africanism: A Short Political Guide*. USA: Frederick A. Praeger Publishers.

Makgoba N.W. (ed.) (1999) *African Renaissance: The New Struggle*. Cape Town: Mafube Publishing.

Meusburger, P. (2015a) 'Knowledge, geography of'. In Wright, J.D. (ed.) *International Encyclopedia of the Social & Behavioral Sciences*, 2nd edition, Vol. 13. Oxford: Elsevier, pp. 91–97.

Meusburger, P. (2015b) 'Education, geography of'. In Wright, J.D. (ed.) *International Encyclopedia of the Social & Behavioral Sciences*, 2nd edition, Vol. 13. Oxford: Elsevier, pp. 165–171.

Meusburger, P., Livingstone, D.N. and Jöns, H. (eds) (2010) *Geographies of Science. Knowledge and Space*, Vol. 3. Dordrecht: Springer.

Narayan, K. (1993) 'How native is a "native" anthropologist?', *American Anthropologist*, 95 (3), 671–686.

Nkoane, M.M. (2006) 'The Africanisation of the university in Africa', *Alternation*, 13 (1), 49–69.

Ogborn, M., Blunt, A., Gruffudd, P. and Pinder, D. (2014) *Cultural Geography in Practice*. New York: Routledge.

Olopade, D. (2014) *The Bright Continent: Breaking Rules and Making Change in Modern Africa*. Great Britain: Houghton Mifflin Harcourt.

Shizha, E. (2014) 'Indigenous knowledge systems and the curriculum'. In Emeagwali, G. and Dei, G.J.S. (eds), *African Indigenous Knowledge and the Disciplines*. Rotterdam: Sense Publishers, pp. 113–129.

Sikes, P. and Potts, A. (2008) *Researching Education from the Inside: Investigations from Within*. Oxon: Routledge.

Teferra, D. and Altbach, P.G. (2004) 'African higher education: challenges for the 21st century', *Higher Education*, 47 (1), 21–50.

Venkatesh, S.A. (2013) 'The reflexive turn: the rise of first-person ethnography', *The Sociological Quarterly*, 54 (1), 3–8.

Warf, B. (ed.) (2006) *Encyclopedia of Human Geography*. USA: Sage Publications.

Warf, B. and Arias, S. (eds) (2008) *The Spatial Turn: Interdisciplinary Perspectives*. New York: Routledge.

Waters, J. and Brooks, R. (2012) 'Transnational spaces, international students: emergent perspectives on educational mobilities'. In Brooks, R. et al. (eds), *Changing Spaces of Education: New Perspectives on the Nature of Learning*. New York: Routledge, pp. 21–38.

Wa Thiong'o, N. (1994) *Decolonising the Mind: The Politics of Language in African Literature*. Nairobi: East African Educational Publishers.

World Bank (2000) *Can Africa Claim the Twenty-First Century?* Washington, DC: World Bank. Available at: www.worldbank.org/html/extdr/canafricaclaim.pdf (accessed 18 May 2015).

Zeleza, P.T. (2009) 'What happened to the African renaissance? The challenges of development in the twenty-first century', *Comparative Studies of South Asia, Africa and the Middle East*, 29 (2), 155–170.

2 Do 'African' universities exist?

Setting the scene

Stig Jensen, Hanne Kirstine Adriansen and Lene Møller Madsen

Introduction

The purpose of this chapter is threefold: we want to provide a background for understanding the book as a whole while bearing in mind that the individual chapters are not necessarily based on a common framework. We will outline some of the debates in which the individual chapters are situated and thereby show how the book contributes to and fills gaps in existing research.

Many of the chapters draw on post-colonial critique, which has highlighted how the Global North and Global South are unequally positioned in knowledge-making processes, and how views from the Global North are inherent in knowledge that is claimed to be universal. Thus, this chapter provides background for the analyses in subsequent chapters of the uneven geographies of knowledge production and how neo-imperialism can be inherent in capacity-building efforts. However, our first step in providing a background for the chapters is to outline a short history of African universities. A short version of such a complex history, however, will out of necessity be very broad and general; therefore, focus will be on issues of relevance for the following chapters. Following this, we proceed to outline the international dimension of higher education in Africa, including an introduction to issues of capacity-building efforts related to African higher education. After this institutional perspective on higher education, we shift to looking at different aspects of knowledge production. It is beyond the scope of this chapter to outline the vast fields of research on knowledge production, but we situate the book in some of the debates. We briefly discuss the hegemony of Western thought in education and knowledge production as well as Africanisation of the curriculum. Then, we address knowledge production at universities. In different ways and to various extents, all the chapters in the book draw on the ideas of knowledge as situated. We end the chapter by discussing this and the issue of scientific and local knowledge as different modes of knowledge.

A short history of African universities and higher education

A short history of African universities is difficult for several reasons: firstly, because of the problem of how to define a university; secondly, because of the diverse and complex history of African countries and their higher education institutions. Damtew Teferra and Philip Altbach argue that higher education in Africa is 'as old as the pyramids of Egypt, the obelisks of Ethiopia, and the Kingdom of Timbuktu' (Teferra and Altbach, 2004: 23). James Otieno Jowi's description is less impressive:

> Except for the peculiar instances of Egypt, Ethiopia and South Africa, much of modern higher education in Africa has its roots in the colonial legacy and the consequent adoption of western university traditions, especially those of then Europe, with the assumption, partly still held today, that superior education existed abroad.
>
> (Jowi, 2009: 265)

While there have been learned institutions (most often in connection with religious institutions) in China, India and Africa long before the foundation of University of Bologna in Italy in 1088, Bologna is most often defined as the world's first university. By using Bologna as a point of reference, we want to highlight the 'European-ness' of the university tradition, while also acknowledging the importance of Islamic learned institutions pre-dating Bologna such as Al-Qarawiyyin in Fez (founded 859) and Al-Azhar in Cairo (founded 970).

Consequently, in this book, we apply a notion of a university based on the type of university which developed from the University of Bologna and the University of Paris through the Middle Ages. This means we define a university as a higher education institution that grants academic degrees within a range of subjects. *Uni* has reference to the Latin word 'whole'; thus, a 'classic' university should cover the whole field of knowledge usually by having different faculties. In the early Middle Ages, liberal arts, theology, law and medicine were the most important. Universities in early modern Europe (1500–1800) extended the field of disciplines, with the natural sciences gaining particularly in importance during the Enlightenment period (Adriansen and Adriansen, in press). Another characteristic of the medieval and renaissance university was internationalisation. Students and scholars were quite mobile, partly due to the use of Latin as the medium of instruction, uniform programmes of study and recognition of degrees (De Ridder-Symoens, 1992). Autonomy and academic freedom were also important tenets of the early European university, although not something which came easily (Pedersen, 1997). While autonomy and academic freedom are still important, they remain contested issues not least in a neo-liberal age with increased privatisation and external funding.

There is no unified way of defining a university, neither historically nor geographically. However, institutions need approval and authorisation; they cannot simply proclaim themselves universities. Historically, universities were granted their authorisation by the pope, later by kings and other emperors; today, the state is usually responsible for granting a university its authorisation and ensuring accreditation of its activities (Adriansen and Adriansen, in press). Ranking universities according to age can be difficult because many old learned institutions did not get their university authorisation until a later point in time. The University of Al-Azhar is a case in point. Al-Azhar is sometimes labelled the oldest existing university due to its foundation in 970 (see e.g. Teferra and Altbach, 2004). However, it only gained its authorisation as a university in 1961. The authorisation was granted by the government of Egypt's second president, Gamal Abdel Nasser, and at the same time a range of secular faculties were added, changing it from a religious *madrassa* to a 'classic' multi-faculty university (Skovgaard-Petersen, 2008). Even if Al-Azhar cannot be claimed to be the oldest existing university in the world, there is no doubt that there were ancient learned traditions in Africa, for instance the 2,700 year-old elite education of Ethiopia with an African script called Ge'ez (Woldegiorgis and Doevenspeck, 2013).

Colonialism

With colonialism, the vast majority of those old African institutions, which had not already disappeared, were destroyed (Teferra and Altbach, 2004). As Shizha explains: 'European education falsely portrayed Africa as if it was terra nullius when they arrived and deceptively occupied the continent. Hence Africans were viewed as a people without a history, without philosophical and scientific knowledge' (Shizha, 2014: 1871). Thus, colonisation meant the introduction of European education and this did not serve the interests of African societies but was used as a means of extending colonial ideology (Sall and Ndjaye, 2007–2008). For the colonial administrators, the objective of establishing higher education institutions in the colonies was not to address the socio-economic problems of Africa; rather, it was to facilitate the smooth running of their colonial administration. While the colonial higher education policy varied from one colony to another, there were some common elements mainly grounded in the fact that the colonial authorities were afraid that widespread access to higher education for Africans would lead to a more knowledgeable and thus less controllable population. Therefore, common traits were: limited access for Africans, colonial languages, limited academic freedom and a limited curriculum (Assié-Lumumba, 2006; Teferra and Altbach, 2004).

There were quite a few differences in the colonial approach to higher education as Emnet Tadesse Woldegiorgis and Martin Doevenspeck have outlined in their excellent overview of the changing role of higher education in Africa (Woldegiorgis and Doevenspeck, 2013). The British established universities and higher education institutions – e.g. Uganda Technical College in 1922 (now Makerere University), University of the Gold Coast in 1948 (now University of Ghana) – of which some were or later became affiliated with universities in England. However, the British higher education philosophy was to produce an elite required for the colonial administration, not to educate the African inhabitants in general; consequently, access to higher education was limited to very few individuals. In contrast, the Belgians simply forbade higher education in their colonies. The French and Portuguese approach to higher education in Africa was different from the British model because the primary focus was on providing education in France and Portugal. The French used higher education as an instrument for their colonial policy of assimilation; based on the idea of expanding French culture to the colonies, Africans were considered French citizens as long as French culture and customs were adopted. Instead of establishing higher education institutions in their colonies, both France and Portugal sent a few Africans to be trained at universities in Europe in order to integrate them into the culture and way of life of the colonial power. However, the majority of these Africans did not return after completing their studies (Woldegiorgis and Doevenspeck, 2013). Only a few universities and other higher education institutions were created in the African colonies. One example is the Université de Dakar in Senegal, which was established on a decree from the French Ministry of Education in 1957 and named as the eighteenth university in the French higher education system (Lulat, 2005). The few higher education institutions created in colonies lacked autonomy and freedom to appoint teachers; curriculum and graduation approval was decided by colonial authorities and were extensions of universities in the metropolis. The educational architecture of the colonial powers caused Africans to become structurally dependent on the colonial power and knowledge system (Assié-Lumumba, 2006).

The post-colonial period

Post-independence African states had a few strong higher education institutions that had been part of the English or French education system rather than African e.g. University of Makerere in Uganda and Université de Dakar in Senegal. Generally, however, the former colonies inherited fragile educational systems. To the extent that higher education existed in the independent states, they were left with European models of higher education that had been imposed by the colonial powers, and which had no roots in African history and little social legitimacy (Sall and Ndjaye, 2007–2008). As the Ugandan scholar Mahmood Mamdani describes:

> The new post-independence African university was triumphantly universalistic and uncompromisingly foreign. We made no concession to local culture. None! We stood as custodians of standards in outposts of civilisation. Unlike our counterparts in Asia and Latin America, we did not even speak the cultural languages of the people. The language of the university was either English, French or Portuguese. As in the affairs of the state, the discourse of universities also took place in a language that the vast majority of working people could not even understand. There was a linguistic curtain that shut the people out. None of this was an accident. All of it flowed from a historical process set into motion with colonial occupation.
>
> (Mamdani, 1993: 11)

Moreover, in the 1960s, less than one-quarter of all professional civil-service posts were held by Africans, and only 3 per cent of high school age students received secondary education in British colonies (World Bank, 1991). This means there were very few Africans to take positions in the administration, and very few Africans who could take over the role as knowledge producers at universities or as teachers in the higher education system. In general, and not only with reference to Africa, colonialism involved control over mind and intellect. This means that even though the colonial administrators left with the end of colonialism, their way of thinking remained because the state and educational systems were modelled on the colonial mind (Breidlid, 2013; Chen, 2010). A number of authors from former colonies have analysed this using different approaches. One prominent example is Franz Fanon, a Martinique-born, Afro-French psychiatrist, philosopher and revolutionary, who has inspired anti-colonial and resistance movements all over the world. In *The Wretched of the Earth* (1968), Fanon argues that the colonised have adopted the colonisers' historical perspective, using the concept 'colonial identification' to denote this and similar tendencies whereby the colonised take on the perspective of the colonisers. One can easily revert to a pessimistic perception of the educational system in post-colonial Africa, but Julius Nyerere, Tanzania's first president, had a more positive view on education: in analysing the links between education, knowledge production and the colonial relations of power, he came to the conclusion that if education could be used by the colonial powers to enslave people, then it could also be used by anticolonial powers to liberate people. Julius Nyerere argued that all people had the capacity to produce knowledge, not only the political leaders of the newly independent African nations (Dei et al., 2008). Nonetheless, the role of universities for societal development in post-colonial Africa has been debated.

The role of universities for societal development

The importance of higher education for societal development in Africa varies from country to country and has changed over time. Universities have served as a means for nation-building and as a place for Africanisation (which will be discussed later) (Assié-Lumumba, 2008; Woolman, 2001). A central element in nation-building is a bureaucracy. In order to make the institutions of the independent countries function, the universities were pushed to educate accountants, teachers, doctors, engineers, etc., who were believed to be very important to nation-building. In the 1970s, there were attempts to define and establish an 'African development university' that would emphasise Africanisation, localisation and production of knowledge for 'the amelioration of the conditions of the common man and woman in Africa' (Yesufu, 1973: 40). While this approach led to innovative methodologies and a focus on knowledge production aimed at African conditions and challenges, it was also caught up in nationalist agendas and by an instrumentalisation of research for development purposes only (Singh, 2010).

The role of African universities for societal development is still debated – caught between the classical argument that higher education and knowledge production should serve the public good by contributing to nation building and its social and cultural needs versus the neo-liberal discourse, which sees universities as transformed into market agents rather than development agents (Johnson and Hirt, 2014; Naidoo, 2010). This book also points to some of the other dilemmas for African universities caught between demands for internationalisation and demands for local relevance. As pointed out by the Beninese philosopher Paulin Hountondji (1990), Africa has become trapped in the inequalities of knowledge production by focusing on research of societal relevance. While this sounds like a reasonable demand, it means that Africa becomes a place for applied research, thereby leaving the basic research to the Global North. Another dilemma for African researchers concerns how to produce knowledge of relevance for African societies. Invariably, local relevance includes taking local realities and worldviews into account. We will return to the issue of local knowledge below. Even though African higher education institutions were European constructs, they were perceived as important for the development of the post-colonial nations and for creating an African identity. In higher education institutions, the process of Africanisation has not been easy due to the claimed universal character of knowledge. Thus, African universities even started to engage more and more with European universities in research and scholarship (Assié-Lumumba, 2006).

During the 1980s, an increasing political hegemony of neo-liberal marked ideologies gained influence in many African countries. This initiated considerable reform pressures on all sectors of society, higher education included (Maassen and Cloete, 2006). This meant that higher education institutions became part of national development policies, and African higher education became marginalised in African societies as they were deprived of both international and domestic support due to structural adjustment programmes. During the 1990s, the role of higher education institutions in knowledge production became recognised as one of the most important means for the so-called knowledge economy (Woldegiorgis and Doevenspeck, 2013). The growth of African economy and the popularity of liberal and knowledge based economy have pushed African governments and international financial institutions to reconsider the role of higher education in the economic development of African countries. There is internal pressure on African knowledge based institutions to provide higher education, not only in order to reach the levels of other developing and middle-income countries but also to satisfy the demand of populations that are eager for opportunities to study. At the same time, universities go from being national organisations with multiple social roles to being global players operating mainly on the basis of economic considerations. The growing demand for higher education in Africa has led to an emergence of private higher education as a business enterprise; this is followed by issues of legal status, quality assurance and cost of service (Teferra and Altbach, 2004; Maassen and Cloete, 2006).

Today, some 50 years after many of the African countries gained their independence, it is relevant to ask how independent African higher education has become. To what extent has the curriculum become Africanised? To what extent is knowledge production still exogenous? To what extent are old power relations still reproduced in partnerships between African and European researchers? Are the ties to the old colonial powers still strong or have new players emerged? These are some of the questions we will try to address in this book.

The international dimension of higher education in Africa

Owing to its history and trajectory, higher education in Africa has always been affected by circumstances beyond campus and across national borders (Altbach, 2004; Teferra, 2012). Yet, as argued in a recent book on the international dimension of higher education in Africa (Teferra and Knight, 2008), internationalisation has become a key factor shaping and challenging higher education in African. Therefore, it is relevant to ask whether steps towards greater independence of higher education and knowledge production, towards a more African, national or endogenous agenda, may be difficult to reconcile with this move towards internationalisation of higher education and greater flows of knowledge and people. Internationalisation is linked to processes of globalisation, but the two are not the same. Globalisation can be understood as the increasing flow of money, people and information taking place in the twenty-first century. Internationalisation of higher education, on the other hand, refers to the institutional policies and practices meant to deal with the effects of a global academic environment (Altbach and Knight, 2007). Since the 1990s, political and institutional concern with the internationalisation of higher education has been accompanied by a substantial growth in research on internationalisation. The new types of imperialism within which cross-border interactions in higher education are embedded have been pointed out (Naidoo, 2011), and some have also claimed that internationalisation would lead to a 'restoration of the universal character of science and education' (Knight and De Wit, 1995: 6). This is based on the idea that the national character of universities will decrease with globalisation and increased mobility of staff and students. Further, capacity-building projects have given rise to mobility of academic staff and students (as a number of chapters in the book illustrate). Many researchers have also pointed to the uneven geographies of internationalisation and argued that internationalisation reinforces existing power structures where powerful universities become even more powerful in the production and distribution of knowledge (Altbach, 2004; Altbach and Knight, 2007), and where student mobilities are hampered by geo-politics (Waters and Brooks, 2012).

With regard to internationalisation of higher education in Africa, one of the main questions is the relationship between quality and internationalisation: internationalisation can lead to improved educational programmes, better educated staff and a more comprehensive curriculum, but internationalisation can also be a threat to quality due to dubious international providers (Ogachi,

2009; Oyewole, 2009). Other issues in the internationalisation research about Africa concern mobility (Jowi, 2009), including brain drain (Knight, 2008b; Teferra, 2008), credit transfer systems (Adamu, 2012) and university reform (Sall and Ndjaye, 2007–2008). Focus is also on the relationship between internationalisation and regionalisation (Ogachi, 2009; Oyewole, 2009) and on inter-regional and intra-regional collaboration (Adamu, 2012). The research shows that south-to-south cooperation, partnerships and networks are increasing (Assié-Lumumba and N'Dri, 2009; Knight, 2008a). Even though a critique of internationalisation efforts from a post-colonial perspective is raised in some of the literature (Johnson and Hirt, 2014; Singh, 2010), the asymmetrical power relations inherent in much of the internationalisation discourse and practice remains unquestioned in large parts of the literature. While focusing on Africa in particular, this body of literature does not explore or theorise 'place', including how conceptions of place are tightly related to the way people come to understand and value certain kinds of knowledge as universal/particular, and as good or relevant. With this book, we will try to fill this gap in the internationalisation literature by emphasising the spatiality of knowledge production in processes of internationalisation.

Private universities are another important international dimension in the African higher education landscape. Private higher education has experienced spectacular growth in Africa in recent years (World Bank, 2010). The effect of privatisation of basic education is discussed by MacPherson et al. (2014). They find that while the involvement of private actors in education is not new, their activities have increased in the last decade both in scale and scope. More importantly, privatisation goes hand in hand with a new conceptualisation of the student as consumer and education as a consumer good, thereby affecting the raison d'être of higher education.

Internationalisation has become an all-encompassing concept covering both for-profit and non-profit activities. In this book, we focus on the non-profit activities, particularly those related to capacity building and development assistance, while acknowledging that other internationalisation activities, especially the for-profit actions related to privatisation of the higher education sector, are also important.

Capacity building and development aid in relation to higher education

Capacity building and development assistance to higher education in Africa can be seen as one aspect of the international dimension of African higher education. While activities such as development cooperation, international academic agreements and student mobility were discussed in terms such as 'international cooperation', 'international relation' and 'international education' 40 years ago, these different activities are now seen as aspects of internationalisation of higher education (e.g. Teferra and Knight, 2008).

The significance of development aid for higher education is disputed. For instance, Teferra and Altbach state that:

The bulk of funding for higher education is generated from state resources. While small variations in the proportion of resources allotted to higher education by country exist, African governments consistently provide more than 90 to 95 percent of the total operating budgets of higher education.

(Teferra and Altbach, 2004: 27)

Lulat on the other hand argues that:

Foreign assistance has been a vital part of higher education including university development in Africa. For any country higher education is extremely costly and therefore, it is not surprising that development of modern higher education in Africa has always been dependent upon external assistance.

(Lulat, 2005: 379–380)

Another aspect of this is the allocation of funding from the Global North. A study from The World Bank in 2010 estimates that during the period 2002–2006 external donors (both bilateral and multilateral) allocated approximately US$600 million annually to higher education in sub-Saharan Africa. However, less than 30 per cent of this amount directly benefited African universities because most of the money never made it to sub-Saharan Africa; it was primarily spent in donors' universities to compensate for the cost of educating African students (World Bank, 2010: 94).

With respect to development assistance to higher education in Africa, three major phases can be identified: post-independence (1960s and 1970s), structural adjustment period (1980s to 1990s) and the knowledge society era (from 1990s till today). Development agencies do not simultaneously change their policies overnight, so there are some overlaps, but these phases serve the purpose of a rough overview. After interdependence, foreign aid to education was primarily focused on basic, primary education and there was limited assistance to higher education in Africa (Lulat, 2005). External funding came mainly from governments and was based on bilateral agreements, multilateral institutions and non-governmental organisation. In the 1960s, the former colonial powers played a vital role with aid; however, soon the Cold War changed the development aid landscape and also the bilateral support for higher education in Africa to become predominantly ideologically based. Altbach has provided this telling description:

The era of the Cold War was characterised by the efforts of the major powers to dominate the 'hearts and minds' of the peoples of the world. The Soviet Union, the United States, and others spent lavishly on student exchanges, textbook subsidies, book translations, institution building and other activities to influence the world's academic leaders, intellectuals and policymakers. The goals were political and economic, and higher education was a key battlefield. The rationale was sometimes couched in the ideological jargon of the Cold War but was often obscured by rhetoric about cooperation [...] The result is the same – the loss of intellectual and cultural autonomy by those who are less powerful.

(Altbach, 2004: 9)

Lulat (2005) seems to disagree somewhat with Altbach. According to Lulat, the Soviet support for research and higher education in Africa was more relevant to African countries because the ideologically-driven approach supported both the African countries' political and economic independence. The Soviet support for higher education in Africa was focused on three aspects: '[P]rovide access to higher education to students of working-class and peasant backgrounds. Develop curricula suited to societies in the early stages of industrialisation. Create a pool of graduated alumnus sympathetic to the Soviet Union and its allies' (Lulat 2005: 381). While the Eastern bloc continued their support for higher education for their African allies, those countries supported by the West were met with dire requirements in terms of economic adjustments: the so-called structural adjustment programmes recommended by the World Bank and the International Monetary Fund (IMF).

Due to the structural adjustment programmes, the World Bank was seen as counterproductive rather than supportive of African higher education during the 1980s and 1990s (Emeagwali, 2011; Mohamedbhai, 2014). Powerful international forces promoted a discourse where there was no need for African universities because the return on investment was claimed to be both too low and unjustifiable (Olukoshi and Zeleza, 2004). In African societies, the World Bank was seen as part of the problem as its policies were at least in part accountable for the deterioration of Africa's universities and the decline of higher education in Africa more generally. Samoff and Carrol explain:

As the World Bank assigned high priority to spending on basic education, it told everyone [...] that higher education was too costly, too inequitable, and marginal to national development goals. Accordingly, resources were to be redirected from higher education to basic education. Decay was the result.

(Samoff and Carrol, 2004: 2)

After the end of the Cold War, bilateral aid to higher education in Africa changed both in terms of countries and in terms of the content of the agreements. More importantly, international focus was yet again on higher education. The renewed interest in higher education should be seen in relation to the knowledge society discourse – or what at first was called the information age and seen as the successor of the Cold War era (Knight and De Wit, 1995). For instance, the World Bank's growing focus on the importance of higher education in Africa can be linked to the publication *Constructing Knowledge Societies: New Challenges for Tertiary Education* which signalled the World Bank's renewed attention on higher education (World Bank, 2002). It is based on the perception that education, especially higher education, is essential to economic growth (Samoff and Carrol, 2004).The focus on primary education, however, has remained high on the international agenda as shown in the UN's Millennium Development Goals (MDG). In the debate about the post-2015 MDG Agenda on education, focus has been broadened to include issues related to equitable, quality education and lifelong learning for all, which is seen as a key to sustainable development (UNESCO, 2012; UNICEF and UNESCO, 2013). Traditionally, multilateral, bilateral and non-governmental organisations have all been active within African higher education. They act through different kinds of trans-boundary partnerships which have emerged as the preferred donor paradigm (Koehn, 2013; Obamba and Mwema, 2009; Teferra, 2012).

The chapters in this book mainly analyse and reflect on different issues within African higher education in relation to capacity building based on bilateral donors from the Nordic counties. Even though there is no particular Nordic concept of bilateral capacity building, there are some commonalities which we want to outline (for a more comprehensive review of the Norwegian, Danish and Swedish approaches see e.g. Danida, 2014; Norad, 2012; Sida, 2013). Within the Nordic countries there has been a relatively long tradition for being involved in higher education in Africa due to an overall goal of strengthening research capacity in the Global South. The donor involvement has often been strongly related to personal relationships among faculty members within specific disciplines across the Global North and Global South. More recently, some have also been consolidated as institutional partnerships, for instance between the University of Sokoine in Tanzania and the Agricultural University of Copenhagen, Denmark (Møller-Jensen and Madsen, 2015). During the 1990s and 2000s, a twinning and partnership approach increasingly gained currency in Danish research capacity-building projects (Hjortsø and Meilby, 2013). Recently, bilateral support from Denmark has changed to support South-driven initiatives by providing funds for Southern universities instead of the former indirect support via Northern universities (Danida, 2013; Danida, 2014; Danske Universiteter, 2011).

Non-governmental organisations have been another actor supporting higher education in Africa. Beginning already during colonisation and continuing after the colonial powers had left, they were primarily Christian and philanthropic organisations such as Ford, Rockefeller, Kellogg and the Carnegie Foundation (Sehoole, 2008). Multilateral institutions are the third donor type, with UNESCO and the World Bank as the most relevant institutions. In the 1960s and 1970s, the focus of multilateral institutions was on primary education. The first breakthrough for multilateral institutions' support to higher education in Africa came with the conference Development of Higher Education in Africa, held in 1962 (Sehoole, 2008). This early focus on higher education was replaced by the structural adjustment period where, as described earlier, higher education institutions in sub-Saharan Africa suffered from abandonment and underfunding. It was the UNESCO World Conference on Higher Education in the late 1990s that started a renewed view on support for African higher education, linking the role of universities to development challenges (Mohamedbhai, 2014) and now seeing universities as drivers for social change and knowledge-intensive development (Koehn, 2013).

With the renewed international interest and investment in higher education in Africa, it is relevant to ask how the international dimension affects African universities and academics. Do capacity-building projects become neo-imperialism in disguise? How do new partnership policies affect the power relations between universities and scholars from Africa and the Global North? How does internationalisation affect tendencies to Africanise the curriculum? These are some of the issues we touch upon in the following chapters.

The hegemony of Western thought in education and knowledge production

To various extents, the chapters in this book all reflect (on) the hegemony of Western thought in educational architecture and academic knowledge production. Therefore, it is worthwhile dwelling on the history of these thoughts that are part and parcel of the Enlightenment era in European thought from the seventeenth and eighteenth centuries and embodied in Cartesian-Newtonian science. They entail a mechanistic world view, universal laws of science and a logical-empirical methodological approach to knowledge production, as well as notions of rationality, development and progress inherent in Enlightenment ideals. These ideas became hegemonic during and after colonialism and the spread of capitalist market economy (Breidlid, 2013). While the university as a European institution dates back to 1088, mass education (primary education) is newer, it grew out of developments in social organisation and epistemology in eighteenth-century Europe: 'Mass education is meaningless and in fact practically inconceivable where the primary social unit is the family, clan, village, or other group collectivity' (Boli and Ramirez, 1986: 69). Hence, in most European countries, the first university was established long before the country had a public school system.

School systems and the hegemonic role of Western thought

In his book *Education, Indigenous Knowledges, and Development in the Global South*, the Norwegian educationalist Anders Breidlid sets out to analyse the hegemonic role of what he calls the modernist, Western epistemology (Breidlid, 2013). Thus, Breidlid focuses on epistemologies and argues that the modernist, Western epistemology outlined earlier has shaped the educational architecture across the world. Given the old learned institutions in Africa and elsewhere in the Global South, it may sound strange that European Enlightenment epistemology should have shaped educational systems worldwide. Yet, educationalists seem to agree that the notion of mass education is part and parcel of European thought, and that educational systems and their role in national state identity-formation are marked by a European heritage (see e.g. Boli and Ramirez, 1986; Breidlid, 2013; Smith, 2012). It continues to be a matter of debate, however, whether there is one world culture of schooling or whether the nearly 200 national school systems in the world represent 200 different cultures of schooling (see e.g. Anderson-Levitt, 2003). It is beyond the scope of the present book to go into detail about mass education; however, we want to highlight that both primary and higher education in Africa grew out of a European tradition; therefore, educational institutions are, in various ways and to different degrees, marked by a hegemonic Western epistemology. Breidlid (2013) argues that the differences in epistemology between the mass-schooling system and the indigenous communities mean that children have to pass 'epistemological bridges' on the way to and from school. The Maori writer Patricia Grace even claims that school books might be dangerous for indigenous populations (Grace in Smith, 2012). Based on an analysis of school texts, Grace argues that these do not strengthen the values, customs and identity of indigenous communities; moreover, school books usually only concern other populations, thereby ignoring the existence of indigenous populations. However, when the books include information about the indigenous communities, the information is often untrue or negative, thereby carrying a message that indigenous people are no good.

Africanisation of African school systems and higher education

Africanisation can be understood as a focus on protecting African knowledge, ways of thinking, cultural heritage and identity. The issue of Africanisation of curriculum is also related to the debate about indigenous knowledge, which is discussed later. With reference to education in the post-colonial states, Africanisation has both been related to changing the school curriculum and to replacing Europeans (and other non-Africans) in central positions in e.g. academia and as civil servants. Africanisation has played a significant role in African nationalism throughout the continent and was especially popular among African nationalists in the 1960s and 1970s as a means to reclaim colonial institutions (Woldegiorgis and Doevenspeck, 2013). Yet, according to Crossman: 'Africanisation [...] has been taken up most seriously in South Africa while it has by and large been ignored by institutions across much of Africa' (Crossman, 2004: 331). In South Africa, it became part of the academic discourse in the 1990s and was used as a vehicle of African identity in the period following democratic elections in 1994 where it was linked to frameworks such as the African Renaissance and Ubuntu (Crossman, 2004). The curriculum in particular has been prone to processes of Africanisation. This is because the 'curriculum is power-saturated and involves the power to construct, validate, and legitimize knowledge, and what is acceptable and not' (Dei, 2014: 171). Yet, ironically, while curriculum changes have been claimed necessary in order to refocus knowledge and pedagogy on African perspectives, research has shown that the majority of curriculum changes have been promoted by donors from the Global North (Shizha, 2010). A detailed account of post-colonial curriculum development in primary and secondary education has been made by Woolman

(2001). In higher education, Africanisation of curriculum has been more difficult because the Euro-centric curriculum tends to carry more value in academia (Dei, 2014); Africanisation may thus be seen in relation to the issue of universality versus particularity of scientific knowledge. Moreover, Africanisation of the curriculum may to some extent be in contrast to attempts to internationalise higher education in Africa and the call for adherence to international standards.

In her book *Whose Education for All? The Recolonization of the African Mind*, the Norwegian educationalist Birgit Brock-Utne shows a renewed curriculum dependency caused by capacity-building activities, donor control of project development processes and the denied validity of alternative, indigenous approaches to such tasks (Brock-Utne, 2002). She argues that there is a need to focus on education for all through Africanisation from primary level to higher education. The need for Africanisation or endogenisation, to use the vocabulary of Hountondji (1997), of knowledge production has been pointed out by Mahmood Mamdani some 20 years ago:

> In our single-minded pursuit to create centres of learning and research of international standing, we had nurtured researchers and educators who had little capacity to work in surrounding communities but who could move to any institution in any industrialised country, and serve any privileged community around the globe with comparative ease. In our failure to contextualise standards and excellence to the needs of our own people, to ground the very process and agenda of learning and research in our conditions, we ended up creating an intelligentsia with little stamina for the very process of development whose vanguard we claimed to be.
>
> (Mamdani, 1993: 15)

After having pointed to the hegemony of Western thought in education and knowledge production in Africa, and having discussed the increasing internationalisation of African higher education, it is relevant to ask how these tendencies have affected universities in Africa. Where do we see Africanisation of curriculum? To what extent are African universities embedded in uneven geographies of knowledge production? Are there tendencies to counter the Western hegemony? How has the European influence on school systems influenced African scholars in their learning journeys? These are some of the questions addressed in the subsequent chapters.

Knowledge production within universities – whose knowledge counts?

Production of scientific knowledge can be seen as entailing a struggle over who should define the terms and conditions of legitimate fields of research. This and similar issues have come under close scrutiny over the past 40 years from a number of disciplines. The importance of analysing scientific knowledge in the same way as other types of knowledge has been highlighted from various fields including geography (see Livingstone, 2003) and there has been a call for studies of the researchers themselves, for instance by studying how social factors influence the production of science in laboratories (Knorr-Cetina, 1981; Latour and Woolgar, 1986). These thoughts were developed in the mid-1970s as a response to Thomas Kuhn and his 'revolutionary' view of science (Kuhn, 1962). The increased interest in knowledge production has stimulated new sub-disciplines with a special focus on knowledge production e.g. sociology of scientific knowledge (SKK) and science and technology studies (STS) (Madsen and Adriansen, 2006).

Alongside debates about the production of scientific knowledge, researchers (notably anthropologists) have criticised the fact that Western, scientific knowledges are considered 'universal', whereas other kinds of knowledge – often named 'local', 'traditional' or 'indigenous' – are deemed 'particular' (e.g. Horton, 1974; Winch, 1964). Following these debates, there is an increased tendency to view knowledge, also scientific knowledge, as *situated* (Haraway, 1988). When conceived of as situated, the production of academic knowledge cannot be seen in isolation from *where* it is produced (Connell, 2007; Livingstone, 2003); or, expressed differently, knowledge is always from 'somewhere' (Gupta and Ferguson, 1997). This book should be seen in this context, as a contribution to the studies of knowledge production, and more precisely to the emerging field of the geography of knowledge and education (Brooks et al., 2012; Hanson Thiem, 2009; Jöns, 2007; Kraftl, 2013; Livingstone, 2003), a field which hitherto has mainly focused on the Anglo-Saxon hegemony.

Knowledge can be conceived of and classified in many ways. In the following sections, we will outline three ideas of knowledge based on or in debate with the Enlightenment thoughts already mentioned. Numerous other ways of under-standing knowledge could be mentioned, but we focus on the debates within which different chapters are situated. Many of the chapters draw on post-colonial critique, which has highlighted how the Global North and Global South are unequally positioned in knowledge-making processes, and how views from the Global North are inherent in knowledge that is claimed to be universal (Chen, 2010; Connell, 2007; Hountondji, 1995; Smith, 2012). Some of the chapters draw on the uneven geographies of internationalisation (Waters and Brooks, 2012) and neo-imperial connotations underlying capacity-building efforts (Naidoo, 2011).

Scientific knowledge as spatially situated

We have already argued that the chapters in this book are based on a common view of knowledge as situated; this also applies to scientific knowledge. It is important, however, to further elaborate on how we see knowledge as situated and where the main contributions of the book are. We draw on three main sources for this perspective: the Northern Irish geographer David Livingstone's *Putting Science in Its Place: Geographies of Scientific Knowledge* (2003); the Beninese philosopher Paulin Hountondji and his 'Producing knowledge in Africa today' (1995) and 'Scientific dependence in Africa today' (1990); and, the Australian sociologist Raewyn Connell and her *Southern Theory* (2007). Even though Hountondji and Connell do not have an explicit geographical perspective, they do have spatial views on knowledge production which we find inspiring and well suited to supplement Livingstone's arguments.

When talking about the geography of knowledge, it may be tempting to view scientific knowledge as 'Western' and local knowledge as 'African'. But that would be very wrong. Local knowledge or indigenous knowledge is produced all over the world. Likewise, scientific knowledge is produced worldwide. In fact, all knowledge is local at first: 'New knowledge always starts as local knowledge. It is created in particular places and contexts. Local knowledge becomes regional and global knowledge only if it is understood and accepted elsewhere' (Meusburger, 2015: 91). Although scientific knowledge is often thought of as universal, the majority of scientific knowledge is in fact particular and situated. We apply two notions of spatially situated: the first is that the production of scientific knowledge always takes place somewhere – even if this knowledge is thought to have universal value, it is produced in a specific place (we will elaborate on that below); the second notion of spatially situated knowledge is phrased by Livingstone:

> Scientific theory evidently does not disperse evenly across the globe from its point of origin. As it moves it is modified; as it travels it is transformed. All this demonstrates that the meaning of scientific theories is not stable; rather, it is mobile and varies from place to place. And that meaning takes shape in response to spatial forces at every scale of analysis – from the macropolitical geography of national regions to the microsocial geography of local cultures.
> (Livingstone, 2003: 4)

By taking his point of departure in the geography of science and analysing historically the development of science, Livingstone shows that science has been marked by what he terms 'regional particularity'. In doing so, he finds that it is not only the use of scientific knowledge in different places that has been appropriated differently and put to different uses, but also that the very meaning of a particular scientific theory or text has shifted from place to place. Livingstone argues that 'science has been, and continues to be, promoted as a universal undertaking untouched by the vicissitudes of the local' (Livingstone, 2003: 134). Hence, the geography has had a profound influence in the production of scientific knowledge and in its movement around the globe. As such, he contests that scientific knowledge is transcendent, neutral and disembodied, and further opposes 'that its [scientific knowledge] claims have ubiquitous validity; and that its diffusion is simply a consequence of its inherent universality' (Livingstone, 2003: 140). By drawing upon a wide range of examples, he shows how the movement and diffusion of knowledge is highly embedded in the local knowledge systems. In this book, we are mainly concerned with the first notion of spatially situated knowledge. It is also this notion that Hountondji and Connell apply.

Livingstone uses geography as the lenses through which he analyses how scientific knowledge is situated. Hountondji and Connell use different lenses but reach the same conclusion: that production of scientific knowledge takes place in different places and cultures, and that these interact with the knowledge produced. Hountondji and Connell supplement Livingstone's argument with a critical perspective on the uneven geographies of knowledge production. For Hountondji and Connell it is power that makes knowledge production spatially unequal. As long as power is unevenly spatially distributed, we will see uneven geographies of knowledge production. Hountondji (1990) applies classic concepts, arguments and theories from development research such as dependency, centre-periphery and world-system to argue that research in Africa is 'extroverted'. By this he means that research is dependent on the Global North in a number of ways and not related to the local situation in Africa. This is similar to the industrial economies in Africa that are oriented towards the Global North, dependent on the capitalist markets there instead of being oriented towards the African continent and national and regional needs and economies. Hountondji's main concern in regard to scientific knowledge production is that the Global South remains a data mining site, while theorising takes place in the Global North. The central aspect of scientific activity is theorising, which is why this division of labour is so detrimental to African universities, leaving them in a dependency relationship with universities and research institutions in the Global North.

The Australian sociologist Raewyn Connell writes about social theory and knowledge production (Connell, 2007). Throughout her book, Connell provides numerous examples of how sociological theory developed in the Global North, e.g. by Foucault or Giddens, is happily applied in the Global South under the (implicit) assumption that these theories possess universal qualities despite being derived in a European context: '[O]n close examination, mainstream sociology turns out to be an ethno-sociology of metropolitan society. This is concealed by its language, especially the framing of its theories as universal propositions or universal tools' (Connell, 2007: 226).

Connell further argues that theories developed in the Global South are generally overlooked, and that if they are being addressed by other researchers, these theories are not perceived to have universal qualities. Instead, theories developed by researchers from the Global South are seen as particular theories. Even though the title of the book could lead the reader to assume Connell's argument would be based on simple notions of the Global North versus Global South, this is not the case. She points to the fact that many researchers from the Global South are educated in the Global North and thus may not be easily positioned. Towards the end of the book, Connell deliberately deconstructs the usual centre-periphery, East–West, North–South global divisions, combining them in new ways in order to illustrate the dynamic positioning of people and places. Australia, for instance, can both be seen as place of the coloniser and of the colonised. And 'Southern' scholars, she argues, may belong to the metropolis rather than the periphery – thus employing new types of binaries. Hence, by arguing that knowledge is spatially situated, we want to point to the importance of taking African experiences and cultures into account in scientific knowledge production, while at the same time not localising African scientific knowledge.

Local knowledge and academia

A number of excellent edited volumes have addresses issues related to indigenous knowledge and (African) universities (Dei, 2011; Emeagwali, 2006; Emeagwali and Dei, 2014; Semali and Kincheloe, 1999; Shizha and Abdi, 2013). While we find the issue very important, we only touch briefly upon the issue of indigenous or local knowledge in some of the chapters, as it has been eloquently treated in the volumes mentioned above. Yet, why do we want to point to the importance of paying attention to local knowledge in a book on higher education and academic knowledge production? There are three primary reasons for this: the first is that local knowledge holds wisdom that should not be ignored; the second is related to this, namely to ensure the relevance of higher education for the surrounding community; and the third is to de-imperialise knowledge production. In the words of George Safa Dei: '[T]he introduction of African Indigenous knowledge systems in the university curriculum should be viewed as a project of the Africanisation of the academy' (Dei, 2014: 169). Before going into detail with these arguments, we need to conceptualise indigenous knowledge, this is defined by Gloria Emeagwali as 'the cumulative body of strategies, practices, techniques, tools, intellectual resources, explanations, beliefs, and values accumulated over time in a particular locality, without interference and impositions of external hegemonic forces' (Emeagwali, 2014: 1). We would prefer to follow Hountondji (1997) and others and use the term 'endogenous' to denote knowledge that is also known as local, indigenous, or traditional knowledge. Unfortunately, the term 'endogenous' has not caught on. We find the term 'indigenous' slightly contentious and therefore we use the notion local experience-based knowledge. In this book, we are mainly interested in the distinction between experience-based knowledge and scientific knowledge, where the latter is derived through systematic, analytical inquiry, but which is also spatial as already argued. It is important to note that local experience-based knowledge is fluid and dynamic since it develops as an integral part of the surrounding society (Escobar, 2001). The focus on people's own views and understanding began in the 1960s, when researchers, mainly anthropologists, 'became increasingly interested in understanding people's own perceptions and interpretations of the world [...] because they form the appropriate context in which to analyse people's actions and decision-making process' (Milton, 1997: 484). The increasing interest in local knowledge can also be seen as an attempt to produce more effective development strategies after the failure of top-down development (Briggs and Sharp, 2004). Local knowledge has therefore been accredited increasing importance and wisdom. Including this wisdom in academia is important as well as difficult given the differences in epistemologies.

Our second reason for addressing local knowledge was related to the issue of local relevance of higher education. As argued in the previous sections, the increased funding for higher education in Africa was based on a premise of the societal relevance of the knowledge production and education of graduates. This relevance necessitates taking local experiences into account, otherwise we risk decoupling academia and society, as argued by Mamdani (1993). Our third concern for local knowledge was the need to de-imperialise knowledge production. In this we are inspired by the Maori professor and educationalist Linda Tuhiwai Smith from New Zealand. Smith has a particular interest in the ways local or indigenous knowledge is treated. With her book *Decolonizing Methodologies*, Smith wants to provoke revolutionary thinking about knowledge and how institutions, hierarchies and production of knowledge are involved in societal transformation. By decolonising methodologies, Smith intends to critically question research production: 'Whose research is it? Who owns it? Whose interests does it serve? Who will benefit from it? Who has designed its questions and framed its scope? Who will carry it out? Who will write it up? How will its results be disseminated?' (Smith 2012: 10). The problems in regard to integrating or combining local experience-based knowledge and scientific knowledge, as seen in studies about environment, sustainability and climate change in Africa, are to some extent due to the differences in epistemologies. In order to be able to treat both types of knowledge with respect without subsuming one over the other, it may be useful to consider them as different types or modes of knowledge (Adriansen, 2008).

Different modes of knowledge

Pivotal to the arguments developed in this book is the idea that different modes of knowledge exist (sometimes also called knowledge systems, repertoires or types of knowledge). Hence, the chapters all build on Haraway's (1988) concept of partial and situated knowledges – a concept that has been widely embraced and further developed (e.g. Mountz, 2002; Rose, 1997). It is central to these thoughts that certain constructions of knowledge or modes of knowledge function in particular ways, and, when asking a particular question, different modes of knowledge will provide different information. Hence, knowledge is partial and linked to the contexts in which it is created (Nightingale, 2003). With the belief that knowledge is socially constructed and situated, it follows that there is no single 'truth' (Nygren, 1999) or objective knowledge. Yet we are searching for 'true' knowledge within each mode of knowledge, and within different modes of knowledge there are different ways of validating this. Moreover, this does not mean that all modes of knowledge are equally useful or valid in the context of a particular research question.

The idea that scientific knowledge is subject to change and does not just constitute the building blocks of truth is not a legacy of postmodernism. Kuhn (1962), for instance, discussed this in his *The Structure of Scientific Revolutions*. He also showed how research is conducted within a certain construction of knowledge with its own set of rules. The chapters in this book use the term 'modes of knowledge' for covering knowledge constructed within one set of ideas – these being 'indigenous/local' or 'scientific'. Hence, scientific knowledge can be seen as one mode of knowledge, or as many different modes, depending on whether it has been constructed within one set of ideas or is the outcome of different sciences. The competition between different scientific modes of knowledge is analysed in the acclaimed *The Lie of the Land*, edited by Leach and Mearns (1996), in which a number of scholars criticise and challenge the so-called received or conventional wisdom on the African environment; the authors call for a sharper focus on local knowledge and argue that this should be included in order to understand both present and future land use. Consequently, local knowledge can be considered as another mode of knowledge. Similar to scientific knowledge, local knowledge is not just one knowledge mode. Different 'local people' have different world views and thus different modes of knowledge.

When studying knowledge production in an African higher education context, it is relevant to ask whose knowledge counts. How can a view on scientific knowledge as spatially situated contribute to our understanding of knowledge production at African universities? Can and should local experience-based knowledge be included in the curriculum at African universities? And how can this be done? To what extent should societal needs drive research at African universities? The chapters will try to address these questions in different ways.

Do 'African' universities exist? Concluding remarks

As this chapter has illustrated, history deems it incorrect to talk about African universities as a certain type of university. The chapters in this book will show that due to the different colonial heritage, the higher education systems have developed differently throughout Africa, with differences not only between countries but also within countries. As discussed in Chapter 1, we do not want to essentialise Africa or African universities. Yet, there are commonalities among universities on the African continent, related to the European roots of universities in Africa and thus the difficulties of using universities as instruments for national development, as pointed out by N'Dri Assié-Lumumba (2006). Also, universities in Africa are facing some of the same challenges, such as struggling with quality and excellence defined in terms of intellectual codes and norms from the Global North (Dei, 2014) – a problem that is not unique to Africa and applies to academia globally. The main struggle related to the European heritage of the university is that what counts as legitimate, relevant and valuable knowledge is measured by the same standard as in the Global North – a standard presented as universal when in fact it is shaped in a particular context, historically in a Western European context, and currently most often in an Anglo-American context.

This chapter has pointed to a number of different yet interrelated debates within the field of education and knowledge. Internationalisation of higher education in Africa cannot be discussed without also focusing on the (counter) trend: Africanisation. Yet, Africanisation is related to issues such as indigenous knowledge and societal relevant knowledge production. Researchers such as Hountondji (1990, 1995) and Mamdani (1993) have argued that the African higher education system is largely exogenous and ought to be more endogenous – directed towards local needs and understanding. With the increased focus on internationalisation of higher education, the question is how African higher education will change in the future. The chapters in this book will offer some perspectives on this. With the book *Asia as Method*, the Taiwanese professor of cultural studies Kuan-Hsing Chen (2010) argues that knowledge production is one of the major sites in which imperialism operates, and consequently calls for a de-imperialisation of knowledge. He argues that this can be done by taking history and geography into account. This book can be seen as a contribution to the de-imperialisation of knowledge in an African context.

References

Adamu, A.Y. (2012) 'Internationalisation of higher education in Africa: introducing credit accumulation and transfer system', *International Journal of Public Policy*, 8 (4), 199–213.

Adriansen, H.K. (2008) 'Understanding pastoral mobility: the case of Senegalese Fulani', *The Geographical Journal*, 174 (3), 207–222.

Adriansen, H.K. and Adriansen, I. (in press) 'Geopolitics of the university: a geo-historical study of universities in the Danish monarchy'. In Meusburger, P., Jöns, H. and Heffernan, M. (eds) *Geographies of the University*. Volume 12, Knowledge and Space Book Series. Springer Verlag.

Altbach, P.G. (2004) 'Globalisation and the university: myths and realities in an unequal world', *Tertiary Education and Management*, 10 (1), 3–25.

Altbach, P.G. and Knight, J. (2007) 'The internationalization of higher education: motivations and realities', *Journal of Studies in International Education*, 11 (3&4), 290–305.

Anderson-Levitt, K.M. (2003) 'A world culture of schooling?'. In Anderson-Levitt, K.M. (ed.) *Local Meanings, Global Schooling: Anthropology and World Culture Theory*. New York: Palgrave Macmillan, pp. 1–26.

Assié-Lumumba, N.T. (2006) *Higher Education in Africa: Crises, Reforms and Transformation*. Dakar: CODESRIA.

Assié-Lumumba, N.T. (2008) 'Higher education as an African public sphere and the university as a site of resistance and claim of ownership for the national project'. *12th General Assembly: Governing the African Public Sphere*. Yaoundé, Cameroon, 7–11 December 2008. Dakar: CODESRIA, pp. 1–30.

Assié-Lumumba, N.T. and N'Dri, T. (2009) 'African universities, imperatives of international reach, and perverse effects of globalisation', *ÖFSE Edition*, 15, 33–49.

Boli, J. and Ramirez, F. (1986) 'World culture and the institutional development of mass education'. In Richardson, J.G. (ed.) *Handbook of Theory and Research for the Sociology of Education*. Westport: Greenwood Press, pp. 65–90.

Breidlid, A. (2013) *Education, Indigenous Knowledges, and Development in the Global South: Contesting Knowledges for a Sustainable Future*. Sabon: Routledge.

Briggs, J. and Sharp, J. (2004) 'Indigenous knowledges and development: a postcolonial caution', *Third World Quarterly*, 25 (4), 661–676.

Brock-Utne, B. (2002) *Whose Education for All? The Recolonization of the African Mind.* New York: Falmer Press.

Brooks, R., Fuller, A. and Waters, J.L. (2012) *Changing Spaces of Education: New Perspectives on the Nature of Learning.* Croydon: Routledge.

Chen, K.H. (2010) *Asia as Method: Toward Deimperialization.* Durham: Duke University Press.

Connell, R. (2007) *Southern Theory, the Global Dynamics of Knowledge in Social Science.* USA: Polity Press.

Crossman, P. (2004) 'Perceptions of "Africanisation" or "endogenisation" at African universities: issues and recommendations'. In Zeleza, P.T. and Olukoshi, A. (eds) *African Universities in the Twenty-first Century, 2.* South Africa: CODESRIA, pp. 319–340.

Danida (2013) *Building Stronger Universities Phase II (BSU-II): Programme Document.* Denmark: Ministry of Foreign Affairs, Technical Advisory Services. Available at: http://dfcentre.com/wp-content/uploads/2014/02/BSU-phase-II-PD-document.pdf (accessed 27 January 2015).

Danida (2014) *Strengthening Research Capacity: Strategic Framework for Danish Support for Development Research 2014–2018.* Denmark: Ministry of Foreign Affairs and Danida. Available at: http://um.dk/da/~/media/UM/English-site/Documents/Danida/Partners/Research-Org/Strategi_DevelopmentResearch_web.pdf (accessed 27 January 2015).

Danske Universiteter (2011) *Building Stronger Universities in Developing Countries: First Phase, August 2011 – July 2013. Inception Report November 2011.* Denmark: Danske Universiteter. Available at: http://dkuni.dk/English/Our-Work/~/media/Files/Internationalt/BSU/Inception%20report%20introduction.ashx (accessed 27 January 2015).

De Ridder-Symoens, H. (ed.) (1992) *A History of the University in Europe. Volume 1: Universities in the Middle Ages.* Cambridge: Cambridge University Press.

Dei, G.J.S. (2011) *Indigenous Philosophies and Critical Education: A Reader.* New York: Peter Lang.

Dei, G.J.S. (2014) 'Indigenizing the school curriculum'. In Emeagwali, G. and Dei, G.J.S. (eds) *African Indigenous Knowledge and the Disciplines.* Rotterdam: Sense Publishers, pp. 165–180.

Dei, G.J.S., Hall, B.L. and Rosenberg, D.G. (2008) *Indigenous Knowledges in Global Contexts: Multiple Readings of Our World.* Toronto: University of Toronto Press.

Emeagwali, G. (2006) *Africa and the Academy: Challenging Hegemonic Discourses on Africa.* New Jersey: Africa World Press.

Emeagwali, G. (2011) 'The neo-Liberal agenda and the IMF/World Bank Structural Adjustment Programs with reference to Africa'. In Kapoor, D. (ed.) *Critical Perspectives on Neoliberal Globalization, Development and Education in Africa and Asia.* Rotterdam: Sense Publishers, pp. 3–13.

Emeagwali, G. (2014) 'Intersections between Africa's indigenous knowledge systems and history'. In Emeagwali, G. and Dei, G.J.S. (eds) *African Indigenous Knowledge and the Disciplines.* Rotterdam: SensePublishers, pp. 1–17.

Emeagwali, G. and Dei, G.J.S. (2014) *African Indigenous Knowledge and the Disciplines.* Rotterdam: SensePublishers.

Escobar, A. (2001) 'Culture sits in places: reflections on globalism and subaltern strategies of localization', *Political Geography,* 20 (2), 139–174.

Fanon, F. (1968) [1961]) *The Wretched of the Earth.* New York: Grove Press.

Gupta, A. and Ferguson, J. (1997) *Anthropological Locations: Boundaries and Grounds of a Field Science*. USA: University of California Press.

Hanson Thiem, C. (2009). 'Thinking through education: the geographies of contemporary educational restructuring', *Progress in Human Geography*, 33 (2), 154–173.

Haraway, D. (1988) 'Situated knowledges: the science question in feminism and the privilege of partial perspective', *Feminist Studies*, 14 (3), 575–599.

Hjortsø, C.N. and Meilby, H. (2013) 'Balancing research and organizational capacity building in front-end project design: experiences from DANIDA'S ENRECA programme', *Public Administration and Development*, 33 (3), 205–220.

Horton, R. (1974) 'African traditional thought and Western science'. In Wilson, B. (ed.) *Rationality*. Oxford: Blackwell, pp. 131–171.

Hountondji, P. (1990) 'Scientific dependence in Africa today', *Research in African Literatures*, 21 (3), 5–15.

Hountondji, P. (1995) 'Producing knowledge in Africa today. The Second Bashorun MKO Abiola Distinguished Lecture', *African Studies Review*, 38 (3), 1–10.

Hountondji, P. (1997) 'Introduction'. In Hountondji, P. (ed.) *Endogenous Knowledge: Research Trails*. Dakar: Codesria, pp. 1–34.

Johnson, A.T. and Hirt, J.B. (2014) 'Universities, dependency and the market: innovative lessons from Kenya', *Compare: A Journal of Comparative and International Education*, 44 (2), 230–251.

Jöns, H. (2007) 'Transnational mobility and the spaces of knowledge production: a comparison of global patterns, motivations and collaborations in different academic fields', *Social Geography*, 2 (2), 97–114.

Jowi, J.O. (2009) 'Internationalization of higher education in Africa: developments, emerging trends, issues and policy implications', *Higher Education Policy*, 22 (3), 263–281.

Knight, J. (2008a) *Higher Education in Turmoil: The Changing World of Internationalisation*. Rotterdam: Sense Publishers.

Knight, J. (2008b) 'Africa in relation to other world region'. In Teferra, D. and Knight, J. (eds) *Higher Education in Africa: The International Dimension*. Accra: African Books Collective, pp. 533–552.

Knight, J. and De Wit, H. (1995) 'Strategies for internationalisation of higher education: historical and conceptual perspectives'. In De Wit, H. (ed.) *Strategies for Internationalisation of Higher Education: A Comparative Study of Australia, Canada, Europe and the United States of America*. Amsterdam: European Association for International Education (EAIE) in cooperation with the Programme on Institutional Management in Higher Education (IMHE) of the Organisation for Economic Cooperation and Development (OECD) and the Association of International Education Administrators (AIEA), pp. 5–32.

Knorr-Cetina, K. (1981) *The Manufacture of Knowledge: An Essay on the Constructivist and Contextual Nature of Science*. Oxford: Pergamon Press.

Koehn, P. (2013) 'Donor-supported transnational higher education initiatives for development and research: a framework for analysis and a call for increased transparency' *Higher Education Policy*, 26 (3), 349–372.

Kraftl, P. (2013) *Geographies of Alternative Education: Diverse Learning Spaces for Children and Young People*. Bristol: The Policy Press.

Kuhn, T. (1962) *The Structure of Scientific Revolutions*. Chicago: University of Chicago Press.

Latour, B. and Woolgar, S. (1986) *Laboratory Life, the Construction of Scientific Facts*, 2nd edn. Princeton: Princeton University Press.

Leach, M. and Mearns, R. (eds) (1996) *The Lie of the Land: Challenging Received Wisdom on the African Environment*. Exeter: James Currey and Heinemann.

Livingstone, D. (2003) *Putting Science in Its Place: Geographies of Scientific Knowledge*. USA: University of Chicago Press.

Lulat, Y.M. (2005) *History of African Higher Education from Antiquity to the Present: A Critical Synthesis*. Portsmouth: Greenwood Publishing Group.

Maassen, P. and Cloete, N. (2006) 'Global reform trends in higher education'. In Cloete, N. et al. *Transformation in Higher Education – Global Pressures and Local Realities*. The Netherlands: Springer, pp. 7–33.

Madsen, L.M. and Adriansen, H.K. (2006) 'Knowledge constructions in research communities: the example of agri-rural researchers in Denmark', *Journal of Rural Studies*, 22 (4), 456–468.

Mamdani, M. (1993) 'University crisis and reform: a reflection on the African experience', *Review of African Political Economy*, 20 (58), 7–19.

MacPherson, I., Robertson, S. and Walford, G. (2014) *Education, Privatisation and Social Justice Case Studies from Africa, South Asia and South East Asia*. Oxford: Symposium Books.

Meusburger, P. (2015) 'Knowledge, geography of'. In Wright, J.D. (ed.) *International Encyclopedia of the Social & Behavioral Sciences*, 2nd edn, Vol. 13. Oxford: Elsevier, pp. 91–97.

Milton, K. (1997) 'Ecologies: anthropology, culture and the environment', *International Social Science Journal* 49 (154), 477–495.

Mohamedbhai, G. (2014) 'Massification in higher education institutions in Africa: causes, consequences, and responses', *International Journal of African Higher Education*, 1 (1), 59–83.

Møller-Jensen, L. and Madsen, L.M. (2015) 'Becoming and being an African scholar: a 15 year perspective on capacity building projects in Ghana', *Forum for Development Studies*, 42 (2), 245–264.

Mountz, A. (2002) 'Feminist politics, immigration, and academic identities', *Gender, Place and Culture*, 9 (2), 187–194.

Naidoo. R. (2010) 'Global learning in a neo-liberal age'. In Unterhalter, E. and Carpentier, V. (eds) *Whose Interests Are We Serving? Global Inequalities and Higher Education*. Hampshire: Palgrave/Macmillan, pp. 66–90.

Naidoo, R. (2011) 'The new imperialism in higher education: implications for development'. In King, R., Marginson, S. and Naidoo, R. (eds) *A Handbook on Globalization and Higher Education*. Cheltenham: Edward Elgar, pp. 40–58.

Nightingale, A. (2003) 'A feminist in the forest: situated knowledges and mixing methods in natural resource management' *ACME*, 2 (1), 77–90.

Norad (2012) *NORHED – The Norwegian Programme for Capacity Development in Higher Education and Research for Development*. Available at: www.norad.no/en/support/ norhed;jsessionid=651D812B699F94DE6A2B46F6EDCB5DD5 (accessed 27 January 2015).

Nygren, A. (1999) 'Local knowledge in the environment–development discourse: from dichotomies to situated knowledges', *Critique of Anthropology*, 19 (3), 267–288.

Obamba, M.O. and Mwema, J.K. (2009) 'Symmetry and asymmetry: new contours, paradigms, and politics in African academic partnerships', *Higher Education Policy*, 22 (3), 349–371.

Ogachi, O. (2009) 'Internationalization vs regionalization of higher education in East Africa and the challenges of quality assurance and knowledge production', *Higher Education Policy*, 22 (3), 331–347.

Olukoshi, A. and Zeleza, P.T. (2004) 'The struggle for African universities and knowledges'. In Zeleza, P.T. and Olukoshi, A. (eds) *African Universities in the Twenty-first Century*, Vol. 12. South Africa: CODESRIA, pp. 1–18.

Oyewole, O. (2009) 'Internationalization and its implications for the quality of higher education in Africa', *Higher Education Policy*, 22 (3), 319–329.

Pedersen, O. (1997) *The First Universities: Studium Generale and the Origins of University Education in Europe*. Cambridge: Cambridge University Press.

Rose, G. (1997) 'Situating knowledges: positionality reflexivity and other tactics', *Progress in Human Geography*, 21 (3), 305–320.

Sall, H.N. and Ndjaye, B.D. (2007–2008) 'Higher education in Africa: between perspectives opened by the bologna process and the commodification of education', *European Education*, 39 (4), 43–57.

Samoff, J. and Carrol, B. (2004) *Conditions, Coalitions, and Influence: The World Bank and Higher Education in Africa*. Prepared for presentation at the Annual Conference of the Comparative and International Education Society Salt Lake City, 8–12 March 2004. Available at: www.eldis.org/vfile/upload/1/document/0708/doc17679.pdf (accessed 29 April 2015).

Sehoole, C.T. (2008) 'Issues, policies, and developments of internationalization in Africa: comparative analysis'. In Teferra, D. and Knight, J. (eds) *Higher Education in Africa: The International Dimension*. Accra: African Books Collective, pp. 515–532.

Semali, L.M. and Kincheloe, J.L. (eds) (1999) *What is Indigenous Knowledge? Voices from the Academy*. New York: Garland Publishing.

Shizha, E. (2010) 'The interface of neoliberal globalization, science education and indigenous African knowledges in Africa', *Journal of Alternative Perspectives in the Social Sciences*, 2 (special issue), 27–57.

Shizha, E. (2014) 'Rethinking contemporary Sub-Saharan African school knowledge: restoring the indigenous African cultures', *International Journal for Cross-Disciplinary Subjects in Education (IJCDSE)*, 4 (1), 1870–1878.

Shizha, E. and Abdi, A.A. (eds) (2013) *Indigenous Discourses on Knowledge and Development in Africa*. Sabon: Routledge.

Sida (2013) *Review of Sida's Programme for Development Research, Final Report*. Sida Decentralised Evaluation 2013: 46. Available at: www.sida.se/contentassets/4c411257fa694deeaba7996af14a700e/review-of-sida8217s-programme-for-development-research_3734.pdf (accessed 27 January 2015).

Singh, M. (2010) 'Re-orienting internationalisation in African higher education', *Globalisation, Societies and Education*, 8 (2), 269–282.

Skovgaard-Petersen, J. (2008) 'Al-Azhar, modern period'. In Fleet, K., Krämer, G., Matringe, D., Nawas, J. and Rowson, E. (eds) *Encyclopedia of Islam*, 3rd edn. Leiden: Brill, pp. 208–212.

Smith, L.T. (2012) *Decolonizing Methodologies: Research and Indigenous People*. Croydon: Zed Books.

Teferra, D. (2008) 'The international dimension of higher education in Africa: status, challenges and prospects'. In Teferra, D. and Knight, J. (eds) *Higher Education in Africa: The International Dimension*. Accra: African Books Collective, pp. 44–79.

Teferra, D. (2012) 'Partnerships in Africa in the new era of internationalization', *International Higher Education*, 67, 19–21.

Teferra, D. and Altbach, P.G. (2004) 'African higher education: challenges for the 21st century', *Higher Education*, 47 (1), 21–50.

Teferra, D. and Knight, J. (eds) (2008) *Higher Education in Africa: The International Dimension*. Accra: African Books Collective.

UNESCO (2012) *Education and Skills for Inclusive and Sustainable Development beyond 2015. UN System Task Team on the post-2015 UN Development Agenda*. Available at: www.un.org/en/development/desa/policy/untaskteam_undf/thinkpieces/4_education. pdf (accessed 28 May 2015).

UNICEF and UNESCO (2013) *Making Education a Priority in the Post-2015 Development Agenda: Report of the Global Thematic Consultation on Education in the Post-2015 Development Agenda*. Available at: www.unicef.org/education/files/Education_ Thematic_Report_FINAL_v7_EN.pdf (accessed 28 May 2015).

Waters, J.L. and Brooks, R. (2012) 'Transnational spaces, international students: emergent perspectives on educational mobilities'. In Brooks, R., Fuller, A. and Waters, J. L. (eds) *Changing Spaces of Education: New Perspectives on the Nature of Learning*. Croydon: Routledge, pp. 21–38.

Winch, P. (1964) 'Understanding a primitive society', *American Philosophical Quarterly*, 1 (4), 307–324.

Woldegiorgis, E.T. and Doevenspeck, M. (2013) 'The changing role of higher education in Africa: a historical reflection', *Higher Education Studies*, 3 (6), 35–44.

Woolman, D.C. (2001) 'Educational reconstruction and post-colonial curriculum development: a comparative study of four African countries', *International Education Journal*, 2 (5), 27–46.

World Bank (1991) *The African Capacity Building Initiative: Toward Improved Policy Analysis and Development Management*. Washington: World Bank.

World Bank (2002) *Constructing Knowledge Societies: New Challenges for Tertiary Education*. Washington: World Bank.

World Bank (2010) *Financing Higher Education in Africa – The International Bank for Reconstruction and Development/The World Bank*. Washington: World Bank.

Yesufu, T.M. (1973) *Creating the African University: Emerging Issues in the 1970s*. Ibadan: Oxford University Press.

Part I

Capacity building of African universities

Asymmetrical power relations?

3 Dilemmas of knowledge production in Ugandan universities

Michael Whyte and Susan Reynolds Whyte

Introduction

One way to discuss knowledge production in African universities would be in terms of binary oppositions: endogenous vs exogenous, universal vs local, the Global North vs the Global South, Africa vs the West. That might be attractive because it would allow us to generalise about big pictures, large-scale trends and intellectual issues. In this chapter we choose a different approach, inspired by the philosophy of pragmatism, the methods of ethnography and our own long experience of working with two universities in Uganda. We analyse knowledge production in relation to sets of dilemmas confronting institutions and individuals. That is to say, we concentrate on tensions and contradictions within, rather than oppositions between, settings. We are attentive to the ways actors deal with difficult alternatives. The dilemmas we examine are two: how to achieve excellent research and teaching while managing on scarce resources; and how to meet both international standards and local needs for research.

Pragmatic philosophy (Bernstein, 1997; Rorty, 1991) provides an overall frame for our approach by emphasising situated action rather than timeless principles. It encourages us to consider how people deal with problems and assess the outcomes in on-going processes. Importantly, it sees knowledge as emergent from practice, and as tentative, revisable and multiple. Historical circumstances and practical challenges are fundamental for understanding the generation and use of ideas. This kind of approach fits well with ethnographic methods, which demand specificity and contextualisation in order to analyse phenomena. Progressive contextualisation helps us move from the narrow and specific to more general patterns. But starting from practice in specific conditions makes us aware of diversity and change in the realities we study.

Those realities cannot be reduced to a simple 'local' knowledge practice that exists in opposition to a 'universalistic' one. Nor can they be adequately understood in terms of the difference between 'European' and 'African' universities. To make that contrast is to generalise at the expense of ignoring the contradictions within particular university settings. The realities of knowledge production are infused with conflicting values and they exist within political economies and specific histories that combine to encourage certain processes of knowledge production and constrain others.

In this chapter we build on 25 years of involvement off and on with university capacity-building within social sciences. That long engagement has encouraged our recognition of incongruities and specificities. By formulating situations in terms of dilemmas, we hope to avoid reducing conditions to categorical characteristics or even caricatures. We will try to present our colleagues as we see ourselves: attempting to navigate tensions and contradictions. We want to learn about these dilemmas and consider how cooperation works with the specificities of universities in Africa. Only in this way can we hope for the kind of mutuality for which Nyamnjoh and Nantang (2002: 21) call in their introduction to a special journal issue on African universities in crisis.

It was our good fortune that the country where we conducted our first long-term research later came to be prioritised by the Danish International Development Agency (Danida). This has allowed us to continue working in Uganda from the time we were green PhD students ourselves through the years when we have had the privilege of supervising Ugandan PhDs and continuing research with Ugandan colleagues. Beginning in 1989, when Danida launched its Enhancement of Research Capacity (ENRECA) programme, until now as we struggle with Danida's Building Stronger Universities framework, we have worked with six different projects of collaboration with Ugandan universities. They have been anchored at two different institutions: Makerere, one of Africa's large old distinguished universities, located in the capital Kampala, and Gulu, a small young public university in northern Uganda. Working for so long in the same country means that we have followed changes over more than 40 years. It does not necessarily mean that we can say with authority just what characterises universities in Uganda.

We have found ourselves, and still find ourselves, trying to appreciate what is specific to Ugandan universities, and to Makerere and Gulu. We wonder how we can respect what is unique to them, while still providing useful resources based on our own Danish university culture. We are aware of forces that tend to veil differences. The much-appreciated support for our collaboration comes from the Danish state, from Danida under the Ministry of Foreign Affairs. Although the frameworks set by the funders provide a certain amount of latitude, they still have some of the elements of state-based planning described by James Scott (1998) in his seminal *Seeing like a State*. That kind of seeing entails the use of telescopes pre-focused on certain given criteria and on ends already envisioned by the planner. Referring to Scott, Van Rinsum writes: 'Cooperative programs, aimed at reinforcing local universities, tend to be evaluated according to the terms and criteria of Western academia, and implicitly, of the Western epistemology with its "high modernity" ideology' (Van Rinsum, 2002: 39).

In fitting one size, or one plan, to all, local realities, knowledge and specificities are ignored. There is a danger that 'building stronger universities' as a Danida development strategy can come to mean simply ameliorating a lack identified from the top, looking down. A focus on 'catching up' with universities in the

Global North, rather than trying to understand realities on the ground and how they have changed may limit the capacity of the programme to support more appropriate developments in given settings.

Specificities of Ugandan university history

In a sense, 'African universities' do not exist. At least, it is useful to dismiss the notion of African universities as one type. For there is an enormous range of universities in Africa today, a half century after the great push to independence in the 1960s. There are national institutions established early in the colonial era, large and small more or less specialised public universities, as well as new private institutions whose owners expect to make a profit. They are, sure enough, universities in Africa and as such they share certain characteristics and problems. But they are also products of specific social, political and economic contexts. They have distinct histories and their teachers and researchers have different social experiences. This is so even for universities within the same country. To understand what these institutions are, how they function and – above all – where they might be heading, demands specific knowledge.

Uganda's university history is part of its political history, beginning in the time of the Uganda Protectorate (see Opio-Odongo, 1993). Early education emphasised moral formation and technical skills needed for administration and practical functions (this was also the case elsewhere, as described in Chapter 2). Makerere was established as a trade and technical school in 1922 and became a college of the University of London in 1950 as the University College of East Africa (Dinwiddy and Twaddle, 1988: 195). At its inception, Makerere, like the other African universities of its generation, was extroverted in the sense of externally oriented (Hountondji, 1995). It was based on a British model and was intended to produce a cadre of elite intellectuals and professionals who would lead Uganda to independence and continue to run the country within the framework built up in the colonial period. The function of higher education in that era was knowledge consumption rather than production. There was a need for competence to run the state apparatus, and that was transmitted through teaching in the mode of the metropolitan institution, the University of London.

As the oldest university in East Africa, Makerere enjoyed distinction in the 1950s and 1960s; it did indeed produce elites and leaders not only for Uganda, but for the whole region. It consolidated and expanded after Ugandan independence in 1962, gaining independent university status in 1970. The Makerere Institute of Social Research (MISR), to which we were affiliated during our PhD fieldwork from 1969–1971, was a vibrant centre of knowledge production, attracting foreign and Ugandan scholars.

In the 1970s universities across Africa were being oriented towards objectives of national development. They were not merely extroverted, but turned towards their own endogenous problems and plans. 'The goal was to appropriate these, in origin colonial exogenous, institutions so that they could play a central role in the development and modernising of postcolonial Africa' (Van Rinsum, 2002: 35).

But Uganda's national history took a different turn with Idi Amin's coup in 1971 and the ensuing 15 years of misrule, conflict and economic decline. In the era of 'the regimes,' many academics fled the country. Those who remained struggled to maintain standards in conditions of low or no pay, and an atmosphere of political menace. University staff members, formerly part of the economic elite, were at pains to manage:

> [D]uring the 1970s, as in the 1960s, a Makerere university teacher's status could be measured roughly by the altitude of his or her residence on Makerere hill. But, whereas under Obote's first government one went up the hill as one's career and family expanded, under the Amin regime the most desirable residences became the ones at the very bottom of the hill and movement, such as there was, was therefore to where water still reached the taps, and where gardens were large and fertile enough for staff to grow more of their own food, as the value of salaries declined with inflation.
>
> (Dinwiddy and Twaddle, 1988: 196)

Stories are told of university lecturers who grazed their cows on campus and sold the milk; some taught their classes only in the morning so they could drive their vehicles as taxis in the afternoon.

With the advent of the National Resistance Movement (NRM) in 1986 under its leader Yoweri Museveni, stability slowly resumed for most of the country. Inflation, which had been extremely high for many years, entered single digits in the mid 1990s, but civil service living standards never returned to pre-Amin levels. For example, the base salary (including housing allowance) for a senior lecturer at Makerere University was $160 a month in January 1994. Tuition in a good Kampala primary school at this time was over $200 a term per child (Whyte, 1994: 4). The problem remains to this day, not least in universities, where official salaries are simply not enough to meet soaring educational expenses at elite schools – the kind that can be expected to provide children with the same advantages that their parents enjoyed. In their recommendations for further reform at Makerere, Musisi and Muwanga (2003: 62) point to the need for new approaches to educating the children of its staff. 'Class reproduction' requires additional incomes, whether from inside or outside the university system.

In the new political climate of increased liberalisation in the late 1980s and 1990s, two forms of privatisation transformed higher education, which had always been a government enterprise. One was the growth of privately established and funded institutions. The first private university in Uganda, Islamic University in Mbale, opened in 1988. Others followed so that by 2011 there were 26, accounting for a third of student enrolment (Mugabi, 2012). About half of these were faith-based, offering curricula infused with religious principles (Muslim, Catholic, Anglican and Seventh Day Adventist). With a rapidly growing population and budget cuts to the public universities, there is an enormous market for higher education, not least among those who did not meet the standards for government stipends in public universities.

The second form of privatisation occurred within the public universities themselves. In dire financial straits, Makerere began to take privately sponsored students in 1992 (Musisi and Muwanga, 2003: 16–17); while this may not have restored it to its former glory, it transformed the university: 'Substantial revenues from this source were responsible for the revitalization of Makerere University – the Makerere miracle – after decades of neglect owing to civil war' (Munene, 2009: 262).

In addition to privatisation, the growing demand for university education was addressed in a geographical mode by the NRM government. In line with its hallmark policy of decentralisation, it established regional universities: in the west, Mbarara University, 1993; in the north, Gulu University, 2002; in the east, Busitema University, 2007. The trend continues as these establish campuses and constituent colleges within their catchment areas.

Makerere still dominates the university landscape in size, infrastructure and prestige. But the emergence of peripheral universities in the process of decentralisation has created new local centres, at least partially oriented to their regions as well as to Makerere and universities in the Global North. Gulu University, with which we are working, is a good example. Its specific history belongs to that of north central Uganda. As stability came to the southern part of the country after 1986, disorder continued in the north for two more decades. The NRM government fought the Lord's Resistance Army in a war that subjected people to atrocities from both sides. For nearly ten years, the national army interned almost the entire population in camps, impoverished and dependent on humanitarian aid.

It was in these conditions, when the war was at its height, that Gulu University was established in 2002. The town itself was relatively secure and swollen with displaced people. But the surrounding countryside was a war zone; travelling to the displaced people's camps was dangerous. Coming from the capital Kampala, buses and vehicles risked attack and moved in convoys once they crossed the Nile into the Acholi sub-region. The new university found it hard to attract teachers, many of whom had to travel from the southern part of the country. Resources were scarce and research was hardly a possibility. It was not until 2008, two years after the Cessation of Hostilities Agreement, when the camps were closed and life began to return to normal, that the university could start to grow. A Danida-supported enhancement of research capacity programme began to support Gulu University in 2009 and others were coming in at the same time. The recent regional history, still evident in the crumbling huts of the emptied camps and the lack of rural infrastructure, gives special poignancy to the university's motto: 'For Community Transformation'.

Gulu was and is peripheral to Makerere. Many of its faculty members were trained at Makerere and in the first years some were seconded from there. Kasozi (2003: 126) describes the dependence of new universities on Makerere for teaching services. As the oldest tertiary institution, Makerere is synonymous with university education. In early 2015, we attended a 'thanksgiving' to celebrate the Master's degree of one of our students. As part of the festivities, six small children sang in Acholi: 'Let us study hard and we too can reach Makerere.' But the 600 guests were giving thanks for the degree he had just completed from Gulu University. Those who are going on for PhDs must seek supervisors or co-supervisors from Makerere, because there are so few qualified to supervise on the Gulu faculty. Makerere offers many more disciplines; Gulu, for example, lacks programmes in sociology, anthropology, political science and philosophy. Makerere is a mass university with 40,500 students; Gulu is growing but still small with about 6,000. Moreover, Makerere is located in the capital city where many Gulu faculty members have houses and families. They frequently make the arduous six- to eight-hour journey on a bad road to spend some days in the country's largest city.

Gulu is peripheral to Makerere, but it is central for three other institutions of higher learning in the region: it has a constituent college in Lira and campuses in Kitgum and Hoima. It is *the* university for Northern Uganda, well integrated into local networks of politicians and civil servants. The difference in scale means that Gulu University has a prominent place in regional society, while Makerere operates in a national arena. Gulu University is known and respected by people of the area; it is on the way to becoming 'our' university for northerners. But Makerere has an iconic status; even in the north, the children sing about Makerere, not Gulu University.

Dilemmas of knowledge production and economic constraints

The production of knowledge, like any production, is constrained by the economy in which it exists. The first dilemma is found in the effort to achieve high standards in research and teaching, while struggling to manage in current political economic conditions. As public universities, Makerere and Gulu are subject to similar general trends. Government budget support to higher education, upon which public universities were once totally dependent, has fallen drastically. But the historical circumstances and the differences in age and size are important for the way dilemmas are played out. With privatisation and student fees, Makerere is now one of the country's biggest taxpayers, rather than being a major recipient of taxpayer resources. Gulu struggles to cover its expenses, especially when the central government is slow in transferring the agreed funds for undergraduate education.

Mahmood Mamdani addresses this dilemma in his book *Scholars in the Marketplace* (2007) tracing the history of 'reform' at Makerere and its consequences for research and teaching. He points out that the university faced severe underfunding in the 1980s and early 1990s because of the financial crisis of government and its prioritisation of primary over higher education. The decision to admit private fee-paying students alongside those on government stipends was a kind of survival strategy embraced by faculty and students, and warmly supported by the World Bank and government (Mamdani, 2007: 3). Initially, privatisation was vitalising because student fees went directly to the departments where they were enrolled; the money was used to top up teachers' salaries and improve department facilities. Suddenly teaching became attractive again and academic staff met the rapidly growing number of students in day, evening and night classes.

Mamdani argues that privatisation may be acceptable and even beneficial as long as the priorities of the university are publicly set and remain sound. But privatisation became commercialisation as the university subordinated its goals to the market. In order to attract more fee-paying students, departments began to offer courses that would sell, even if they did not have the capacity to teach them at a high enough academic standard. There were turf wars between faculties and between departments over who could teach which lucrative course, and there was poaching of staff between faculties in order to gain teaching capacity in the profitable areas. The Faculty of Arts, which had low student numbers and a weak economy at the outset of the 1990s, took advantage of the new possibilities. It developed vocationally oriented degrees in fields such as Environmental Management, Tourism, Mass Communication and Organisational Studies that attracted large numbers of students hoping for jobs in NGO and donor programmes. The professional faculties like Law, Medicine, Technology and Agriculture were much less involved in developing new commercially based courses.

How were postgraduate education and research affected by the commercialisation? The university and the government stopped support to postgraduate studies in 1994. These courses became fee-based and postgraduate students had to find their own funding. Departments and faculties pursued two alternatives. They developed 'taught' Master's courses in attractive fields for fee-paying students. And they turned to donors, especially for the funding of PhD education. The former strategy continued commercialisation beyond the Bachelor's degree; for fee-paying students, research training was often minimal and students hoped mainly to get a job or to qualify for promotion. The strategy of seeking donor support has other problems according to Mamdani. He claims that donors tend to set the research agenda, and that they encourage applied, more than basic, research. We return to this issue shortly, but for the moment, we take the point that public universities have been not only privatised, but also commercialised. Research, whether basic or applied, is heavily dependent on external sources for funding.

It was in the 1990s and the early 2000s that foundations like Rockefeller and bilateral programs like Danida and SIDA (Swedish International Development Cooperation) began to support postgraduate education and collaborative research. There followed a rush of agreements between Ugandan faculties or departments and universities in Europe and North America. Makerere was by far the biggest beneficiary of these programmes, while Mbarara University came second. Johane Crane, who worked at Mbarara University, uses the phrase 'scrambling for Africa' to describe the efforts of research organisations from North America and Europe to make collaboration agreements with African universities. She suggests that the trend is particularly salient within the field of global health, where partnerships provide exogenous medical researchers access to poor and sick populations. But as she also points out, the relationship is not simply one of dominant Western interests and subordinate African science. Mbarara researchers had their own agendas and the relationship was one of 'friction' in Anna Tsing's sense of abrasive interaction between diverging interests and perspectives, rather than smooth implementation of a North American programme (Crane, 2013: 12).

Research collaboration has continued, and it is also present, albeit on a more modest scale, at a new university like Gulu. Involvement in such arrangements has been attractive to Ugandan universities on many grounds – idealistic, academic, intellectual and social. But certainly one major appeal was economic. These collaboration agreements offered much needed facilities and income not provided by their own government. Budgets included research infrastructure like computers, internet, library facilities and vehicles for transport to the field. Impressive new buildings appeared on Makerere hill. There were stipends for Masters and PhD students, funds for fieldwork, salary top-ups and transport allowances. For the faculties that had not benefitted from commercially successful courses for fee-paying students, such partnerships were a particular boon. For individual staff members, the extra income was most welcome. Their salaries were insufficient, costs of living rose constantly, they had large extended families and they had aspirations for their children.

Research enhancement capacity programmes were not the only source of funding for academic work. Beginning in the 1990s, international donors increasingly called on national scholars to carry out appraisals, baselines, evaluations, background studies and training for their activities. Such contracts often pay quite well but the timeframes are tight. A consultancy syndrome has emerged at universities that Mamdani (2007) would probably also consider a form of commercialisation. There is a market for Ugandan consultants with academic qualifications and connections (and sometimes even a pattern of paying kickbacks to the organisation officials who provide contracts). As Mamdani emphasised in relation to teaching, some topics are more attractive than others. For example, there is demand in the areas of public health, gender issues and conflict resolution – fields in which NGOs, bilateral and multilateral agencies have activities. Here too the difference in scale between Makerere and Gulu is marked. Makerere staff members do consultancies and studies in the national arena, including in northern Uganda. Gulu faculty members find opportunities with the organisations that work in their own region, including the many donors with humanitarian and development projects in the conflict and post-conflict situation.

In many cases, individual staff members take on this kind of work in addition to teaching. They carry it out themselves, sometimes with the help of student research assistants. Another pattern is for the unit – a department or research centre – to take on a contract and form a team for the work. This can mean some overhead for the unit and extra income for team members. During our collaboration with the Child Health and Development Centre at Makerere, it was undertaking such assignments for organisations. In 2002, for example, the

Annual Report shows that our partner hosted seven consultancies and projects funded by: University of California, World Bank, GTZ (German Technical Cooperation Agency), USAID, UNICEF, WHO/TDR (Special Programme for Research and Training in Tropical Diseases) and the Rockefeller Foundation. The work and report writing provided learning experiences for younger scholars, brought groups out to the field, familiarised them with different districts in the country, encouraged discussion and built team spirit.

Obviously this is not basic research and often it does not produce really new knowledge. The Terms of Reference define the output; there is a tendency to use methods mechanically – a certain number of Focus Group Discussions and Key Informant Interviews that get reduced to selected quotations in reports that lack historical depth and local context. But here too, it is important to differentiate. Some consultancy assignments allow more latitude in terms of empirical focus, methods, and analysis. When the Child Health and Development Centre undertook a study about the feasibility of introducing the HPV (human papilloma virus) vaccine to prevent cervical cancer, they built on and expanded their earlier studies on adolescent girls and attitudes towards sexuality and medicines. The contract lasted for some years and they were able to follow through from planning to the actual introduction of the vaccine for schoolgirls. The current Director of the Child Health and Development Centre, Anne Katahoire, is discriminating about which externally financed projects to take on. Some, like the HPV study, provide scope for enhancing competence in key areas and are of longer duration; others are 'quick and dirty' and she does not think the Centre should bid for them.

There are assignments that fall between academic collaboration and short-term consultancies. For instance, in 2012 the Office of the UN Resident Coordinator in Uganda supported a conference on peace building in northern Uganda, organised largely by our colleagues at Gulu University. Funds covered the publication of a book (Ovuga, 2012) printed in Uganda, in which three of the seven chapters were written by scholars involved in our collaboration and concerned our common research focus on post-conflict reconstruction.

Financial constraints for university staff and postgraduate students make it attractive, even necessary, to take on externally financed projects, whether they be research enhancement collaborations or consultancies. Perhaps inadequate financing of universities is the most basic problem, but in everyday activities it is experienced as constant shortage of staff and of time (see also Kagoda and Katabaro (2013) on this problem in faculties of education). This is most pronounced at Gulu University, where resources are scarcest. Our colleagues there have heavy teaching loads both during the week and on weekends, when many MA courses are held. Scarce senior academic staff must also devote time to attend university committees and meetings, to deal with university politics and to supervise postgraduate students.

Moreover, all our academic colleagues have heavy responsibilities for large extended families whose members are poorer and less well connected than they are. They are constantly trying to help with family problems and are obliged to attend family events like funerals and weddings. All of these university and family obligations exist in addition to the demands of consultancies, projects and international activities and squeeze the budgeting of time (see Chapter 9 for an account of life as an African scholar).

Protected time for research, reading and publishing is scant. In a recent conversation, an older highly respected professor at Makerere exclaimed: 'There is a disease called telephonitis! When we are home in Uganda, the phone is constantly ringing. There is no time to think. It's only when we have study visits at European universities that we can read and write.' Under these conditions, the production of knowledge is inhibited. We see it even in very concrete situations involving our PhD students. When they go back to Uganda for fieldwork after spending some months in Denmark, the agreement is that they should devote themselves full time to their research projects. Nevertheless, it has happened that Gulu PhD students take on a consultancy to earn extra money or are assigned to teach a course because there is a shortage of staff.

In such circumstances, scholars face dilemmas about how to prioritise personal and institutional needs for resources in relation to the kinds of knowledge production and teaching they might like to do. Mamdani (2007) takes the view that economic dependence means that donors set the research agenda. But our experience is that some academic collaboration is quite broad in terms of topics. This may have been more true earlier on than it is today. Certainly the first ENRECA project (1989), in which Copenhagen University collaborated with Makerere Institute of Social Research, allowed PhD students to choose their own topics. In 1994, negotiating the TORCH project with the Child Health and Development Centre, we met Ugandan partners who refused some of our suggestions; we spent two weeks talking until we reached an agreement on the research focus of the programme that met the needs and visions of both sides. Three of the four projects we have had with Gulu University had topical themes (e.g. land conflicts, governance and trust), but they were discussed with our partners before applications were submitted and there was a good deal of room for PhDs to define their own projects. In terms of the degree of freedom to define one's own research topic, the conditions of our Ugandan partners are not so different from our own. We too respond to calls by funding bodies for applications under given themes; we too experience that opportunities for free individual research grants are declining.

One feature that consultancies, applied research, collaborative research and postgraduate training opportunities share is a focus on useful knowledge. This orientation may be seen in terms of what Cooper (2006), referring to Etzkowitz, calls the 'third mission' of universities (the first two being teaching and basic research), emerging at the end of the twentieth century. 'Use-inspired basic research' is responsive to socio-economic development and collaboration with civil society, although not 'applied' in the sense of addressing a pre-defined set of requirements. Cooper suggests a restructuring of PhD education in South African universities to better undertake such use-inspired research, while leaving actual applied research consultancies to non-academic organisations. He places PhD training in the context of historical developments in North American and European universities. But he does not mention economic constraints; it seems that the University of Cape Town had no need of external funding to create a PhD programme, nor any need for the income that consultancies provide for departments or individuals. In this South Africa is the exception.

The situation is different in Uganda, and in most other Sub-Saharan African countries. Underfunding necessitates externally financed PhD education; it is the reason for the many donor programmes supporting capacity development. As for consultancies, policy and applied research tasks defined by 'clients' provide welcome additions to institutional and family budgets. (Such contracts are more common in countries like Uganda with many international NGOs and donor-funded development projects.) Dilemmas arise because it is difficult to reconcile economic necessities and high standards for research and research education. The challenge is how to combine the 'use-inspired' with the depth and breadth that a solid grounding in basic research requires. In our experience, there is general consensus that research should be 'useful'; the social science and public health studies in which our colleagues engage are all related to some or another identification of Ugandan needs.

Dilemmas of international standards and Ugandan needs

This brings us to another dilemma in the production of knowledge at Makerere and Gulu Universities, one that has a long history in debates about university teaching and research. To what extent should they be oriented to international standards rather than the needs of the regional and national societies in which they exist?

In its 1945 report, the Asquith Commission, which recommended upgrading Makerere to university status, was careful to acknowledge the need for 'useful service to the community'. But it also endorsed the idea of a liberal education at international standards: 'An institution with the status of a university which does not command the respect of other universities brings no credit to the community it serves' (quoted in Dinwiddy and Twaddle, 1988: 197). It seems to us that this tension between international orientation and local needs is related to, but not identical with, the discussion about extroverted (or 'universalistic') and endogenous kinds of knowledge (Hountondji, 1995). The latter contrast requires a great deal of care, since all knowledge production and exchange is localised, as Livingstone (2003) suggests. It is placed both socially and geographically, but it is transmissible and changing, without one clear origin or owner. We think that framing the debate and dilemma in terms of standards and needs more accurately reflects the concerns of our Ugandan colleagues.

The significance of international standards is reflected in the requirements for faculty promotion at both Makerere and Gulu. Publications in international peer-reviewed journals form one important criterion for advancement up the academic ladder. Obtaining a PhD degree is another. Most on the Gulu faculty do not have the latter qualification. If they are not fortunate enough to get a

PhD stipend from a foreign funded enhancement of research capacity project, they struggle on their own to develop a concept paper and then a proposal. Getting time to do the research is difficult; finding a supervisor usually means identifying someone at Makerere, because so few faculty members at Gulu are qualified. Under these conditions, PhDs take many years, if they are completed at all.

Those who do obtain their PhD degrees are respectfully addressed and referred to as Doctor. The prestige is great for those who study and obtain their qualifications from universities abroad. It is recognised that facilities, supervision and academic milieu are strong in European and American departments. Opportunities there are sought after. When Danida changed its policy in 2007 and required those on stipends to register for Masters and PhD degrees in their own countries, it was something of a disappointment, even though it was understood that PhD programmes should be strengthened in African universities. Fortunately, study stays at Danish universities are still financed, and these are so valued that some parents are even willing to leave small children in the care of others for months in order to spend time in an international milieu. Danida does not pay for African scholars to bring their families, even if they are in Denmark for a whole year, so the opportunity comes at the price of a considerable personal sacrifice.

Ugandan students want to expand their horizons with an international educational experience, in the same way as students from the academic North. Being part of an international community of scholars is valued and that is one of the reasons why the collaborative projects we know have been so well received at Makerere and Gulu. It is noticeable too that knowledge, approaches and connections acquired by those who spent time abroad during their PhD studies are brought back by them. The links between them and their northern university hosts can be reactivated as we have seen in many instances.

At the same time, the colleagues with whom we have worked are committed to engagement with local communities and local problems. When PhD students have been free to choose their own topics, they identified issues that were of concern in Uganda. This was not only because Danida expected them to do research in their own country, as Mamdani (2007) suggested. In the years of collaboration with the Child Health and Development Centre, we were impressed with efforts to work with districts, to listen to local leaders, to bring back to 'stakeholders' whatever was learned in a research project. At one point the unit was thinking of itself as a resource centre for district health and community development officials. There were close relations with Ministry of Health officers and more than once our colleagues took us to government offices to discuss our joint work.

At Gulu University with its motto 'For Community Transformation', there is a strong assumption that research should be applicable to local problems and that knowledge and skills should be shared with frontline local actors. An example is the course on 'patientology' that colleagues from Health Sciences recently offered for nurses and clinical officers in the area where we are collaborating on a long-term health surveillance project. The rootedness of the university in local society is strong, with local leaders, including the District Council Chairman, registered for Masters degrees and Gulu University graduates employed in local administration and NGOs. When we go into the field together with our Gulu colleagues, we meet their students manning sub-county offices and running development projects.

The problem is that spending too much energy on serving the local community and engaging in applied research may not further publishing in international peer reviewed journals. In principle, applied social science research can certainly be worked up for publication, but in practice the written records of these efforts often end as reports that few others ever see. It is hard to translate these empirical experiences into the conceptual frameworks, theoretical approaches and comparative perspectives that are necessary for exchange in the international marketplace of academic journals. If the opposition between international standards and meeting local needs is to be transcended, perhaps Gulu should add some of its own standards to criteria for promotion – such as developing and carrying through projects 'for community transformation' in which non-university actors are involved. In other words, the international standards may not be sufficient as a measure of the production of relevant knowledge.

The tension between meeting local needs and striving for international standards was an issue of concern for the late Chango Macho, when he was Eastern Regional Tutor for Makerere. He addressed it provocatively in a lively debate carried on in the pages of the Uganda Argus in 1970. Government, at that time headed by Milton Obote, was proposing a new medical curriculum of highest international standard in order to increase the numbers of Ugandan doctors in the country. Chango Macho argued that what Uganda needed were personnel trained to work in local dispensaries and to help to expand health services to local communities. Such people – including doctors – should be prepared for the job at hand rather than to 'international' standards. When it was argued that such medical qualifications would not be recognised 'internationally' Chango Macho agreed. This was his point. Training doctors to Ugandan, rather than to an international professional, standard would impact health issues at home and also solve the problem of brain drain. Forty years later these views seem naive and would be offensive to top Ugandan academics. But in his argumentative way Chango Macho pinpointed an issue that permeates the production and reproduction of knowledge in Ugandan universities. Tertiary education should train people to work – and to find work – in today's Ugandan reality. An excessive focus on 'international' standards by programmes financing university development may force attention away from local needs.

Chango Macho called for skepticism about 'international standards' – indeed about any set of standards that claimed to be true. His criticism of the colonial enterprise was clear, but it did not inspire him to promote the wholesale return to 'African traditions'. His eyes were fixed firmly on Ugandan's present, on Ugandan needs rather than international standards. In our view, this remains the heart of the issue. But the questions are these. First, what are local needs? Second, who has the authority to identify them?

President Yoweri Museveni seems in no doubt. An article from 2015 in the *Sunday Monitor*, a national newspaper, has him criticising 'educationalists for promoting arts courses which he says are responsible for the high level of unemployment of university graduates'. The president refers to 'unmarketable courses like conflict resolution and psychology' while praising Mbarara University of Science and Technology where he claimed that no graduate is unemployed (Wandera, 2014). Here, and in other public comments, the president seems keen to promote 'science' as opposed to courses (psychology and conflict resolution here, and also development studies) that focus simply on 'thinking' (Tumushabe, 2014). Kasozi (2003) argues as well that Ugandan universities need to concentrate more on the natural sciences in order to contribute to national development.

Our job here is not to debate the relevance or irrelevance of arts courses or science courses. It may be that science graduates are more apt to find jobs in today's Uganda (though there is no evidence offered to back the proposition). But does this then demonstrate what Uganda needs? It seems that the identification of needs is a matter of disagreement. The very courses that the President dismissed as unmarketable are the kinds that had a good market among Makerere students, who saw job possibilities in them.

Not only is it debatable what kinds of education best suit the Ugandan market, it is also not clear what local needs really are. The many NGOs and aid agencies identify local needs for which their activities are the answer. Different members of local society may have their own views on the matter. Given the liberty to choose their own research projects, postgraduate students have a wide range of ideas about 'relevance'. So too do the northern funders of research capacity enhancement programmes. Hountondji sees the orientation to international standards as extroversion entailing the unfortunate effect that 'research programs, units and facilities are still not aimed at answering the needs and concerns of the societies that host them' (Hountondji, 1995: 4). He first made this point in earlier publications, and it may not hold so clearly now. The two Ugandan universities we know entertain both the values of international scholarship and the commitment to local needs. However, local needs are multiple, and can be used to justify many different kinds of research and teaching.

In his analysis of dilemmas of South African sociology in a global context, Burawoy (2004) offers a distinction between four kinds of sociology oriented towards academic or extra-academic audiences and falling within instrumental or reflexive knowledge traditions. Distinguishing so many dimensions makes for an elaborate framework, but the important thing is that Burawoy tries to avoid over-generalisation. In an exemplary appreciation of the history of South African social science and the diversity of universities within the country he writes:

> An externally driven professionalism and a market driven research agenda creates an ever deeper divide between the historically white universities

whose comparative advantage lies in professional and policy sociology and the historically black universities whose comparative advantage lies in their proximity to local communities and therefore to a critical and public sociology.

(Burawoy, 2004: 24)

He concludes by summarising a dilemma that resembles the one we have identified. South African universities cannot isolate themselves from hegemonic US sociology, but they must appropriate elements from it that can be incorporated within a South African sociology 'on terms defined by South African priorities' (Burawoy, 2004: 26). Like Burawoy, we see the dilemma of international standards and local needs as one that must be analysed with respect to historical and institutional locations, rather than endogenous and extroverted structures.

Conclusion

In this chapter, we have shown how two Ugandan universities experience dilemmas of knowledge production somewhat differently because of their particular historical, political and geographical locations. Our perspective on these differences is based in our participation in capacity-building efforts funded by the Danish International Development Agency. Like other donors, Danida treats universities as development projects. It requires that objectives and milestones be set and it has a framework that determines in general what activities, expenditures and procedures can and should be undertaken. Although university capacity enhancement programmes vary, with more flexibility and possibilities for local adaptation in some, there is a general tendency to work towards international standards for the recipient universities. PhD courses, completed degrees, research facilities and publications are the kinds of activities that typify building stronger universities. The danger is that a general template does not recognise that peripheral universities may have other histories, other roles to play and other needs.

As we have argued, international standards are not simply 'exogenous'. That may have been the case at some earlier historical point, but they have certainly been 'endogenised' for many decades now. That is why we prefer to speak of dilemmas faced by our Ugandan colleagues. The question is not whether knowledge production is about exogenous or endogenous content and methods. It is rather about what kinds of knowledge and ways of learning specific universities should be helped to enhance. Should there be an emphasis on basic research, policy research, strategic research, applied research or action research? In some Ugandan contexts, perhaps building stronger university projects should recognise consultancies and applied research as ways of producing knowledge and enhance capacity to do it in more innovative and critical ways. If community transformation is the mission of a university, then objectives and indicators should be set accordingly. Successful outreach projects might merit the same value as publications in peer-reviewed journals.

56   *Whyte and Whyte*

The terms 'exogenous' and 'endogenous' are more relevant for describing sources of funding than knowledge and values. For most universities in Africa, with the exception of South Africa, economic dependence on external funding for research is a fact. That is why a clear recognition of the political economic conditions for knowledge production is a necessary starting point. But instead of simply seeing universities in Uganda as dependent on funding from the Global North, we argue that programmes and policy must dig deeper, starting with ethnographic analyses of the economic and career challenges of academic life in context. In this light, we included an account of the dilemma that economic constraints present for colleagues engaged in knowledge production.

In emphasising dilemmas of knowledge production, we wish to orient attention towards the challenges that any attempt at mutual understanding and collaboration must meet. We must consider how to learn about these dilemmas and how to develop cooperation that works with the specificities of universities in Africa. Only in this way can we hope for the kind of mutuality that might exist despite inequalities in resources.

We argue that appreciating differences is crucial, not least when designing donor driven collaboration. University collaboration works best when it is based in mutual knowledge and experience or, the more usual situation, where there is clear recognition that one or more parties in the collaboration lacks such specific and grounded understanding. In other words, not understanding one another can be a fruitful starting place, so long as this condition is recognised and so long as dealing with the understanding gap becomes part of the collaboration itself. Where such grounded understanding is lacking, universities may spend money and provide resources, but collaboration in the sense of encouraging sustainability is less likely.

References

Bernstein, R.J. (1997 [1988]) 'Pragmatism, pluralism and the healing of wounds'. In Menand, L. (ed.) *Pragmatism: A Reader*. New York: Vintage Books, pp. 382–402.
Burawoy, M. (2004) 'Public sociology: South African dilemmas in a global context', *Society in Transition*, 35 (1), 11–26.
Cooper, D. (2006) 'International restructuring of higher education: comments on implications of global trends, for restructuring of sociology in South Africa', *South African Review of Sociology*, 37 (2), 260–292.
Crane, J.T. (2013) *Scrambling for Africa: AIDS, Expertise, and the Rise of American Global Health Science*. Ithaca: Cornell University Press.
Dinwiddy, H. and Twaddle, M. (1988) 'The crisis at Makerere'. In Hansen, H.B. and Twaddle, M. (eds) *Uganda Now*. Oxford: James Currey.
Hountondji, P. (1995) 'Producing knowledge in Africa today, the second Bashorun M.K.O. Abiola Distinguished Lecture', *African Studies Review*, 38 (3), 1–10.
Kagoda, A.M. and Katabaro, J. (2013) 'Funding teaching practice in two East African Universities: its influence on the behaviour and practices of a supervisor', *Africa Education Review*, 10 (1), 117–133.

Kasozi, A.B.K. (2003) *University Education in Uganda: Challenges and Opportunities for Reform*. Kampala: Fountain Press.

Livingstone, D.N. (2003) *Putting Science in its Place: Geographies of Scientific Knowledge*. USA: University of Chicago Press.

Mamdani, M. (2007) *Scholars in the Marketplace: The Dilemmas of Neo-liberal Reform at Makerere University, 1989–2005*. Kampala: Fountain Press.

Mugabi, H. (2012) 'The role of private universities in the provision of higher education in Uganda: growth and challenges', *Africa Education Review*, 9 (2), 213–229.

Munene, I.I. (2009) 'Anticipated developments: East Africa's private universities and privatisation of public universities in the global context', *Africa Education Review*, 6 (2), 254–268.

Musisi, N.B. and Muwanga, N.K. (2003) *Makerere University in Transition 1993–2000: Opportunities and Challenges*. Oxford: James Currey.

Nyamnjoh, F.B. and Nantang, B.J. (2002) 'Introduction to a Special Issue: African universities in crisis and the promotion of a democratic culture: the political economy of violence in African educational systems', *African Studies Review*, 45 (2), 1–26.

Opio-Odongo, J.M.A. (1993) *Higher Education and Research in Uganda*. Nairobi: African Centre for Technology Studies.

Ovuga, E. (ed.) (2012) *Peace and Peacebuilding: Concepts and Perceptions in Northern Uganda*. Kampala: Gulu University and United Nations Uganda.

Rorty, R. (1991) 'Method, social science and social hope'. In Rorty, R. *Consequences of Pragmatism*. Hertfordshire: Harvester Wheatsheaf.

Scott, J. (1998) *Seeing Like a State: How Certain Schemes to Improve the Human Condition Have Failed*. New Haven: Yale University Press.

Tumushabe, A. (2014) 'Arts courses to blame for joblessness – Museveni', *Daily Monitor*, 24 October 2014.

Van Rinsum, H.J. (2002) '"Wipe the blackboard clean": academization and Christianization – siblings in Africa?' *African Studies Review*, 45 (2), 27–48.

Wandera, D. (2014) 'Arts courses are useless – Museveni', *Daily Monitor*, 14 August 2014.

Whyte, M. (1994) *Inventory of Current Anthropological and Sociological Scholarship and Research In Uganda*. Sweden: Stockholm University: Development Studies Unit, Department of Social Anthropology.

4 Collaborative education across continents

Lessons from a partnership on sustainable resource management education

Bevlyne Sithole, Torben Birch-Thomsen, Ole Mertz, Trevor Hill, Thilde Bech Bruun and Thuita Thenya

Introduction

This chapter brings together a multi-disciplinary group of authors drawn from partner universities from southern Africa and east Africa, who are collaborating with the Danish Universities Consortium for Environment and Development – Sustainable Land Use and Natural Resource Management (DUCED-SLUSE), to analyse partnerships over collaborative education and capacity building in Africa. The aim of the collaboration is to enhance teaching and research as an interdisciplinary exercise within the area of development, environment and natural resource management (Treue et al., 2004). The SLUSE initiative was launched and funded by the Danish Government for collaborations with Malaysia (Malaysian University Consortium on Environment and Development-MUCED); Thailand (Thai University Consortium on Environment and Development-TUCED); and with the Southern African Consortium of Universities for Development and Environment (SACUDE). In 2012, the programme was extended to east Africa in Kenya where DUCED-SLUSE is collaborating with the University of Nairobi, Wangari Maathai Institute (WMI) (Kenya-SLUSE) which also co-funds the project. Funding for DUCED-SLUSE started in 1998 and continued for eight years. The SACUDE-partnership was only funded for three years (2002–2005), whereas in Southeast Asia (MUCED-SLUSE and TUCED-SLUCE) it started earlier (1999 and 2000) and was funded over a longer period of time. Therefore, the Southeast Asian consortia are more established and have assumed a more consolidated form as the courses have been devolved, adapted and integrated within local curricula. In recently involved countries like Kenya, the programme provides an interesting insight of expansion, based on long-term experience from other countries. Experiences from TUCED-SLUSE and MUCED-SLUSE demonstrate that collaboration can continue beyond external funding and Magid et al. (2005) argue that the continued interest for such programmes in Asia and Africa demonstrates their importance in a globalising world. Thus, the need for courses of a more applied nature, where students are exposed to a wide array of development issues and are trained as development practitioners, is obvious. In this chapter, we explore experiences from southern and eastern Africa and show the importance of working with diverse partners in diverse situations to develop a self-sustaining programme.

As already outlined, the various SLUSE consortia have evolved under diverse institutional and political settings and have been running for different durations between various partners, giving rise to variable experiences, perceptions, practices and understandings of partnerships and how they should be formulated and work. According to Traynor et al. (2007) there is no one SLUSE model or experience, rather there are several, due to the high degree of local adaptation needed each time a new consortium or partnership is formed. A strength is the cognisance of the variability and difference that adds to the nature and complexity of the relationships between DUCED-SLUSE and partners from the Global South. In this chapter, we differentiate between experiences and opinions from the newly established programme in Kenya-SLUSE and the more established programme of SACUDE-SLUSE. Further, we analyse reflections from key interviews conducted by the lead author with a small sample of students and lecturers/partners structured around three open-ended questions on experiences and opinions about collaborative education. The key questions were: a) what do you think are the big outcomes for you from collaborative education? b) what was your experience of the collaboration through SLUSE? and c) what do you think of the outcomes of it? Responses from the key interviews are presented alongside views drawn from existing data in the project especially from SACUDE-SLUSE to achieve balance in the analysis as most of the responses from the key interviews were collected from the DUCED-SLUSE and Kenya-SLUSE staff and students. Responses during the key interviews are organised into the following four thematic questions and these create the organising framework for the chapter:

- How do partners in SACUDE-SLUSE and in the Kenya-SLUSE perceive partnership with DUCED-SLUSE?
- How do partners and students view learning together in the joint field course?
- How do partners and students view partnerships with communities where the field course work is conducted?
- How do partners work together to produce employable graduates for the environment and development sector?

Data from on-going self-assessment processes within the programme are used as the basis for exploring issues across a wider group. The lead author is an outsider to the programme and draws on her social science background and experience of higher education in southern Africa to add to the existing and ongoing analyses.

Collaborative education across continents

In 1996, the Danish parliament identified human resource development through university cooperation as an area of priority. In response to this, the DUCED-

SLUSE was formed. The aim of the DUCED-SLUSE was to facilitate the development of the human resource base in participating universities in Denmark and recipient countries. The main objective was to develop capacity in education and research on an interdisciplinary basis, in areas of development and environment and natural resources management in particular regions chosen by the Danish Environment and Development Assistance (DEDA). According to Traynor et al. (2007) the preliminary objective during the pilot phase of the programme was threefold; first to strengthen the Danish resource base within interdisciplinary environmental research, second to develop an interdisciplinary environmental postgraduate training programme and third to prepare the establishment of collaboration with universities and research organisations in DEDA countries. Later the purpose of the collaboration was amended to focus on addressing development challenges regionally while making targeted interventions to inform policy and governance decision makers.

One of the key principles of the collaborative programme was the acknowledgement that the synergy between practical and theoretical knowledge can produce both academic qualifications and practical solutions that will enhance sustainable land use (Traynor et al., 2007). To achieve this synergy, interdisciplinary learning and teaching approaches are used to make it clear to students that there are no perfect answers to problems. However, they offer a range of perspectives, opportunities and concerns, which are often contradictory in settings that are highly differentiated and socially contested. Figure 4.1 illustrates how the interdisciplinary approach can provide a comprehensive understanding of problems that can lead to improved policy decisions.

Hill et al. (2008a) explain that the collaboration with SACUDE-SLUSE is developed around the joint field course in the hosting countries, which is devised, implemented and assessed together. Elements of the field-based course are broken up into three stages: the first stage is called the preparatory stage at the host university lasting 4–5 days. The second stage of the course is fieldwork conducted over 8–11 days. The third stage is called course conclusion and lasts 4–5 days at the host university with an examination.

Collaboration among universities through joint education programmes is not new (Aarts and Greijn, 2010; Gaillard, 1994; Teferra, 2012). Higher education in Africa has always been a collaborative and an international affair, owing to its history and trajectory (Teferra, 2012). Higher education partnerships are diverse, complex and numerous; they are, however, not always successful or effective (Hettne, 2001; Kwaramba, 2012). Some are very successful and effective in their delivery and impacts, witnessed by knowledge development and transfer. Hessels and van Lente (2008) find that African universities face the dual imperative of engaging in a new knowledge society and contributing to basic development within their own societies. In the current global realities, where global is local and local is global, mutual benefits of collaborations should not be underestimated or overlooked. The rise in partnerships between universities in the Global North and Global South has transformed the production, utilisation and creation of knowledge (Kwaramba, 2012; Teferra, 2012). The importance of higher

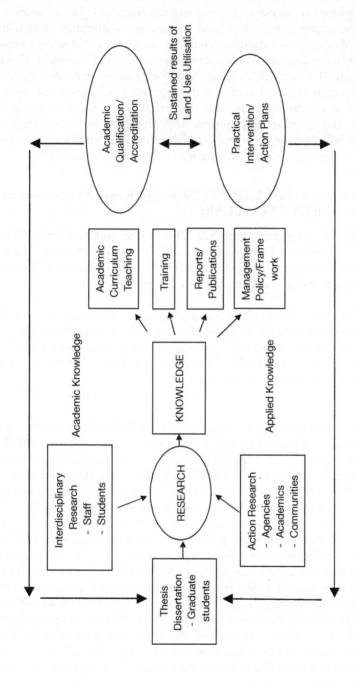

Figure 4.1 SLUSE concept model (developed by SLUSE consortia partners)

education for socio-economic development particularly in Africa has become more obvious (Aarts and Greijn, 2010; Friesenhahn, 2014; Materu, 2007; Muller, 2000). Development agencies, regional organisations and nation states are placing new expectations on higher education institutions, demanding production of new types of graduates who have the requisite skill sets to operate in a global world and are relevant to socio-economic needs of the region (Knight and Yorke, 2003). Otara (2012) argues that if we want to move development forward, then there is a need to change the approach to educating and training graduates from overtly academic and theoretical orientations to workplace educational and training programmes. The challenge for these types of partnerships will be how to organise collaborative education in a way that learning globally contributes to local capacity (Aarts and Greijn, 2010).

How do partners in SACUDE-SLUSE and in Kenya-SLUSE perceive partnership with DUCED-SLUSE?

DUCED-SLUSE's partnership with SACUDE-SLUSE and Kenya-SLUSE has been shaped by different partners, events and settings. For example, Traynor (2005) describes the partnership with SACUDE-SLUSE as a journey of discovery where the road is always under construction. She states:

> We have achieved some significant developments. We have discovered the ability to collaborate across universities and academic disciplines. We have found confidence to undertake extended fieldtrips with students from an array of educational and cultural backgrounds and with disparate interests, and mould them into coherent groups.
>
> (Traynor, 2005: 118)

The diversity of university partners within SACUDE-SLUSE means that there are differences in positioning, needs and circumstance relative to higher education experience in the collaboration. This leads to differences in the conception of the collaboration. For example, the perceptions and views of partners in Kenya-SLUSE expose newly formed views regarding the partnership that reflect, to some degree, the newness of the partnership as well as the shifting relationships as partners manoeuvre around each other within the programme. Further, perceptions at this stage may draw on past history and experiences of collaboration on similar projects rather than be based on current experiences from the collaboration with DUCED-SLUSE. Partners in Kenya-SLUSE state that reaching some level of shared understanding about what the partnership should be takes time and, even when this is understood and defined, reality can be different from what is desired. The collaboration opens up new opportunities for academic interaction and effort, builds capacity for both students and lecturers while at the same time develops a shared experience of process and outcomes of the collaborative programme within the context of higher education.

Collaboration in the SACUDE-SLUSE is seen as a relationship where partners have understood and are comfortable with the terms of engagement. In the SACUDE-SLUSE, strong ties have developed among partners leading some partners to suggest that when there are close personal ties the collaboration is strong. In comments made by both the DUCED-SLUSE and the SACUDE-SLUSE, working together is seen as a product of the mutual respect and easy communication among the partners. However, such relationships are not easy to create, there needs to be time, opportunity, resources and spaces where relationships can form. Collaboration can thus be seen beyond the contractual documents, as a product of processes and events crafted in informal arenas where formality and boundaries are not as important. The cost of forming good relationships among partners are rarely supported within the budgets and funding arrangements. The SACUDE-SLUSE experience suggests that synergies between individuals may be as important and in some situations should be afforded greater value than synergies between organisations.

There is general acknowledgement among partners that getting adequate support for programmes is an ongoing challenge for most partner universities in Denmark and those in Kenya and southern Africa. For example, partners in the Kenya-SLUSE express a wish to broaden the scope of the collaboration to include exchange visits for students and lecturers from Africa in the partner DUCED-SLUSE universities. Adequacy of local and external resources to participate effectively in the programme influences the dynamics in the programme. A partner from Kenya-SLUSE explains that where there is a dependency on external resources to support local action and processes, this can be the basis for creating imbalances in power among partners. In the SACUDE-SLUSE, partners have worked hard to balance out power relations in the collaboration to a point where Traynor (2005) was calling the programme a southern African programme. She locates the ownership of the programme with the SACUDE-SLUSE and makes an explicit statement regarding the shift in the form, identity and nature of partnership since it was started. This shift in ownership and identity of the programme evident in SACUDE-SLUSE reflects the level of adaptation possible within the programme relative to the general framework and changes that can occur as a programme develops from inception to implementation. While in the SACUDE-SLUSE, ownership has shifted towards the partners in the Global South, in the Kenya-SLUSE, the programme is still in a state of flux, where partners are working to even out the power differentials that may be still evident. For example, a partner in the Kenya-SLUSE programme observes:

> It is how the story is told that concerns us and we want to be part of telling it ourselves, we don't always get that opportunity, but I believe we should tell it so that we don't feel our voice is dwarfed by the Global North. I am not even sure how this collaboration came about, what the expectations were but it has been difficult, it is like we were behind and following, I am not sure if we have caught up with our Northern colleagues yet.
>
> (Key interview, Kenya-SLUSE partner)

The manner by which programmes are initiated and evolve plays an important part in shaping initial perceptions and views regarding ownership at a start of a programme. Creating opportunities in the programme for disclosure where students and partners feel able to function cohesively, coherently and effectively and efficiently is an important part of developing a strong collaboration and a strong joint course.

The DUCED-SLUSE partners see the programme as recognition of mutual interests. A partner from the DUCED-SLUSE working with Kenya-SLUSE observes that it is the opportunity to link up that is important, how it is accessed and seen is left as part of the evolving relationship. The idea that the relationship among the partners should evolve as the programme takes shape to allow its identity to shift as the programme grows is explained in the following comment:

> SLUSE only took off when it's a win-win situation, serves the University programme and the South see an opportunity to link up. There are not many opportunities for them to go to the field and practise science. But we have had to be creative in how we put the programme together because of limited resources. The benefits of the programme became visible after they tried it, they could see it worked and bought into the idea much more, the practice helped.
>
> (Key interview, DUCED-SLUSE partner)

There are challenges facing partners in Africa that influence the nature of the partnership. Dependency on external funding to support research and fieldwork varies among partners in SACUDE-SLUSE and Kenya-SLUSE. Views drawn from DUCED-SLUSE partners indicate a high awareness of the difficult circumstances of the African partners – that is, the heavy teaching loads; the limited local funding to support research; low remuneration packages; and a highly constrained research environment. One of the DUCED-SLUSE partners observes that because of the limited funding available in the collaboration with Kenya-SLUSE, the partners have had to be very creative in the way they have developed and supported the programme. Partners are operating under very different conditions and are driven by different imperatives and thus collaborating under these circumstances can be a big challenge. The differences between the situations of the participating institutions in Global North and Global South play out in the level of participation and engagement feasible in various activities. African counterparts in the collaboration have a different configuration of time and effort dedicated to the collaborations because of their situation both within and external to the higher education institution. One of the partners from the SACUDE-SLUSE acknowledges that while differences among partner universities exist and present difficulties in the partnership, processes and solutions to address them become part of defining the partnership. They state:

> We should not worry about the level of complexity and differences of approach etc. – this is what we want – consider that both North and South

students themselves often come from quite different training and cultures – so we already have a great diversity, added to this we have different degrees/courses/training all coming together in the course. We must not look or aim for common outcomes – the idea in undertaking a joint project between Global North and Global South is that there will always be agendas – recognise and celebrate them – do not seek commonality, even in terms of methods – we can teach the same even use the same books however interpretation and site specificity will alter our lens. I think both North and South staff also develop through the process and we must not lose sight of that in the process as it is an important outcome. It is all about personalities and not material for me – I still believe that without the staff we have it would not work – you cannot force it! We have different points of starting – both sides need to understand this. Both sides bring in new technical skills and also just new approaches to the same techniques – if that makes sense.

(Key interview, SACUDE-SLUSE partner)

Generally, the view in the programme is that real collaboration between partners is feasible despite the diversity within and across consortia. For example, a partner from the DUCED-SLUSE working with Kenya-SLUSE discusses the evolving relationship between partners as follows:

Our collaborators have a different way of doing things, certainly when we started this was very clear to us and there were many misunderstandings, there was something there, but our colleagues are strong and they argue their positions. I would say things have changed now compared to where we started, and each country is different, certainly economic situation and standing matter in how they negotiate and what they negotiate for.

(Key interview, DUCED-SLUSE partner)

In the case of SACUDE-SLUSE, the relationship has matured over time and general consensus is that it works. Having a relationship that is working is explained by a key partner in SACUDE-SLUSE as follows:

Diversity is what makes it unique and it works! Yes there is a difference in participation (idea of interdisciplinarity and passive recipients of an existing process, tour guide!) and collaboration (more proactive and notion of transdisciplinarity, have a voice and it is listened to!) The French call it something like 'bricolage' – in other words – let it play out and we will work with what come sounds so un-structured but seems to work for us at times but that is ok we have some rules but need to adapt and be accepting of this.

(Key interview, SACUDE-SLUSE partner)

Differences between and among partners do not hamper collaborations, rather they are considered as an opportunity for relationships to evolve, mould and thrive based on lessons being learnt. One outcome of this acceptance of difference

Figure 4.2 Students conducting a semi-structured interview with focus on the importance of 'home-gardens' to women's livelihood at SLUSE joint field course (DUCED-and SACUDE-SLUSE), in Swaziland (Zombodze) January 2004

Photo: T. Hill.

is that multiple and different configurations of agreements have been developed over the implementation of the joint field course between the DUCED-SLUSE consortium and partner universities within the SACUDE-SLUSE and Kenya-SLUSE. The idea that one goes into collaboration accepting blurriness and murkiness creates an opportunity for the collaboration to evolve and is the defining feature of this programme. The lack of desire for clearly defined boundaries and definition of concepts and process suggests a preference for a level of elasticity that allows for moulding of different groups and universities as a viable institutional base for the joint field course, producing in the end many varieties of partnerships in the programme.

How do partners and students view learning together on the joint field course?

The joint field course provides an opportunity for students from universities in Denmark and east and southern Africa to work across disciplines and for students to work with others from different university traditions in new environments that are culturally foreign (Treue et al., 2004). Students in the programme come from diverse institutional and geographic backgrounds and represent a variety of cultures and disciplines (Bob et al., 2005). Bob et al. (2005) found that diversity at various levels in the programme, once embraced, brings significant educational benefits creating an opportunity where the dynamic interchange between different life experiences, disciplines, perspectives and identities can define and enrich the learning experience. Partners in the universities in east and southern Africa see the joint field course as an opportunity to provide students and staff with field experience.

Within the joint field course there are differences in how partner universities and consortia address stage 1 of the course when the students are prepared. A partner from the DUCED-SLUSE, who has been working in Kenya found that the challenges may arise because of the differences in the level and type of preparation students receive leading up to attending the joint field course and states:

> We have established a modus operandi, lectures, group work, whereas that part of the course hasn't taken off with our partners. We have discussed it, the issue has come out of the evaluations. When the students meet they are not at the same level, the local students come unprepared but are willing to take part therefore students from the Global North have ideas about the projects and lead. There is a lack of synchrony between the partners on some of the elements of the program.
>
> (Key interview, DUCED-SLUSE partner)

Differences in levels of preparations are generally exposed during the field course when the students are formed into groups. For example, on some courses, students from Kenya-SLUSE found that students from the DUCED-SLUSE had already prepared what they want to do during the field course before they arrived and it was difficult for the local students to 'get them to open the box and add to it'. So it was sometimes difficult for local students from Kenya to contribute or participate. As a result students could be in a group but work individually to meet their course requirements for the assessments. One of the students from the DUCED-SLUSE describes how differential preparation for the joint field course affects group dynamics and morale during the joint field course in this comment:

> The Kenyan students were keen to learn and to see how we work, they knew the context, there were students from different disciplines, and after discussing we came to an understanding for the things that we may not have thought about, it was stressful because it was difficult to agree. There was not enough local preparation or interdisciplinary interaction, there was no similar preparation to what I got in the north for students in Kenya, there were a lot of things new to them, but it was different for different students, we have to produce a report, they don't. Maybe if they are asked to write a similar report they would be more involved and contribute more during fieldwork, rather than helping with fieldwork. The interpretation of data

could benefit with more involvement from the local students. They don't get the same benefit we did, they did not get involved in all the aspects as we did.

(Key interview, DUCED-SLUSE student)

Comments about unequal preparation and requirements raise questions about how the joint field course is perceived. Currently, the students from the DUCED-SLUSE who participated in the programme in Kenya feel that the differences in level and type of preparation places them in a privileged position with respect to how they participate in the joint field course. Consequently, Hansen (2013) finds that the lack of synchrony between requirements for the course among the SLUSE partner universities can influence the dynamics among the students that can be seen during the joint field course. For example, Bob et al. (2005) observe that students from the University of Swaziland did not follow a specific preparation course and did not write a synopsis while students from the University of KwaZulu-Natal participate on a voluntary basis, and often sacrifice part of their holidays to participate in the joint field course. Students from the University of KwaZulu-Natal got credit simply by participating in the field course and did not have to present and defend a formal report. In the Kenya-SLUSE, where the programme is starting, the requirements for participation are that local students can get credit from participating and generating a report from the fieldwork. Bob et al. (2005) also found that because the students in the SACUDE-SLUSE did not have the same amount of preparation as the students from the DUCED-SLUSE and were not required to deliver a final report at the end of the fieldwork, this gave them a different stake in the course. Mlipha and De Neergaard (2005) attribute some of the problems in the group work to what they term north–south differentiation in pre-fieldwork training. For example, they find that while the students in the DUCED-SLUSE have two months preparatory field preparation course, their counterparts in the SACUDE-SLUDE do not go through the same courses or preparation process. Thus, Mlipha and De Neergaard (2005) conclude that Southern African students in the programme do not have the same feeling of ownership as the DUCED-SLUSE students. They state:

> Students might feel forced to work on a research project defined by their counterpart, without having had any influence on it. Since southern African students often have much better knowledge of the context than the Danish students, they can strongly resent the fact that they have not had more influence on the writing and the synopsis.
>
> (Mlipha and De Neergaard, 2005: 50)

Mlipha and De Neergaard quote a statement from a student in Botswana who indicates that they were now starting to feel ownership because they felt they had a choice and no one was telling them what to do anymore. Mlipha and De Neergaard (2005) identify time as a big constraint to forming good relationships among students. Regardless of the difficulties, one of the students from the

SACUDE-SLUSE quoted in Hill et al. states: 'The group work and fieldwork is hard, exciting, difficult, interesting and frustrating and you learn a lot about culture, methods, each other and most importantly about yourself' (Hill et al., 2008a: 122). They observe that the most highly rated aspect of the course was student cooperation during group work, though a minority of the students encountered difficulties.

Generally, opinions among students from DUCED-SLUSE who participated in the Kenya-SLUSE courses indicate both awareness and discomfort with some of the asymmetries in the groups. For example, a DUCED-SLUSE student who participated in the Kenya-SLUSE states:

> I get the feeling the students in the other universities are under prepared and just assist us in our ideas and projects. They comment and contribute, I would call it participation not collaboration. I would like to see joint preparation for the course together, maybe they come here, we identify the problems together and decide on the tools together. We had separate living arrangements, I would have preferred for us to be together, we were quite separate.
>
> (Key interview, DUCED-SLUSE student)

Some students from DUCED-SLUSE described the type of participation of local students in groups during the field course in Kenya as 'just assisting us' or 'just following and doing what we wanted to do'. This description of participation as 'just following' raises important questions at conceptual and practical level about the nature and level of integration achieved in groups. In the joint field course, efforts are made to provide positive reinforcement on the students' individual strengths to encourage them to share their skills in their groups. This has the triple effect of encouraging the lateral, horizontal and vertical understanding of problems being addressed, but there are differences that influence the internal group dynamics (Hill et al., 2008b). Some comments from students in the SACUDE-SLUSE in Botswana suggest that students are mostly optimistic and exhibit a desire to work together despite cultural discomforts. One of the students from the DUCED-SLUSE describes his participation in a field course in Swaziland as life changing in ways that he had not expected; he learnt more than he had anticipated at an academic and cultural level. Bob et al. (2005) find that constituting groups is always a big challenge as the partners must balance many factors and this combined with requirements for different outcomes leads to a tendency for the DUCED-SLUSE students to work as a sub-group and to dominate their counterparts, who have difficulties negotiating an equal footing. Magid et al. (2005) explain that whereas students from DUCED-SLUSE are often freshmen, partner country students may often be mid-career professionals pursuing their Master's degree with extensive knowledge of the field of study or related issues. However, while local students may have the upper hand they may be trapped in conventional modes of approaching development problems while some of the freshmen may have the advantage of looking at problems from a new angle. At times, partners in the Kenya-SLUSE note that students working in the groups sometimes operate in parallel and this can be due to how students' preparation is handled by partner universities. They find that for some thematic areas, collaborating in groups works perfectly well and there is a good dynamic in the groups and among the lecturers, while in other cases, there is division and the groups do not work well. Reviews of the SLUSE consortia are generally positive with partners and students acknowledging that the ability to work in groups is challenging but a necessary skill. As more field courses are being run collaboratively, partners in the Kenya-SLUSE have found that some of the asymmetries evident in the field course in the earlier courses are being addressed and the field course is starting to run more smoothly. One student from the DUCED-SLUSE who participated in the field course in Swaziland and is quoted in Bob et al. (2005) was initially sceptical of his role and responsibilities in the group during the fieldwork but states:

> I left the village and the trip as a whole having learnt so much more than I anticipated. We were all filled with warm satisfaction at having learnt to live with each other and people from a vastly different reality from the one we know.
>
> (Bob et al., 2005: 64)

Most comments from students and partners in the joint fieldwork underline the high value students placed on the exposure to interdisciplinary research and being exposed to learning in an intercultural learning in the field. One of the students from the DUCED-SLUSE who participated in the field course in Kenya states that:

> It was really good, a brilliant experience not only academic, I tried out quantitative and qualitative methods, it was a good chance to do that, what mainly stuck in my mind was the social environment, the bringing together of our team. Five northern and three local students, it was an intense experience but very challenging and unexpected. Challenging because I always thought I was easy to get on with but suddenly it was different, very striking experience for me as a student. We had a topic – livestock we had no background. Local students were veterinary students. We got on well together and we were complementary, they could fill in a lot of the context, we were from different backgrounds so it worked out. Preparations were different for us and for the local guys, they handled it with different purpose, we learnt a lot from them and we had lots of questions and they knew a lot.
>
> (Key interview, DUCED-SLUSE student)

Students from the DUCED-SLUSE relied heavily on students from local partner universities, as they lacked sufficient background and familiarity with the country and community situations they were working in and the problems that they were addressing during the field course. Some comments made by the DUCED-SLUSE

Figure 4.3 Student group presenting their findings to the community at the end of the field course at SLUSE joint field course (DUCED- and SACUDE-SLUSE) in Swaziland (Zombodze) January 2004

Photo: A. De Neergaard.

students, who participated in the field course in Kenya, suggest that participation could be seen in terms of the dominance of students from the DUCED-SLUSE in theoretical knowledge versus dominance of students from the SACUDE-SLUSE and the Kenya-SLUSE who had extensive practical experience. Students from the SACUDE-SLUSE felt that years of theory in the classroom had prepared them adequately for the field course.

How do partners and students view partnerships with communities where fieldwork is conducted?

During the field course, much time is spent living and working in rural community settings to give students a real learning experience. For each joint course, arrangements are made by partners to select a location for the field course. The SLUSE consortium enters into agreements with the local communities hosting the field based course (Traynor, 2005). Before each field course, partners visit the proposed field sites to engage with the communities and other stakeholders to identify research problems and organise logistics. Mlipha et al. (2005) find that over the years the selection process has been altered and adjusted to suit the local and external partners. Experience in the SACUDE-SLUSE demonstrates the importance of working in communities where there is a clear structure or organisation. This organisation then becomes the local host and partner institution during the field course. On some field courses, the community and organising committees are paid and enter into the agreement as business partners. These agreements are brokered by the partner universities. In the Kenya-SLUSE, students and the host families are well informed of the negotiation and are also briefed extensively on what to expect from each other. While clearly agreements are brokered and the permission is granted by the community to be part of the joint field course, it is important to note that in some instances those granting permission may not communicate with the wider population, and second, the process of permission giving may itself be contested. These factors can complicate the dynamics within the community and change the architecture of the joint field course where the relationships are shifting relative to the community members' view of the permission.

Problem identification and formulation of research questions are an important part of the field course. After a few years, the programme has developed a number of core topics that are tested for relevance each year (De Neergaard, 2005). De Neergaard acknowledges that although the objectives of the course are educational rather than developmental, the field course constitutes a significant effort in identifying some of the challenges the communities face. Some DUCED-SLUSE students felt uncomfortable and disconnected with the community because of the requirement to identify a topic before they got to the field and state:

> It's a bit funny because in the course we are talking about problem focus and responding to the communities/policymakers or others, but really we go there with an idea of what we have to do, we plan how we are going to do and even think about and make the tools. So when we are there really it is our questions and our tools. I cannot see how the information I collected can be used by the community it was just for my report.
>
> (Key interview, DUCED-SLUSE student)

One of the students from the DUCED-SLUSE found that he only felt comfortable to be learning in a community, once his group had learnt to work within the rhythms set by the community. Working to the rhythms of the community is a challenge as the field course has a fixed duration. During the field course, a delicate balance must be achieved where the research must be linked to students' own needs and educational purposes, but at the same time be focused on the needs and pace of the community. De Neergaard (2005) finds that the expectations from the community are therefore high. According to Traynor (2005), communities ask about the results of the research that the students carry out, therefore feedback meetings are conducted at the end of the field course to provide an opportunity for the community to hear from the students on issues relevant to them. But in the SACUDE-SLUSE experience, De Neergaard (2005) suggests a need to be very cautious during the feedback as he argues that it is neither realistic nor recommendable for results to be considered as advice to communities as there might be a risk that recommendations may propose solutions based on a superficial understanding of the local problem and context or an inadequate grasp of the relevant discipline. Consequently, during the feedback the students stress the educational role rather than the developmental role in their feedback. De Neergaard observes that even when care is taken communities can still interpret the presence of the students and lecturers in their own way. Some of the students who participated in the field course in Kenya expressed concern, because the joint field course has a problem focus without the requisite resources or support for communities to address the problems.

There are significant benefits to communities and these should not be downplayed. These can include material benefits including wages and purchases (Hill et al., 2008a; Traynor, 2005). Hill et al. (2008a) shows that the joint field course can yield significant benefits to the community where the results and analysis of research activities can be aligned with a particular development activity as happened in Madlangala, South Africa, where local people provided accommodation and catering for students during the field course as part of an effort to build capacity to manage a community based tourism venture. The Madlangala example demonstrates how working in partnership with a community organisation can extend the experience of learning for the students while benefiting the community. Host organisations involved in negotiating arrangements for the field course benefit from their interactions and gain confidence in planning and executing responsibilities associated with the field course. The income derived from hosting has become the basis for developing other projects in the community or, in the case of Swaziland, the money was used to purchase inputs for farming. However, despite the clear benefits derived by communities, there does seem to be a moral dilemma expressed by the DUCED-SLUSE students who participated in the field course in Kenya about how to help the host communities more. For example, some of the students from the DUCED-SLUSE in partnership with the students from the Kenya SLUSE have initiated a goat project. The goat project is supported from funds raised by a cohort of DUCED-SLUSE students in collaboration with students Kenya-SLUSE from the same field course. The implementation of the goat project has been difficult because as one of the students from the DUCED-SLUSE states:

> Benefits to communities are definitely something we should talk about more in the course ... we are raising expectations, what are we doing there, even with the goat project, there were more people waiting ... in the whole context the goats are small I think, SLUSE should be talking and thinking about this. Local people didn't really benefit. I didn't think of it like that to be honest I assumed the lecturers have taken care of that, maybe the local university who found the site.
>
> (Key interview, DUCED-SLUSE student)

Figure 4.4 Student group, translator and the project manager visiting a community
poultry project financed by the municipality. SLUSE joint field course
(DUCED- and SACUDE-SLUSE), in South Africa (Pepele sub-village,
Madlangala, Eastern Cape) March 2007

Photo: T. Birch-Thomsen.

Students from the Kenya-SLUSE who are also involved in the goat project
acknowledge the challenges involved through initiating projects with the
communities where the field course occurs. One of the challenges is deciding
who gets the goats and finding enough resources to meet the demand from the
farmers and of ensuring that aspirations and expectations are managed carefully.
Once established, even though external to the course, the goat project can act to
redefine relations between the SLUSE partners with the community should the
joint course return to the same site. A partner from the SACUDE-SLUSE
observes: 'The issue of what we leave behind will always be there – we just need
to be careful of "burden of promises" – students saying they can deliver and forget
the educational reason' (key interview, SACUDE-SLUSE partner).

While doing field work in a community setting is an important and exciting
part of being on the course, it also challenges the students' conception of what a
learning space should be and questions their understanding of what is right and
required when learning in a community setting where the local communities are
essentially active research actors and potential beneficiaries of the knowledge
that is generated.

How partners work together to produce employable graduates for the environment and development sector?

Much thinking has gone into developing a course that addresses some of the skill sets needed to produce an employable graduate. The intention by partners in the DUCED-SLUSE to extend the collaborative education programme across continents is driven by a northern need to expose students from partner universities in Denmark to a wide array of issues and locations in developing countries. Partners from the SACUDE-SLUSE and from the Kenya-SLUSE identify a need to provide their students with access to a course that provides them with fieldwork experience and opportunity to learn in an intercultural and interdisciplinary setting alongside students from the Global North. Available materials and publications about the programme explain the type of capacity building the joint field course is aiming to achieve such as producing qualified manpower for the environmental sector, development practitioners who are able to deal with scientific and technical aspects of natural resources management problems. The intention is to develop university Master courses across continents that are of a more applied nature where students are exposed to a wide array of development issues and are able to work with local partners (Birch-Thomsen et al., 2004).

The aim of the programme explicitly mentions building capacity to produce development practitioners or consultants as described by Treue et al. (2004). Hill et al. (2008a) observe that there is a need to train students effectively and efficiently as development practitioners because:

> the society demands (and students clamour for) university courses of a more applied nature. Such courses must offer the learners 'real life' experiences where students can develop transferable skills that are of benefit in the labour market. Conditions that are conducive to achieving these aims can be created through courses that are field based, problem oriented and interdisciplinary in nature.
>
> (Hill et al., 2008a: 122)

Similarly, Treue et al. (2004) describes the types of skills sets required as follows:

> Danish students may in some respects have a stronger theoretical background, but in a problem oriented learning situation the professional experience of the local students, who are also familiar with context, becomes very valuable to the group. An additional quality of the joint fieldwork is that it closely resembles the conditions under which consultants in the natural resources management and development sector work: terms of reference are externally given, a group of people with different professional and cultural background approach the task in collaboration, a professionally high quality product must be produced and the time pressure is considerable, thus making the learning environment very close to the real working life experience.
>
> (Treue et al., 2004: 212)

The focus on developing practitioners and consultants is interesting given the prevalent views on effects of consultancy work on scholarship in Africa. Sawyerr (2004) confirms the involvement of senior scholars in consultancies and states, unfortunately more typical is the senior scholars who are too distracted by consultancies and project oriented work to devote adequate time to student supervision and mentoring. Involvement in consultancies is seen as impacting of the quality of research and the effectiveness of involvement of local partners in partnerships.

Most comments from the students about the programme indicate that taking the field course was an important step towards employment in research on sustainable natural resources and development in African and other developing nations. Most students felt positive that they had an edge on their compatriots because of having attended the joint field course. For example, one student from DUCED-SLUSE stated that he found that the course developed two key interaction skills that have been vital in his work with communities: first now he knows what to do around communities and secondly he now felt comfortable working in project teams with different partners and foreigners. Another student

Figure 4.5 Student group presenting their results regarding the use and management of medicinal plants to the chief and village representatives at the SLUSE joint field course (DUCED- and SACUDE-SLUSE) in South Africa (Pepele sub-village, Madlangala, Eastern Cape) March 2007

Photo: T. Birch-Thomsen.

from DUCED-SLUSE describes how working on the field course was 'a real life experience' and was a realistic example of how it could be when students obtain employment and go and conduct research projects in the field. A student from a partner university in Africa describes the field course as a great experience of working in a multi-disciplinary research group and preparation for the future in agricultural research and development. The student explained that he found the course was a good proxy for how to work in research and the communities were ideal as a training ground for real work experience. The students get first-hand experience of having to collaborate with colleagues from different cultural and academic backgrounds to solve a specific assignment (an experience that they are likely to experience also in their future professional careers) while the lecturers gain useful insights into other academic structures and other ways of curriculum development (Treue et al., 2004). One of the students from the DUCED-SLUSE insisted that the real value of the course was not what was written down or described in the course or presented in lectures. It was what one learnt on the ground, the difficulty to describe skill sets that shaped behaviour towards team members, the community, the ways of talking and sometimes listening, questioning and being challenged every day in the way one viewed people, issues and society.

Discussion

The question of what is the nature of partnerships in collaboration on educational programmes across continents is an important one in a globalised world. Partnerships evolve and take shape depending on the configuration of partners who are involved and in relation to the socio-cultural and political setting where the partner university is located. Imperatives to collaborate are different, but as has been the experience in SLUSE, differences become the basis of defining mutually benefiting relationships through the joint field course. Defining relationships in terms of collaboration or participation highlights the ongoing challenges of interpreting meaning and nuance where understandings are filtered through underlying broader conceptual lenses defining Global North/Global South relationships. While the joint field course was originally conceived as a Danish programme, the way it has been allowed to evolve and mould itself as a shared joint course with the SACUDE-SLUSE has resulted in a shift in ownership and identity. In the Kenya-SLUSE, the programme is slowly assuming an identity and though it cannot yet be called a Kenyan programme, partners in the programme feel that a shared experience and alignment of interests is becoming more visible. The shift in ownership of a programme initiated in the Global North to the Global South is atypical of projects where the identity of the programmes remains located with originators. Dambisa Moyo's argument in *Dead Aid* is that external support for programmes should be terminated within a specified period and then the programme should be left to find its feet and left to evolve with local and other resources (Moyo, 2009). Such a trajectory is possible and has been seen for some of the partners in the SACUDE-SLUSE and also seen in Asia with TUCED-SLUSE and MUCED-SLUCE. In the Kenya-SLUSE where local support is already being used in the project, sustainability is feasible based on current experience and levels of support.

Students appreciate learning together in the joint field course and their comments reflect a desire to broaden the scope of the collaboration as well as synchronise preparatory courses for the joint field course. The extreme weakness of graduate study programmes in most universities in Africa makes these collaborative courses very important and significant to produce highly qualified graduates (Jansen, 2003; Sawyerr, 2004). Participation of students in a collaborative education programme such as the SLUSE that combines African experience and external expertise constitutes an effective form of capacity building (Jansen, 2003). The current imbalance in accessing preparatory courses reflects on one level the challenges of financing education in the Global South at similar levels as in the Global North. Further, patterns and conditions for funding arrangements facilitate as well as constrict symmetry in the way benefits and activities in a collaborative programme can be balanced. Generally, there is a perception that asymmetries in a programme portray the typical Global North/Global South collaboration where the Global North appears to benefit more. This perception is more common among some universities in the Global South. Galliard (1994) finds that partnerships between Global North and Global South are conditioned by clear differences, but that collaboration is feasible between unequal partners.

Developing courses in a different way and thinking about employability of graduates are the hallmarks of the new global trends in higher education where the challenge is not just to improve delivery and quality of education but also focus on the employability of graduates. The joint field course is a good example of a course that addresses some of the key thinking and objectives of higher education. In Africa, some universities have embraced an approach to higher education where there is the formation of hybrid knowledge constructs, and where there is a greater merging of vertical (disciplinary) knowledge with horizontal (work or community-based) experiential competencies (Kraak, 2000). Based on current understanding and practice, the joint field course contains many of the elements of the new type of educational experience advocated for African graduates and addresses some of the parameters for employability identified by Knight and Yorke's (2003) model for what attributes employable graduates should have. Students perceive their employability to be enhanced and the existing tracer study cited in the evaluation report prepared by Traynor et al. (2007), though limited, indicates positive outcomes. However, Aarts and Greijn (2010) find the success of these collaborative education programmes will need to be considered based on the capability of the students to tap knowledge from the global knowledge economy and apply it effectively to their local situations for sustainable development. Aarts and Greijn argue that one of the ways in which students can gain this ability is to contextualise global knowledge as a problem focus and this is a key component of the joint field course. The joint field course sets out to produce a development practitioner or consultant to work in development work. This is a big sector both in the Global North and Global South, but the reality is that in the Global South, this sector is still dominated by expatriate researchers and consultants (Kagwanja, 2000). Some of the graduates from this course will likely end up in this sector, though the number of students from the course, who will be employed in the sector, will not significantly shift the dominance of expatriate experts.

While the joint field course is quite specific about its target market for the graduates, it is impossible to ignore the need for capacity building to extend to strengthening the staff in the partner universities who participate as collaborators in the joint field course. Though not covered in this case study, one of the big challenges for building stronger collaborative education programmes is obtaining experienced and capable staff from partner universities in Africa. Jansen (2003) finds that universities in Africa suffer from institutional incapacity and he points to an urgent need to strengthen the lecturers and target what Mkandawire (1995) calls third generation scholars that are weak, dispirited and overburdened and are products of weakened higher education systems. Jansen (2003) is very specific about what is needed and is looking for a young academic, who grows among the best minds available both in the Global North and in the Global South, and learns the art of scholarship within a community of peers drawn from a wide spectrum of disciplines, who will be a critical thinker and learn reflection, research and reproduction over a period. While what Jansen is looking for is a skill set to build capacity within the universities themselves, some if not most of the skill sets he describes are similar to those developed under the joint field course. The joint field course clearly has wider relevance beyond the development sector.

Conclusion

The last few decades have seen a transformation of the courses and knowledge producing spaces for higher education through collaborative programmes involving partners in the Global North and Global South. The significance of these joint courses for Global North and Global South is clear, yet even as there is that acknowledgement, looking at elements of the joint course in the context of wider issues and trends in higher education highlights some important conjunctions and disjunctions. For example, looking at student participation in terms of dominance of theoretical knowledge over practical experience conforms to current critiques of Global North/Global South education systems and adds weight to supporting the de-colonising discourse which argues to shift the dominance of northern based theory in scholarship. At the same time, that same dominance in theory is a strong argument for capacity building and justifies continued African interest in collaborating with universities in the north. The joint field course underscores the importance of complementary capabilities across cultures, disciplines, places and experience. Collaboration and participation developed on the basis of strong personal relationships, mutual trust and in informal arenas challenge conventional formulations of partnerships in joint projects where synergies at a personal level are valued as much if not more than those at an organisational level. An important lesson from the self-assessment process among partners and students has been the importance of flexibility, sincerity, honesty, absence of prejudice, lack of definitive boundaries and welcoming opportunities to raise old and new questions while ensuring that lessons become the basis for growing the programme. Processes of course making, course shaping and course delivery are different every time, with every student cohort and in every field site making it a very organic programme.

References

Aarts, H. and Greijn, H. (2010) 'Globalization, knowledge and learning: developing the capacities of higher education institutes'. In Teferra, D. and Greijn, H. (eds) *Higher Education and Globalisation – Challenges, Threats and Opportunities for Africa*. The Netherlands: Maastricht University Centre for International Cooperation in Academic Development (MUNDO), pp. 9–18.

Birch-Thomsen, T., Buch-Hansen, M., Hill, T., Oksen, P. and Magid, J. (2004) 'Integrating knowledge systems for developing sustainable natural resources management'. In Finchham, R., Georg, S. and Holm Nielsen H. (eds) *Sustainable Development and the University: New Strategies for Research Teaching and Practice*. South Africa: Brevitas Publishers, pp. 73–86.

Bob, U., Moodley, V., Traynor, C.H., Gausset, Q. and Chellan, N. (2005) 'Embracing difference and diversity: interdisciplinary, cross cultural and group dynamics'. In Traynor, C.H. (ed.) *The SLUSE Model of Natural Resource Management: From Theory to Practice through Field Based Training – Experiences from Southern Africa*. Scottsville: SACUDE-SLUSE, pp. 59–81.

De Neergaard, A. (2005) 'Problem identification and formulation'. In Traynor, C.H. (ed.) *The SLUSE Model of Natural Resource Management: From Theory to Practice through Field Based Training – Experiences from Southern Africa*. Scottsville: SACUDE-SLUSE, pp. 35–47.

Friesenhahn, I. (2014) 'Making higher education work for Africa, facts and figures'. *Science Development Network*. Available at: www.scidev.net/global/education/feature/higher-education-africa-facts-figures.html (accessed 25 February 2015).

Gaillard, J. (1994) 'North and South research partnership is collaboration possible between unequal partners: knowledge and policy', *The International Journal Transfer and Utilisation*, 7 (2), 31–63.

Hansen, C.P. (2013) 'Towards constructive alignment of the interdisciplinary land use and natural resource management course'. In Ulriksen, L., Solberg, J. and Hansen, C.P. (eds) *Improving University Science Teaching and Learning: Pedagogical Projects*. IND's skriftserie 5 (1). Department of Science Education, pp. 231–240.

Hettne, B. (2001) 'The international university – and the Centre for African Studies'. In Närman, A. and Ewald, J. (eds) *Göteborg University in Africa – Africa in Göteborg University*. Göteborg: Centre for African Studies, pp. 27–29.

Hessels, L.K. and van Lente, H. (2008) 'Rethinking new knowledge production: a literature review and research agenda', *Science Direct, Research Policy*, 37 (4), 740-760.

Hill, T.R., Birch-Thomsen, T., Traynor, C.H., De Neergaard, A. and Bob, U. (2008a) 'Problem based interdisciplinary field based courses: reflections from the southern African experiences', *South African Geographical Journal*, 90 (2), 122–133.

Hill, T.R., Traynor, C.H., Birch-Thomsen, T., De Neergaard, A., Bob, U., Myanyatsi, A.M. and Sebego, R.J. (2008b) 'Clear the mind of pre-conceived ideas and get your hands dirty! An approach to field based courses: the SLUSE–southern Africa experience', *Journal of Geography in Higher Education*, 32 (3), 441–457.

Jansen, J.D. (2003) 'On the state of South African Universities', *South African Journal for Higher Education - SAJHE/SATHO*, 17 (3), 9–12.

Kagwanja, P.M. (2000) 'Post industrialism and knowledge production: African intellectuals in the new international division of labour', *CODESRIA Bulletin*, 3, 5–11.

Knight, T.P. and Yorke, M. (2003) 'Employability and good learning in higher education', *Teaching in Higher Education*, 8 (1), 1–16.

Kraak, A. (2000) *Changing Modes: New Knowledge Production and Its Implications for Higher Education in South Africa*. Cape Town, South Africa: Human Sciences Research Council, Social Science Publisher – HSRC Press.

Kwaramba, M. (2012) 'Internationalisation of higher education in southern Africa as a major exporter', *Journal of International Education and Leadership*, 2 (1), 1–23.

Magid, J., De Neergaard, A., Birch-Thomsen, T., Saarnak C. and Juul, K. (2005) 'Intercultural and interdisciplinary experiences, challenges and outcomes from joint field courses conducted between Danish, Southeast Asian and southern African universities on sustainable land use and natural resource management', *Providing Our Graduates with a Global Perspective through Real and Virtual Student Exchange: ICA – NASULGC*. Vienna: BOKU – University of Natural Resources and Applied Life Sciences, 9–12 April, pp. 123–134.

Materu, P.N. (2007) *Higher Education Quality Assurance in Sub Saharan Africa: Status, Challenges and Opportunities and Promising Practices*. Washington DC: World Bank Paper no. 124.

Mkandawire, T. (1995) 'Three generations of African academics: a note', *Transformation* (28), 73–83.

Mlipha, M. and De Neergaard, A. (2005) 'The fieldwork planning process'. In Traynor, C.H. (ed.) *The SLUSE Model of Natural Resource Management: From Theory to Practice through Field Based Training – Experiences from Southern Africa*. Scottsville: SACUDE-SLUSE, pp. 48–58.

Mlipha, M., Manyatsi, A.M., Hill, T.R., Kgabung, B.T. and Chellan, N. (2005) 'Site selection'. In Traynor, C.H. ed. *The SLUSE Model of Natural Resource Management: From Theory to Practice through Field Based Training – Experiences from Southern Africa*. Scottsville: SACUDE-SLUSE, pp. 25–34.

Moyo, D. (2009) *Dead Aid. Why Aid Is Not Working and How There Is a Better Way for Africa*. New York: Farrar, Straus and Giroux.

Muller, J. (2000) 'What knowledge is the most worth for the millennial citizen?' In Kraak, A. ed. *Changing Modes: New Knowledge Production and Its Implications for Higher Education in South Africa*. Pretoria: Human Sciences Research Council, pp. 70–88.

Otara, A. (2012) 'The future of education and its challenges in Africa', *International Journal of Humanities and Social Science*, 2 (9), 151–156.

Sawyerr, A. (2004) 'African universities and the challenge of research capacity development', *JHEA/RESA*, 2 (1), 211–240.

Teferra, D. (2012) 'Partnerships in Africa in the new era of internationalization', *International Higher Education*, 67 (3), 1–6.

Traynor, C.H. (2005) *The SLUSE Model of Natural Resource Management: From Theory to Practice through Field Based Training – Experiences from Southern Africa*. Scottsville: SACUDE-SLUSE.

Traynor, C.H., De Neergaard, A. and Magid, J. (2007) *SLUSE and Evaluation – University Collaboration on Outreach across Cultures and Interdisciplinary Capacity Building for Sustainable Land Use and Natural Resource Management*. Denmark, University of Copenhagen: SLUSE, Department of Agricultural Sciences, Faculty of Life Sciences.

Treue T., Mertz, O. and Oksen, P. (2004) 'Teaching interdisciplinary land use and natural resource management'. In Fincham, R., Georg, S. and Nielsen, E.H. (eds) *Sustainable Development and the University. New Strategies for Research, Teaching and Practice*. South Africa, Howick: Brevitas, pp. 192–214.

5 The Confucius Institute at the University of Zambia

A new direction in the internationalisation of African higher education?

Peter Kragelund and Godfrey Hampwaye

Introduction

In the past decade, China has intensified its engagement in the internationalisation of higher education in Africa via the establishment of Confucius Institutes. The aim of this chapter is to shed light on the differences between Chinese support for higher education and 'traditional' partnerships, and what the implications of these differences are for the chances of producing locally relevant knowledge in Africa. This is done through a case study of the newly established Confucius Institute at the University of Zambia in Lusaka, Zambia. This case enables us to further our understanding of how the Confucius Institute operates, how it is governed and, more importantly, how it affects the University of Zambia's room for manoeuvre in determining (and funding) its own vision and strategy.

Almost without exception, all African higher education institutions grew out of collaboration with European institutions. Only at Independence did these institutions become sovereign bodies. Sovereignty, however, did not mean that they were *de facto* independent. The history of African higher education institutions – and in particular African universities – is also the history of external support, academic partnerships and adherence to the standards of the Global North that have directly and indirectly shaped African universities today (Samoff and Carrol, 2004) (see Chapter 2 for a more detailed description of the influence of the colonial powers in shaping educational systems in Africa).

However, European countries were not alone in collaborating with African universities. For two decades – beginning in the 1960s – the Soviet Union, China, Cuba and a number of Eastern European countries expanded their collaboration with African universities. Nevertheless, since the end of the Cold War, external funding for African universities has been provided almost exclusively by countries in the Global North, either directly by bilateral and multilateral agencies funded by large donors in the Global North, or from private foundations based in countries in the Global North.

These donors have, to a large extent, shaped African educational policies through financing (Samoff and Carrol, 2004). This is especially the case for the World Bank and institutions within the UN family (UNDP, UNESCO and

UNICEF). On the one hand, the structural adjustment programmes of the 1980s and 1990s focused on increasing efficiency via cost reductions and the abolition of subsidies. This hit higher education in Africa especially hard, causing large-scale budgetary deficits that resulted, *inter alia*, in the deterioration of working conditions, the relocation of staff and declining academic standards (Obamba and Mwema, 2009). On the other hand, the important role of the knowledge-driven economy in most donor countries has resulted in a revision of the role of higher education in development. Since the 1990s, major bi- and multilateral development organisations have promoted higher education as a vehicle to spark social and economic development in the Global South[1] (Naidoo, 2011). Despite this, however, funding remained limited, which essentially meant that African universities had to boost their partnerships with foreign universities in order to finance their activities. This also happened in Zambia, where the Ministry of Education's 1996 policy paper entitled *Educating our Future* called for increased funding for secondary and tertiary education from non-governmental organisations and private entities (Samoff and Carrol, 2004; Takala, 1998).

The past decade has seen a waning of the Global North's domination of funding to, and influence over, Africa's higher education, as a number of donors from the Global South have intensified their funding to Africa, including to higher education. This has led to what Naidoo (2011) calls a critical disruption in the inter-hegemonic rivalry between 'traditional' and 'emerging' political and economic actors that may lead to major changes in the economic and political order, as well as in the direction of higher education. The most important Global South donor to Africa is China (King, 2013).

Chinese aid in Africa has received quite a lot of scholarly attention lately. Although China's aid to Africa is repeatedly portrayed as different from that provided by the Global North, it is often analysed from two opposing ends of a continuum: either as fuelled mainly by foreign policy concerns (see Eisenman and Kurlantzick, 2006), or as offering a more equal relationship (Li, 2008). What is more, the great majority of these studies have analysed Chinese aid at a rather aggregate level (see e.g. Biggeri and Sanfilippo, 2009), and only recently have in-depth studies been conducted of Chinese aid practices and their effects in Africa. Among the latter are King (2013), who has studied Chinese aid to education and training in Africa, providing an impressive overview of the history of this aid and its various modalities, and Wheeler (2014), who has studied the perceptions of purpose and learning objectives of Confucius Institute students and staff at the University of Nairobi, Kenya. Likewise, Nordtveit (2011) has looked at the differences and similarities between Chinese education models and Global North education models, analysing how Chinese models have been implemented in Cameroon. The other side of this relationship has also been studied – namely, how China has once again become an attractive study abroad destination for African university students and how African students have fared in this milieu (see Gillespie, 2001; Haugen, 2013). None of these studies, however, has examined whether Chinese aid to higher education differs significantly from traditional aid to the sector and whether any such differences affect the 'local' production of knowledge at African universities.

In that connection, a growing body of literature argues that the renewal of China and other Southern partners' interest in Africa will increase African countries' room for manoeuvre, as more money will be available, enabling them to choose between different development models (Chin, 2012). This chapter follows this recent trend in studying Chinese educational aid to Africa. It uses the newly established Confucius Institute at the University of Zambia as a case to shed light on whether Chinese support for African higher education differs significantly from the continent's traditional partnerships; and whether this new type of collaboration can enable the University of Zambia to carve out policy space vis-à-vis traditional partners, thereby enabling it to regain control over research strategies and curriculum development. We thereby seek to scrutinise whether this instrument in China's relations with Africa is an example of soft power rather than South–South collaboration, while simultaneously analysing whether the extra resources from the Confucius Institute indeed enable the University of Zambia to develop a curriculum that is more relevant to local needs than the curricula and research funded by actors based in the Global North.

In this chapter, soft power is defined as the power to shape what other nations do through attraction and agenda-setting rather than brute force. South–South collaboration is defined as joint development achieved through collaboration among countries of the Global South (the two concepts will be discussed later).

This chapter proceeds as follows: section two sets out to provide an overview of the internationalisation of higher education in Zambia, arguing that the partnership with a Chinese university to establish the Confucius Institute is by no means exceptional. Rather, it follows a long tradition of external actors' influence over the development of Zambian universities. We point out that these partnerships – despite their seductive label – are actually based on unequal power relations. Hereafter, section three takes us to the Confucius Institute at the University of Zambia. It tells the story of the Institute's founding, its development and its current position in the Zambian higher education system. Section four compares two somewhat fuzzy concepts often associated with the Confucius Institute: namely, 'South–South collaboration' and 'soft power'. Based on a disaggregation of the concepts and an analysis of the inner workings of the Confucius Institute at the University of Zambia, it is argued that the Confucius Institute resembles soft power more than South–South Collaboration. Section five presents the conclusions.

Internationalisation of higher education in Zambia

There is little doubt that internationalisation, i.e. the integration of international aspects in the teaching, research and service functions of an institution, is closely related to the development of higher education in Sub-Saharan Africa. Depending on which definition of internationalisation is chosen, the concept may be used to refer either to a phenomenon that began during the colonial period, or to the establishment of universities that occurred at Independence (see Knight, 1997, 2008 for further discussion and definition of the internationalisation of higher education). Ever since then, internationalisation has been a major buzzword in higher education – in the Global South as well as in the Global North. It has come to signal an efficient way of dealing with the socio-economic challenges of the twenty-first century and may refer to changing teaching standards, delivery of teaching services to institutions located in other countries, the use of ICT to offer programmes previously located in one country in another country, academic mobility, collaborative research programmes, etc. (Jowi, 2009; Oyewole, 2009).

Internationalisation is driven by different rationales in different parts of the world and in different types of institutions. A number of classifications of such rationales have been proposed, which all revolve around a distinction between political (higher education as a diplomatic foreign policy tool), economic (higher education as a means to increase competitiveness), academic (achievement of international standards) and cultural (promotion of national culture) rationales for internationalisation (Knight, 1997, 2008). These rationales seem to differ according to context. According to Jowi (2009), for instance, economic rationales have dominated the internationalisation of higher education in Europe, while African institutions have been driven more by academic rationales, notably the need to strengthen institutional and academic capacity.

However, rationales change over time, as do the actors involved in the internationalisation process. In Sub-Saharan Africa, post-independence internationalisation of higher education has been linked closely to development aid from bi- and multilateral donor agencies. This internationalisation has been driven by the Global North and has been characterised by uneven power relations and an unequal balance in the exchange of knowledge, skills and resources (Knight, 2008). Of late, this situation has changed somewhat. First and foremost, intra-African internationalisation has moved up the agenda of many higher education institutions in Sub-Saharan Africa. Second, South-driven internationalisation has moved up the agenda. Currently, for instance, a number of East Asian countries are using partnerships in higher education both to open and cross borders (Chapman et al., 2010). This is also the case in Africa, where China and India have taken major steps in this direction.

The role of external actors in the development of University of Zambia

These general trends concerning higher education in Africa are, to a large extent, mirrored in the Zambian case. The University of Zambia Act, i.e. the law that paved the way for the establishment of the University of Zambia, was passed in Parliament in 1965, and teaching began one year later. Academic standards were inspired directly by the British Higher education system and, due to shortages of Zambian staff, almost half of the academic staff were British and only two were Zambian (the rest were mainly from South Africa, the US, India and New Zealand). Initial funding for the construction of the University of Zambia came, among others, from the British and Japanese governments (Phiri, 2001). Not surprisingly, therefore, the first linkages formed by the University of Zambia were with British universities. These linkages sought to enhance research and teaching capacity through the exchange of lecturers. The University of Zambia is an autonomous entity funded, by and large, by the Treasury through Parliament. Hence, the university can form any partnerships and accept any funding it can obtain as long as it fulfils its overall aims. With the rapid growth of the university at the beginning of the 1970s, in terms of students, staff and faculties, the University of Zambia leadership sought to expand its partnerships with foreign universities to include continental Europe and the US. Most of these partnerships were directly linked to development aid (Siwela, 1995).

The economic downturn of the late 1970s and the 1980s changed the situation for the University of Zambia. Structural adjustment and stabilisation programmes set in motion by the World Bank and IMF meant that subsidies for education – including higher education – were slashed. Research projects could no longer be serviced and many staff members left the university. Most partnerships, therefore, focused on seconding short- and long-term staff from donor countries and the few research programmes that did continue were all funded by external sponsors (Phiri, 2001; Siwela, 1995).

In this period, the University of Zambia also developed partnerships with universities in the Global South. Most prominently, the University of Zambia and the University of Dar es Salaam, Tanzania, initiated a student exchange programme and in the mid-1990s it also established research and capacity-building linkages with South African universities. Partnerships with universities in the Global North, however, still dominated and at the beginning of the 1990s the University of Zambia had 15–20 such partnership arrangements (Rawoo, n.d.). Although the formation of partnerships became a central part of the 1994–1998 strategic plan for the University of Zambia, the number of partnerships declined slightly and by 1995 the University of Zambia only had active partnerships with ten foreign universities, all of which were funded directly by bilateral donors (Siwela, 1995).

In line with internationalisation strategies elsewhere, the aim of the University of Zambia's partnerships with foreign universities is, according to the University of Zambia's former Vice-Chancellor Professor Andrew A. Siwela (1995), to enrich and broaden the academic environment and thereby raise the academic level at the university. This is achieved by sending University of Zambia staff abroad for career development through research collaborations, by gaining access to research facilities in foreign universities and by providing funding for applied research. Although the aim of all the partnerships is the same, their design and financing differ from case to case. With universities in the Global South, costs are shared equally between the two partners; in some partnerships with universities in the Global North each university pays for its staff to visit the other university; and in the remaining partnerships donors pay/supplement the salaries of the involved staff, pay for infrastructure development, provide ICT equipment and/or provide funds for research directly. In the words of Professor Siwela, these partnerships 'to a large extent, determine the research priorities' (Siwela, 1995: 203) of the university. This contrasts with the ideal situation where the University of Zambia has 'enough of its own resources to pursue collaborative links as demanded by its own academic policy, but that, of course, is impossible' (Siwela, 1995: 204).

At the turn of the millennium, the situation changed for the University of Zambia. Internally, the University of Zambia was almost completely broke and, according to Phiri (2001), this scenario worsened radically due to the University of Zambia's decision to raise salaries by 50 per cent from one day to the next, which essentially meant that the university faced insolvency. Matters deteriorated even further when traditional donors, displeased with the situation, withheld their support (Phiri, 2001). This situation coincided with the Government of Zambia's change of priority focus from higher education to primary education. Almost overnight, other internal and external funds for teaching and research dried up. Still, despite the changed focus and rapidly vanishing funds, donors in 2003 still paid for approximately half of the 115 staff development fellows affiliated to the University of Zambia Staff Development program (Carmody, 2004).[2]

Since then, the situation has 'normalised' and the University of Zambia administration has initiated measures to cut costs. The Government of Zambia, inspired by the global focus on higher education, made higher education a priority once again and donors' willingness to fund partnerships returned. The university is now eager to strengthen these collaborations. In fact, within the context of the current Strategic Plan (2013 to 2017), under strategic direction 10, the University of Zambia is encouraged to establish partnerships for university functions such as teaching, research, consultancy and public service. According to this plan, the overall objective is to promote beneficial partnerships (UNZA, 2012). In the first ten months of 2013 the University of Zambia signed a total of 100 Memoranda of Understanding (MoUs) for partnerships. Most of these are local, but approximately 10 have been signed with foreign universities including a Norwegian, a Malaysian, a South African and a Zimbabwean university. According to the current Deputy Vice-Chancellor, the main purpose of the MoUs with universities of the Global North is exchange of students, but teaching, research partnerships and infrastructure development are also highly prioritised (personal communication, Professor Mwase, Lusaka, 17 October 2013).

As already outlined, the internationalisation of higher education has been a fundamental part of higher education in Zambia since the inauguration of the University of Zambia half a century ago. The University of Zambia has been staffed with foreign professors, research has been funded and initiated by external actors and large portions of the budget have been subsidised by donors. Although the intention has always been for the university to define its own research and teaching priorities, the economic reality has resulted in partnerships characterised by highly unequal power relations, which basically means that external partners have determined the direction of the University of Zambia.

The Confucius Institute at the University of Zambia

The most important partnership in recent years is, without a doubt, the Confucius Institute at the University of Zambia. Not only does it affect numerous University of Zambia students directly and indirectly, it has also brought totally new facilities to the University of Zambia and introduced a new way of governing partnerships at the university. In its most simple form, the Confucius Institute is an academic unit located in a host country's university. It is governed and financed by the Office of Chinese Language Council International (often shortened to Hanban) in Beijing and functions like a non-profit organisation. In official parlance, it seeks to intensify educational cooperation, support the development of Chinese language education and increase mutual understanding (Starr, 2009). According to Gill and Huang (2006), the Confucius Institutes are set up to spread Chinese culture and the teaching of Mandarin throughout the world and thereby to 'present a kinder and gentler image of China to the outside world' (Gill and Huang, 2006: 18). This is done via short- and long-term teaching programmes in Chinese, the Hanyu Shuiping Kaoshi international Chinese Proficiency test, the equivalent of the TOEFL English language test (Test Of English as a Foreign Language), Chinese culture courses and the like. Moreover, the Confucius Institute sponsors a wide variety of extracurricular activities such as film screenings, art exhibitions and sports, and it sometimes also acts as a consultancy firm for individuals and organisations interested in China.

To be precise, Hanban administers two types of Confucius collaboration: namely, the Confucius Institute and the Confucius Classroom. They share the same aims but have different setups. While the former are established within host universities, the latter are aimed at secondary education institutions. By the end of 2010, a little over half of all the Confucius collaborations established worldwide were Confucius Classrooms (Hartig, 2012). In this chapter, we focus only on Confucius Institutes that are located in universities and governed as university partnerships.

The first Confucius Institute was established in Seoul in 2004,[3] and just one year later a Confucius Institute was set up at the University of Nairobi, Kenya. As of March 2015, the Hanban website listed a total of 38 Confucius Institutes in Africa, located in 27 different African countries (Hanban, 2015). That figure is growing very rapidly. In 2013, Hanban reported a total of 22 Confucius Institutes in 16 African countries and later that year King (2013) put the figure at 33 Confucius Institutes in 26 African countries.

The Confucius Institutes are expected to increase the inflow of foreign students and researchers into China. Furthermore, they aim to make Chinese a global language for teacher training and to foster an increase in trade and investment between the home and the host economy (Pan, 2013; Starr, 2009). Finally, Confucius Institutes are seen as counterbalancing American dominance in the world (Hartig, 2012). Taken together, the establishment of Confucius Institutes 'signifies the first time in the modern period that the Chinese government has sought to establish a significant cultural presence around the world' (Hayhoe and Liu, 2010: 82).

To further our understanding of the Confucius Institutes, a few basic facts have to be established. First, the Confucius Institutes are built on twinning arrangements between two universities – one Chinese and one in the host country. In very rare cases, like the China Institute in New York, the host partner is not a university. Likewise, a few examples exist where more than two universities collaborate to form one Confucius Institute. Second, Hanban operates with three funding arrangements – namely, wholly Hanban-operated and funded units; joint ventures with local partners; and units run and funded fully by local universities but licensed by Hanban (Starr, 2009). The Zambian Confucius Institute falls into the second category, namely that of joint ventures between a Chinese university, Hanban and the University of Zambia. In this format, Hanban provides start-up funding, books and teaching material and pays the salaries of one or two language instructors. Whether this causes the Confucius Institutes to adapt to the local contexts, strategies and visions governing the host universities, or whether it leads them to control and dictate what is taught, and how, is a highly controversial issue (see e.g. Sahlins, 2013) and is most likely also related to the specific funding arrangements in each case. Third, Confucius Institutes are said to be demand-driven, i.e. responding to the increasing demand in e.g. African countries for Chinese language and cultural skills (King, 2013). Fourth, although the teaching of Chinese abroad dates back to the late 1980s, Confucius Institutes are a relatively new phenomenon. We therefore only have limited knowledge of how they operate and how they affect higher education in host countries. What we do know is that their growth rate is phenomenal. As stated above, the first Confucius Institute was established in 2004. As of the end of 2013 a total of 833 Confucius collaborations existed worldwide (of which almost 70 per cent were located in Europe and the United States and less than 4 per cent in Africa) according to the official Hanban website (Hanban, 2013b). Unfortunately, the official Hanban website does not distinguish between Confucius Institutes and Confucius Classrooms. Moreover, the numbers do not necessarily provide a full picture of the scale of the operations as some centres are not (yet) in operation and others are merely one-room offices (Hartig, 2012).

It should be noted, though, that the Confucius Institutes are not the only way that China supports higher education in Africa. Also of importance is the Chinese Government Scholarship Program which aims 'to familiarise scholarship recipients with Chinese culture and build goodwill towards China while assisting recipients in getting higher education' (Dong and Chapman, 2008: 156). The scholarship programme is much older than the Confucius Institutes. In fact, its origins may be traced to the Science Education Team established in 1970 to manage the growing number of exchange students. The first students from Zambia to use this programme began their studies in China in 1972. Since then, the programme has grown and changed incrementally and in 1997 it was taken over by the newly established Chinese Scholarship Council under the Ministry of Education.

The Confucius Institute at the University of Zambia was established on 26 July 2010 and began operating two months later, on 1 September 2010. Teaching of the first class of 20 students began approximately a month later. Since then, more than 2000 students have attended classes at the Institute (Hebei University, 2013) and a further 2000, approximately, have attended classes in the Confucius Classrooms set up elsewhere in Zambia (personal communication, Dr Ngalande, Lusaka, 14 August 2014). As most of these students only come for short-term courses, this figure is highly misleading as an indicator of the actual number of students attending classes at any one time. The real figure is probably closer to 70 (Hanban, 2013a).

The University of Zambia Confucius Institute is the only one in Zambia, but since its inauguration in July 2010, Confucius Classrooms have been set up at the Mulungushi University in Kabwe, the Copperbelt University in Kitwe and most recently at the Livingstone Institute of Business and Engineering Studies. Moreover, the privately owned Chinese International School in Lusaka opened its doors to students in 2009. It offers lessons in Mandarin to students of all ages (from kindergarten to adults) and, like the Confucius Institute, it also offers lessons in the martial arts. Although the Chinese International School is a private entity, the teachers are paid by the Chinese government.

The Confucius Institute is currently located close to the main parking lot, just next to the library, at the University of Zambia. It consists of two newly renovated

Figure 5.1 The main entrance to the University of Zambia

Photo: P. Kragelund.

classrooms, an office and a storage room. Moreover, a small part of the main library is devoted to Confucius Institute related texts. Although the location is by no means ostentatious, it is one of only three units that is signposted at the main gate of the University of Zambia. Likewise, it is the only university institute that boasts its own advertisement at Lusaka International Airport.

The Confucius Institute is soon to become much flashier, though. In late December 2012, the University of Zambia signed a contract with a Chinese construction company, China Nantong No. 3 Construction Group, to build a new and very spacious two-storey building that will not only accommodate the Confucius Institute but also provide office space for staff from the School of Humanities and Social Sciences as well as from the University of Zambia Central Administration. The company began building in the spring of 2014.This entire project is to be financed by Hanban. Thus, funding arrangements at the University of Zambia Confucius Institute have changed from a joint venture model to a wholly Hanban operated and funded unit. The main purpose of the building is to allow for a large-scale expansion of the Confucius Institute's activities that cover numerous short-term courses and, as of last year, a degree programme in Chinese. Currently, eight students are enrolled in the degree programme offered by the School of Humanities at the University of Zambia.[4] They have now completed their first year of studies and the plan is to gradually take in more students (personal communication, Dr Ngalande, Lusaka, 14 August 2014).

Figure 5.2 The new Confucius Institute construction site

Photo: P. Kragelund.

In university terms, the process of setting up the Confucius Institute has been exceptionally fast. The former dean of the School of Humanities at the University of Zambia, Professor Chanda, claims credit for the idea of establishing a Confucius Institute at the university. He knew the scholarship programmes offered by the Chinese government to foreign students but, as a linguist and professor at the school of Humanities and Social Sciences, he was also aware of the difficulties Zambian students faced language-wise when they went to study in China. He therefore contacted the Chinese embassy in Lusaka to inquire about the possibilities of setting up a Confucius Institute at the university. The embassy directed him to Hanban, which offered to help him establish connections with Hebei University of Economics and Business (henceforth Hebei University) in Shi Jia Zhuang City in the province of Hebei, and less than one year later the MoU between the two universities was signed (personal communication, Professor Chanda, Lusaka, 18 October 2013). Exactly who initiated the contact and how the partnership was formed is nevertheless still shrouded in mystery. According to the biggest private newspaper in Zambia, the deal of establishing a Confucius Institute in Zambia was struck alongside other deals, like avoidance of double taxation, when a Chinese delegation led by Chinese State Councillor Dai Binggou met with the president at that time, Rupiah Banda, in June 2010 (Bupe, 2010).

The Confucius Institute is open to the public and access is therefore not limited to the University of Zambia students or staff, but until recently most of the students came from the university, and in order to cater for the students' needs, beginners' classes were offered in the students' lunch breaks until the beginning of the October 2013 term. According to Hoogenbosch (2012), this created several problems for the students and the classes have therefore now been integrated into the School of Education's new language programme and are offered in normal teaching hours. Although the costs of attending language courses is markedly cheaper for the University of Zambia students and staff than for others, the relative share of university students is currently falling. This is because the Confucius Institute cooperates with a number of Zambian private and public institutions as well as Chinese companies located in Zambia in providing basic language teaching for their staff. Most recently, the Confucius Institute has signed an agreement with the Zambian police force to teach Zambian policemen Mandarin as the increasing number of Chinese people living and working in Zambia has meant that an increasing number of them also engage with the police.

As of October 2013, the cost structure for short-term language courses at the Confucius Institute was as follows: ZMW 350 (USD 66) for students at the University of Zambia, ZMW 600 (USD 113) for University of Zambia staff and ZMW 1300 (USD 244) for all others (personal communication, Professor Chanda, Lusaka, 18 October 2013). It should be noted, though, that as of late 2011 most students at the Confucius Institute did not pay for the courses themselves. In the words of Hoogenbosch: '[N]ot all students at Confucius Institute actually pay the tuition fees. They did not know they had to, and were never asked to pay anyway' (Hoogenbosch, 2012: 27). This is supported by the current Zambian head of the Confucius Institute who, in an interview in August 2014, stated that the Confucius Institute is heavily subsidised by Hanban and that 'the tuition fee by no means covers the costs of running the Confucius Institute' (personal communication, Dr Ngalande, Lusaka, 14 August 2014).

The Confucius Institute also offers Chinese tests for primary and secondary school students and a Chinese proficiency test, the so-called HSK international Chinese language examination, which is required to enrol in a Chinese university. Not surprisingly, therefore many of the University of Zambia students see the language classes offered at the Confucius Institute as a stepping stone to a scholarship programme in China (Hoogenbosch, 2012). The Confucius Institute has two directors: one Chinese and one local. Moreover, the board of the Confucius Institute is chaired by the Vice-Chancellor of the University of Zambia. This setup is intended to ensure a more equal relationship between the partners than the traditional partnerships with universities in the Global North. However, like all other Confucius Institutes around the world, this Confucius Institute is regulated by Hanban in Beijing. Hanban offers several different curricula that a recipient university can choose from.[5] They are made up of centrally approved study programmes and text books and do not necessarily correspond to the pedagogy or curriculum in other programmes at the School of Education. Moreover, the University of Zambia has no say over which Chinese teachers are appointed to conduct the teaching. They do not take part in the staff development programme and do not conduct research.

The Confucius Institute at University of Zambia: South–South collaboration or soft power?

Confucius Institutes are often named as examples of South–South collaboration. This is also the case at the University of Zambia where the university management perceives the Confucius Institute to be distinct from traditional partnerships in higher education. In concluding an interview about the internationalisation of higher education in Zambia, the Deputy Vice-Chancellor of the University of Zambia said: '*In South–South collaborations each partner has to contribute. In North–South collaborations only the Northern partner has to contribute*' (personal communication, Professor Mwase, Lusaka, 17 October 2013).

South–South collaboration

This may lead us to believe that South–South collaboration is qualitatively different from North–South collaboration. The challenge, however, is that the concept of South–South collaboration is very ill defined. It is taken to refer to a broad framework for collaboration among countries of the Global South that may include issues related to culture, politics and economics. It is perceived to be organised and initiated by countries in the Global South themselves and may include a variety of actors from these countries. It thus refers to a process whereby two or more countries from the Global South pursue development through cooperative exchanges of, for instance, resources, skills and technical know-how (UNOSSC, 2014). Still, the term itself does not provide us with any idea as to the type, scope and magnitude of the collaboration. Moreover, it often has positive connotations, so that the two-way interaction between countries from the Global South is depicted as a win-win engagement offering 'mutual benefit', reciprocity and 'common development' (see e.g. Mawdsley, 2012).

Even though the concept is analytically vague it has a long history dating back to the 1955 Bandung conference, where 29 leaders from Africa and Asia met to speak the voice of the South. It is thus 'closely related to the liquidation of colonialism in the 1950s and 1960s' (Folke et al., 1993: 22). This paved the way for the Group of 77 established in 1964 as an intergovernmental organisation within the UN to promote developing countries' common interests in the UN and to support South–South cooperation. The establishment of the UN Conference on Trade and Development in 1964 and the subsequent Declaration of a New International Economic Order – a proposal for a new economic and political framework for international relations among equal countries – was another hallmark in the early years of South–South collaboration. The initiatives of these early years came to a sudden standstill, however. The two oil crises in the 1970s and the related recycling of petrodollars meant, first, that the Global South was divided; and second, the region became the focus of the 1980s debt crisis, which further undermined the idea of a collective South. However, the fast growth of big economies like China and India in the past two decades has resulted in a new-found interest in the economic and political potential of South–South collaboration (see Carmody, 2013).

Thus, despite the current rhetoric of 'win-win' and mutual benefit, the concept has political undertones – even in its latest form. This is also the case with regard to the concept of soft power, which is the angle most often used to analyse Confucius Institutes throughout the world – either directly or indirectly as public or cultural diplomacy or as a nation branding campaign (see e.g. Barr, 2012; Hartig, 2012; King, 2013; Yang, 2010).

Soft power

The concept of 'soft power' focuses attention on how a nation may obtain what it wants or how it shapes what other nations do through persuasion and co-operation rather than through brute force. Soft power in the sense of attraction derives from the extent to which a country can make its culture, political values and foreign policies appealing to other countries. Soft power, thus, makes us think beyond coercion and material power to describe the ability to achieve desired outcomes (Kearn, 2011). It also points to the dynamic aspect of power, as soft power is not static but changes frequently in line with the nature of its sources, e.g. culture, political values and foreign policies, including commercial and government policies.

Although the concept is more than 30 years old, it was only picked up in China this millennium. Most forcefully, former President Hu Jintao used it for the first time in 2006 to describe China's international influence, appealing to 'enhance culture as part of the soft power in the country' (cited in Fallon, 2014: 38). Although Confucius has by no means always been a popular figure among Chinese heads of state – indeed he has even at times been seen as a hindrance to social change – the Chinese teacher and philosopher is nowadays used to brand and unify China internally as well as externally: internally, the concepts of equality and opportunity for all via education are applied to keep the increasingly unequal Chinese society together; and externally Confucius offers global brand recognition and is closely associated with teaching and culture (Barr, 2012; Starr, 2009).

Unfortunately, soft power has also become a catch-all concept – used by politicians, journalists, practitioners and academics alike to describe any political mission that does not use brute force to achieve its aims (Kearn, 2011). Regarding China's relations with African countries, the concept is widely used (and abused). This is also the case in the sphere of China-Africa higher education collaboration (see e.g. Pan, 2013; Wheeler, 2014). This intuitively makes sense, as academic and scientific exchanges are central to the soft power concept. This is especially the case for student scholarship programmes, as soft power theory 'presumes that students with pleasant first-hand experiences of life abroad will admire the host country's political system and, in turn, push politics at home in the direction desired by the country they studied in' (Haugen, 2013: 318).

Alas, these studies on soft power and higher education do not bring us closer to defining what constitutes soft power policies nor how they relate to hard power. For instance, they do not distinguish between the various 'tools' used to wield soft power. Whether or not an activity can indeed be classified as soft power has as much to do with the target country as with the country wielding a particular 'tool'. Hence, only if the target finds e.g. that Chinese culture or language is attractive will this have a soft power effect of persuading the target nation to do China's bidding. Also, analysts seldom reflect upon the fact that the doings of individual firms and institutions may contradict a country's overall soft power strategy.

When using the concept of soft power, it is therefore important to recognise that soft power is not only a foreign policy tool but can also be used to shape domestic politics. Furthermore, it is important to bear in mind that as soft power, to a large extent, rests on values and the way these values are expressed (and relate to other values), acts by individual institutions may be counterproductive vis-à-vis a nation's overall soft power strategies. We must also distinguish between the attractiveness of a country's development path at the aggregate level and the attractiveness of individual institutions/policies.

South–South collaboration or soft power?

In the case of China's engagement with other countries in the Global South the distinction between South–South collaboration and soft power is not always clear. This is also the case in relation to higher education partnerships (King,

2013). As outlined earlier, South–South collaboration is characterised by reciprocity, common development and cooperative exchanges. Applied to the case studied here, this would suggest that the University of Zambia had (for the first time) established an evenly balanced partnership in Zambian higher education. This is, indeed, the current Deputy Vice-Chancellor's reading of the partnership (personal communication, Professor Mwase, Lusaka, 17 October 2013). In contrast, soft power is characterised by agenda-setting, branding and attractiveness. This would, conversely, signify an unbalanced collaboration where external partners define the terms and conditions and pay for the collaboration, and where activities are often unrelated to other activities at the university and may even, at times, clash with the host institution's own vision and strategy. Whether the Confucius Institute at the University of Zambia is a real example of South–South collaboration or whether it is yet another example of soft power depends on how the partnership actually functions. Is it really characterised by reciprocity, common development and cooperative exchanges, or does it bear signs of agenda-setting, branding and persuasion? These questions will be addressed below.

To further complicate the analysis, higher education partnerships are often linked to educational diplomacy and the broader concept of cultural diplomacy. In other words, the internationalisation of higher education is often framed as a diplomatic investment in the future. Education and cultural diplomacy have historically been central aspects of Northern interaction with the Sub-Saharan economies. This has not gone unnoticed in China's relations with Africa. In 2006, for instance, China Radio International established an Africa Centre in Nairobi, which broadcasts English language radio to East Africa. This was followed, in 2010, by the launch of CNC world, a 24 hour news channel which aims to present international affairs to the world from a Chinese perspective. The following year, Xinhua launched a mobile newspaper in East Africa distributing Chinese news to East African subscribers via mobile phones. The very same year, Chinese Central Television (CCTV) inaugurated CCTV Africa in Kenya, which offers a Chinese interpretation of local and world affairs via programmes like 'Africa live', 'Talk Africa' and 'Faces of Africa'. On top of this, news and pictures from the Xinhua News Agency are increasingly used by African media houses, as Xinhua offers pictures either for free or much cheaper than Western news agencies (Gagliardone, 2013; Wekesa, 2013). Finally, Chinese media houses seek to cater for the growing Chinese population living in African countries. This is also the case in Zambia where the Oriental Post is specifically aimed at the Chinese population.

The Confucius Institute as a university partnership: more soft power than South–South collaboration?

The Confucius Institute fulfils many of the purposes of university partnerships as defined by the governing body of the University of Zambia: it enhances teaching capacity and develops key infrastructure while simultaneously facilitating the future exchange of students with Chinese universities. This leads the university's Deputy Vice-Chancellor to argue that the partnership with Heibei University benefits the University of Zambia through the expansion of teaching programmes, internationalisation and improved infrastructure (personal communication, Professor Mwase, Lusaka, 17 October 2013). Following this line of argument, King (2013) claims that there is a degree of symmetry between the Chinese and the host university. Hence, it is easy to perceive the partnership as a genuine example of South–South cooperation focusing on reciprocity and common development.

On closer inspection, however, it is not obvious that the Confucius Institute is an example of South–South cooperation. Rather, the Confucius Institute seems to resemble the numerous university partnerships that the University of Zambia has been involved in since its inauguration in the mid-1960s, i.e. partnerships which are dictated by the external partner, exhibit highly uneven power relations and are not necessarily in line with the University of Zambia's vision and strategy.

First, the financing of the new Confucius Institute building points towards an unequal relationship. Although the University of Zambia provided office space for the temporary premises of the Confucius Institute, Hanban has provided full financing for the new two-storey building. In the words of the Deputy Vice-Chancellor of the University of Zambia:

> The Chinese partner even finances the infrastructure. The University of Zambia does not have the funds to finance these kinds of initiatives. The new Confucius Institute building will even accommodate several offices for the University of Zambia administrative staff. This is part of the deal with Hebei University.
>
> (Personal communication, Professor Mwase, Lusaka, 17 October 2013)

Moreover, the new Confucius Institute building has been on the drawing board for a couple of years now and the reason why construction of the building has only just commenced is that the Ministry of Education in Zambia had to make a number of critical decisions first. Most graduates from the School of Education get jobs as secondary school teachers. Until recently, however, no secondary school offered Chinese, so there was no reason to offer a BA programme in Chinese at the University of Zambia and no reason to build new structures to expand the Confucius Institute at the University of Zambia. This changed in 2013, when the Ministry decided to offer Chinese at secondary level in 10 pilot schools – one in each province in Zambia. Immediately after, the first batch of eight students was admitted to the BA programme in Chinese at the University of Zambia. Until the first Zambian students have graduated from the BA programme, teaching will be conducted by Chinese teachers sent from China and paid for by Hanban (personal communication, Professor Chanda, Lusaka, 18 October 2013). Thus, in the future, Mandarin and French will have equal status in the Zambian educational system.

Second, the Confucius Institute has sparked a discussion about quality assurance both inside and outside Africa (Kotzé, 2010; Starr, 2009). In short, host universities, including the University of Zambia, face tremendous challenges monitoring and evaluating the teaching that takes place there. The Confucius Institute undergraduate and postgraduate programmes were all developed at Hanban and hence do not follow the procedures set up by the host university. Related hereto, the Confucius Institute system does not take into account that good language teaching is not only about language fluency but also pedagogical skills and cultural knowledge. Linked to this, suggestions have been put forward to create contextually relevant local teaching material. However, this has not yet been set in motion and currently all teaching material is centrally produced and approved in Beijing. It is important, however, to distinguish between the short-term courses and the degree programme. While the former is wholly developed, paid for and implemented by Hanban, the latter is, in theory, managed partly by the University of Zambia although it is still funded and designed by Hanban.

Third, the Confucius Institute's influence is not limited to teaching, exhibitions and martial arts lessons. Just like other partnerships seek to do, the Confucius Institute aims to be an opinion former, for instance through news reports produced by Confucius Institute staff that feed into the growing presence of Chinese media in Zambia. Journalists from these media houses regularly interview Confucius Institute staff to disseminate information about its progress (Hebei University, 2013). Moreover, the Confucius Institute broadcasts its own show on the University of Zambia Radio. A couple of times a week, a Confucius Institute teacher or student broadcasts a feature on Chinese culture or Chinese business on the university radio station that covers Lusaka and the surrounding suburbs and thus can potentially reach approximately 1.5 million people. Recently, the Confucius Institute at the University of Zambia also formalised an agreement with the Zambia National Broadcast Corporation (ZNBC) to broadcast a television show entitled *Get to Know China*. The idea is to bring in people with a good understanding of China and China-Zambian relations to portray another picture of China to the Zambian people than that painted by CNN and Deutche Welle, for instance.

Apart from being an example of reciprocity and joint development, i.e. South–South collaboration, the establishment of the Confucius Institute at the University of Zambia should therefore be analysed alongside other nations' widespread use of language and cultural encounters as a soft power tool in Africa. The promotion of French, German and English language and culture has been an important task for institutions like the Alliance Française, the Göethe Institute and the British Council since Independence.

The Alliance Française is the main instrument through which French language policy is promoted in Africa. It functions under the French Embassy and operates throughout Africa. In Zambia, it has branches in five major cities. Through these branches, the Alliance Française offers French language lessons to the general public in Zambia. More importantly, however, it targets French teachers in Zambia, giving them the skills to promote knowledge about the

French language throughout the country. In a similar vein, the Alliance Française sponsors postgraduate students studying French at the University of Zambia School of Education. Likewise, the Göethe Institute, the German equivalent of the Alliance Française, has just announced that it has initiated collaboration with the University of Zambia Language Centre to facilitate the spread of German as a foreign language in Zambia. German soft power does not stop here, however. Deutche Welle, Germany's international broadcaster, which is financed by tax revenues in Germany, broadcasts throughout Africa. Its visions and values include communication of German points of view, liberal democratic values and respect for human rights (Deutche Welle, 2013; German Embassy, 2013). Finally, the British Council facilitates Zambian university students' studies in the United Kingdom and offers a range of school-linking programmes intended to further intercultural understanding and networking. Of particular importance is the 'Development Partnerships in Higher Education' programme that has offered funding, exchange of staff/students, capacity building and research collaboration for institutions of higher education since 2006. In Zambia, eight programmes have been funded. Five of these were with the University of Zambia (British Council, 2013).

Conclusions: a new way forward in university partnerships?

This chapter has set out to advance our understanding of the internationalisation of higher education in Zambia through a case study of the recently established Confucius Institute at the University of Zambia. In theory, this collaboration differs from the lion's share of partnerships established in the past 50 years as it is not North-driven. In theory, the establishment of a Confucius Institute at the University of Zambia has also increased the room for manoeuvre of the university governing board, which is now free to choose between different educational models and is no longer obliged to rely only on inputs and inspiration from its Northern partners. In reality, however, it seems that the university is merely following a new set of standards, this time prescribed by Hanban, which defines curriculum development and research priorities at the University of Zambia via funding, teaching material and influence over decisions taken in the Ministry of Education. Put differently: the Confucius Institute, like traditional partnerships, fails to assist the university in implementing its own vision and strategy, including the development of locally relevant curricula and research. Hence, although the funding arrangements between the Confucius Institute and traditional partners in the internationalisation of higher education differ, as does the role of the home government and the governing bodies, the end result is the same: the University of Zambia still has to rely on external funding for teaching and research. Foreign actors thereby influence key aspects of local knowledge production.

The chapter has also argued that the Confucius Institute resembles an example of soft power more than it resembles South–South collaboration. The Confucius Institute is a hotbed for training future Zambian political and economic leaders, and it therefore serves as a breeding ground for opinion shapers capable of communicating Chinese values to the Zambian public. This is supported by recent developments at the Confucius Institute, where the focus is increasingly on teaching Zambian employees of large-scale public and private enterprises rather than only University of Zambia students and staff. Local media initiatives also point in this direction: the Chinese state, through its access to the University of Zambia Radio and the ZNBC, may sway public opinion in Zambia and portray a picture of China that differs radically from that depicted in other media present in Zambia. This strategy smacks of educational diplomacy, as already described, and resembles soft power more than South–South collaboration. The strategy of using higher education partnerships to make the sponsoring country more appealing is not confined to China but is well documented in the literature on the internationalisation of higher education (Knight, 1997; Naidoo, 2011). Likewise, the use of higher education partnerships is a well-documented aspect of certain currently powerful nations' rise to power in global higher education (Altbach and Peterson, 2008).

It should be noted, however, that the Confucius Institute is not the only vehicle used to shape the decisions of Zambian politicians without the use of brute force. In the case of China's relations to Zambia, there is no doubt that China's economic growth path in the past three decades appeals to the Zambian political elite. This is especially the case since the global financial crisis in 2008/2009. Thus, the very fact that China has grown while Zambia's traditional partners have stagnated makes the Chinese model attractive in Zambia.

In conclusion, therefore, it is important to state that despite the 'equal partners' rhetoric of Chinese support for higher education, the Confucius Institute is as donor driven as the other partnerships in which the University of Zambia has engaged historically. Notwithstanding these uneven power relations, the Confucius Institute is, indeed, a result of collaboration between two partners in the Global South. This case therefore questions the notion of positive and symmetrical partnerships built on reciprocity, common development and cooperative exchanges normally alluded to in the case of South–South collaboration. Instead, it shows that these collaborations may also include aspects of asymmetrical power just like North–South collaborations. The case also questions whether the Confucius Institute signals a new era in the history of the university – an era where the University of Zambia defines the premises for its partnerships with foreign universities.

Notes

1 The Global South here refers to people and places affected by poverty and marginalisation regardless of geographical location.
2 Under this programme employees are appointed and supported to pursue graduate degrees up to the PhD level.
3 In fact, a trial institute was set up a couple of month earlier in Tashkent, Uzbekistan, but officially the one in Seoul is regarded as the first.

4 To be precise, all the degree programme students belong to the School of Education but the language courses are offered by the School of Humanities, University of Zambia.
5 It is important to bear in mind, however, that Confucius Institutes only teach *Hanyu*, the language of the Han people – the majority ethnic group in China, i.e. they neither teach *Putonghua*, the 'common speech' language in China, nor the many dialects and languages spoken throughout China.

References

Altbach, P. and Peterson, P.M. (2008) 'Higher education as a projection of America's soft power'. In Watanabe, Y. and Mcconnell, D.L. (eds) *Soft Power Superpowers: Cultural and National Assets of Japan and the United States*. New York: M.E. Sharpe, pp. 37–53.

Barr, M. (2012) 'Nation branding as nation building: China's image campaign', *East Asia: An International Quarterly*, 29 (1), 81–94.

Biggeri, M. and Sanfilippo, M. (2009) 'Understanding China's move into Africa: an empirical analysis', *Journal of Chinese Economic and Business Studies*, 7 (1), 31–54.

British Council (2013) *Delphe Projects*. Manchester: British Council. Available at: www.britishcouncil.org/delphe-projects-1.htm (accessed 30 October 2013).

Bupe, F. (2010) *China Lends Zambia US$53m for Mobile Hospitals*. Lusaka: The Post Online.

Carmody, B. (2004) *The Evolution of Education in Zambia*. Lusaka: Bookworld Publishers.

Carmody, P. (2013) *The Rise of the BRICS in Africa. The Geopolitics of South–South Relations*. London: Zed Books.

Chapman, D.W., Cummings, W.K. and Postiglione, G.A. (2010) 'Transformations in higher education: crossing borders and bridging minds'. In Chapman, D.W., Cummings, W.K. and Postiglione, G.A. (eds) *Crossing Borders in East Asian Higher Education*. Hong Kong: Springer, pp. 1–22.

Chin, G.T. (2012) 'China as a "net donor": tracking dollars and sense', *Cambridge Review of International Affairs*, 25 (4), 579–603.

Deutche Welle (2013) *Mission Statement: Vision and Values*. Bonn: Deutche Welle. Available at: www.dw.de/about-dw/mission-statement/s-8852 (accessed 30 October 2013).

Dong, L. and Chapman, D.W. (2008) 'The Chinese Government Scholarship Program: an effective form of foreign assistance', *International Review of Education*, 54 (2), 155–173.

Eisenman, J. and Kurlantzick, J. (2006) 'China's Africa strategy', *Current History*, 105 (691), 219–224.

Fallon, T. (2014) 'Chinese fever and cool heads: Confucius Institutes and China's national identities', *China Media Research*, 10 (1), 35–46.

Folke, S., Fold, N. and Enevoldsen, T. (1993) *South–South Trade and Development. Manufacturers in the New International Division of Labour*. New York: St. Martin's Press.

Gagliardone, I. (2013) 'China as a persuader: CCTV Africa's first steps in the African mediasphere', *Ecquid Novi: African Journalism Studies*, 34 (3), 25–40.

German Embassy (2013) *German Courses at the University of Zambia*. Lusaka: German Embassy. Available at: www.lusaka.diplo.de/Vertretung/lusaka/en/06/Weshalb__Deutsch__lernen/seite__Deutschkurs__UNZA.html (accessed 30 October 2013).

Gill, B. and Huang, Y. (2006) 'Sources and limits of Chinese "soft power"', *Survival*, 48 (2), 17–36.

Gillespie, S. (2001) *South–South Transfer: A Study of Sino-African Exchanges*. New York: Routledge.

Hanban (2013a) *Confucius Institute at the University of Zambia*. Beijing: Hanban. Available at: http://english.hanban.org/node_12483.htm (accessed 25 October 2013).

Hanban (2013b) *Confucius Institute Online*. Beijing: Office of Chinese Language Council International. Available at: www.chinesecio.com/m/cio_wci (accessed 08 November 2013).

Hanban (2015) *About Confucius Institute/Classroom*. Available at: http://english.hanban.org/node_10971.htm (accessed 11 March 2015).

Hartig, F. (2012) 'Confucius Institutes and the rise of China', *Journal of Chinese Political Science*, 17 (1), 53–76.

Haugen, H.Ø. (2013) 'China's recruitment of African university students: policy efficacy and unintended outcomes', *Globalisation, Societies and Education*, 11 (3), 315–334.

Hayhoe, R. and Liu, J. (2010) 'China's universities, cross-border education, and dialogue among civilizations'. In Chapman, D.W. et al. (eds) *Crossing Borders in East Asian Higher Education*. Hong Kong: Springer, pp. 77–100.

Hebei University (2013) *Confucius Institute at the University of Zambia*. Shi Jia Zhuang City: Hebei University of Economics and Business. Available at: http://web.heuet.net.cn/exchange/ConfuciusInstitute.htm (accessed 17 October 2013).

Hoogenbosch, A. (2012) *'Made-in-China': Chinese as a Commodity and a Socio-economic Resource in Chinese Language Schools in Zambia*. Research Master thesis, Utrecht University.

Jowi, J.O. (2009) 'Internationalization of higher education in Africa: developments, emerging trends, issues and policy implications', *Higher Education Policy*, 22 (3), 263–281.

Kearn, D.W. (2011) 'The hard truths about soft power', *Journal of Political Power*, 4 (1), 65–85.

King, K. (2013) *China's Aid and Soft Power in Africa*. Woodbridge: James Currey.

Knight, J. (1997) 'Internationalisation of higher education: a conceptual framework'. In Knight, J. and De Wit, H. (eds) *Internationalisation of Higher Education in Asia Pacific Countries*. Amsterdam: EAIE/IDP, pp. 5–19.

Knight, J. (2008) 'The internationalization of higher education: complexities and realities'. In Teferra, D. and Knight, J. (eds) *Higher Education in Africa: The International Dimension*. Boston: CIHE/AAU, pp. 1–43.

Kotzé, R. (2010) 'Notes from the recent Confucius Institute Africa regional conference', *The China Monitor*. Stellenbosch: Centre for Chinese Studies, Stellenbosch University.

Li, A. (2008) 'China's new policy toward Africa'. In Rotberg, R.I. (ed.) *China into Africa. Trade, Aid and Influence*. Washington D.C.: Brookings Institution Press, pp. 21–49.

Mawdsley, E. (2012) *From Recipients to Donors. Emerging Powers and the Changing Development Landscape*.London: Zed Books.

Naidoo, R. (2011) 'Rethinking development: higher education and the new imperialism'. In King, R. , Marginson, S. and Naidoo, R. (eds) *Handbook on Globalization and Higher Education*. Cheltenham: Edward Elgar, pp. 40–58.

Nordtveit, B.H. (2011) 'An emerging donor in education and development: a case study of China in Cameroon', *International Journal of Educational Development*, 31 (2), 99–108.

Obamba, M.O. and Mwema, J.K. (2009) 'Symmetry and asymmetry: new contours, paradigms, and politics in African academic partnerships', *Higher Education Policy*, 22 (3), 349–371.

Oyewole, O. (2009) 'Internationalization and its implications for the quality of higher education in Africa', *Higher Education Policy* 22 (3), 319–329.

Pan, S.Y. (2013) 'Confucius Institute project: China's cultural diplomacy and soft power projection', *Asian Education and Development Studies*, 2 (1), 22–33.

Phiri, B.J. (2001) *The Crisis of an African University: A Historical Appraisal of the University of Zambia, 1965–2000.* Denver: International Academic Publishers Ltd.

Rawoo (n.d.) *Supporting Capacity Building for Research in the South. Recommendations for Dutch Policy.* Advisory Council for Scientific Research in Development Problems. Publication no. 10. Available at: www.nuffic.nl/en/library/rawoo-publications/view (accessed 28 May 2015).

Sahlins, M. (2013) *China U.* New York: The Nation. Available at: www.thenation.com/article/176888/china-u# (accessed 10 November 2013).

Samoff, J. and Carrol, B. (2004) 'The promise of partnership and continuities of dependence: external support to higher education in Africa', *African Studies Review*, 47 (1), 67–199.

Siwela, A.A. (1995) 'Discussion paper'. In De Gast, W.J. (ed.) *Linkages Revisited. Higher Education and Development Cooperation: An Assessment.* The Hague: Nuffic, pp. 194–208.

Starr, D. (2009) 'Chinese language education in Europe: the Confucius Institutes', *European Journal of Education*, 44 (1), 65–82.

Takala, T. (1998) 'Making educational policy under influence of external assistance and national politics – a comparative analysis of the education sector policy documents of Ethiopia, Mozambique, Namibia and Zambia', *International Journal of Educational Development*, 18 (4), 319–335.

UNOSSC (2014) *What Is South–South Cooperation?.* United Nations Office for South–South Cooperation. Available at: http://ssc.undp.org/content/ssc/about/what_is_ssc.html (accessed 10 December 2014).

UNZA (2012) *Strategic Plan 2013–2017.* Lusaka: University of Zambia.

Wekesa, B. (2013) 'Emerging trends and patterns in China–Africa media dynamics: a discussion from an East African perspective', *Ecquid Novi: African Journalism Studies*, 34 (3), 62–78.

Wheeler, A. (2014) 'Cultural diplomacy, language planning, and the case of the University of Nairobi Confucius Institute', *Journal of Asian and African Studies*, 49 (1), 49–63.

Yang, R. (2010) 'Soft power and higher education: an examination of China's Confucius Institutes', *Globalisation, Societies and Education*, 8 (2), 235–245.

Part II

Researching and teaching climate change in Africa

Whose reality counts?

6 Power of knowledge under changing conditions

Lessons from a Sahelian village under climate change

Jonas Østergaard Nielsen, Marie Ladekjær Gravesen and Stig Jensen

Introduction

This chapter reflects on the so-called 'crisis of knowledge' discussion (Dei et al., 2002). This discussion highlights how external factors, such as globalisation and commodification, often have negative implications on the way in which the 'localised knowledge' is contested, negotiated, constructed and applied. The main focus of this chapter is to add some new dimensions besides globalisation and commodification to this discussion. In particular, we argue that issues related to climate change bring new challenges to social conditions and constructions of the localised knowledge because knowledge is negotiated often in the light of such phenomena (Ahlborg and Nightingale, 2012).

Herein, the point of digression is a specific local context. Following Livingstone (2003, 2012), we want to show that 'cultural spaces' are the places where knowledge about climate change is generated and employed. By 'particularising climatic experience' (Livingstone, 2012: 93), we hence contend that although climate change is a global phenomenon, its actual consequences and negotiations are always profoundly local (e.g. Cruikshank, 2005). By local cultural spaces, we imply, again following Livingstone (2003), a social space for everyday life embedded in wider social, economic, political, environmental, historical and educational relations (see also Chapter 7). As Livingstone (2003) states:

> All of us, in one way or another, are implicated in global transaction. As the Irish poet Seamus Heaney puts it: 'We are no longer just parishioners of the local.' The circulation of goods and commodities, information and data, means that it [the local] is persistently shaped and reshaped by distant influences and agents.
>
> (Livingstone, 2003: 7)

The extent to which these forces influence and change 'the local' is, however, a widely debated topic. For some, like Dei et al. (2002), the external factors, here labelled 'globalisation', have severe impacts on local knowledge systems:

> Globalization has accelerated the flow of cultures across geographical, political, and cultural borders … For indigenous peoples, the 'crisis of knowledge' can be seen in, or has resulted in, the following: fragmentation of traditional values and beliefs; erosion of spirituality; distortions in local, regional, and national ecosystems and economies; and tension related to cultural revitalization and reclamation.
>
> (Dei et al., 2002: 4)

Similar statements can be found in the climate change literature (e.g. Ford and Furgal, 2009; Green and Raygorodetsky, 2010; Salick, 2009). Subsistence farmers in Sub-Saharan Africa have, for example, climate sensitive livelihoods which make them particularly sensitive to climate change. Long histories of neglected and/or oppressive policies imposed upon them by centralised governments have further enhanced their vulnerability to climate change. The combination of ecological and socioeconomic vulnerability has often led to statements entailing the loss of traditional life-ways and, in turn, local knowledge in Sub-Saharan Africa (e.g. Salick, 2009).

Our perspective is slightly different. We, by focusing on the development and production of local knowledge, want to argue that such knowledge cannot be perceived being 'in danger' as this implies an understanding of knowledge as something inherently stable. In the presentation and analysis of ethnographic data from rural Northern Burkina Faso, we illustrate how adaptation to a changing biophysical environment is linked to new knowledge systems associated with the presence of development projects and new educational skills often located among young people. Our data show that climate variability has impacts on established systems of social organisation and knowledge and as such can be seen to represent a 'crisis of knowledge' as understood by Dei et al. (2002). However, we want to move beyond the 'crisis of knowledge' discourse inherent in most of the literature on local/indigenous knowledge. A central point of this paper is to argue that this discourse highlights not only the need to explore what happens to knowledge production when surrounding conditions change, but also, that it does not capture the fluid and negotiated nature of local knowledge production in Sub-Saharan Africa communities (Lefale, 2010).

The chapter is organised as follows. First an overview of current research on the topic 'local knowledge' is presented. Focus is on what we here term local experience-based knowledge and the difference between this and Western knowledge. While we maintain the differences between knowledge modes, a central point is to show how all modes of knowledge are negotiated, context specific and often influenced by outside forces. This is followed by the case study of Biidi 2, a small village in Northern Burkina Faso. A major point of the case is to show that knowledge is locally negotiated but global events often open up for such negotiations. In this case, climate change, declining agricultural production, the presence of development projects in the village and the education of Mamadou, the main instigator and holder of new types of knowledge are intertwined in order to illustrate how such negotiations work out. The insights from the case study and the theoretical framework are our foundation for the concluding discussion. Here, we focus on the 'crisis of knowledge' discourse arguing that what is seen in the study village is not as such a crisis of knowledge but a negotiation of knowledge. A central point is that this negotiation, to a large extend, is controlled by local people with a Western style education. By Western style education, we simply mean education obtained in a school based upon a largely colonial/Western system and with a curriculum focused on the ability to read and write and do basic arithmetic (see Chapter 2).

Theoretical overview

In any given community, localised experience-based knowledge is often anchored in various local authorities, who administer land and norms and practices, for example, in relation to land management (Zimmerman, 2005; Lefale, 2010). Berkes defines this localised experience-based knowledge as:

> [A] cumulative body of knowledge, practice, and belief, evolving by adaptive processes and handed down through generations by cultural transmission, about the relationships of living beings (including humans) with one another and with their environment [...] It includes traditional medicinal, agricultural and ecological knowledge, as well as traditional music, stories and poems, dance, design, and sculpture.
>
> (Berkes in Lefale, 2010: 319)

Thus, the local knowledge category is normally understood as locally founded, orally transmitted, culturally dependent and contextually specific. It is generated through the negotiated field of inter-personal relations, and refers to the authorities within traditional or endogenous institutions (Zimmerman, 2005). Local authorities in Sub-Saharan Africa are often represented by chiefs and elders along with more officially sanctioned systems of governance (Mbiti, 1996). Local knowledge is thus integrated both in the management of economic and social resources, and administrative and more traditional forms of power (Lefale, 2010; Salm and Falola, 2002).

Embedded in these often counterpoised power regimes and dealing with, for example, matters of sociality and land management, the local knowledge can be considered a product of a process in which knowledge constantly evolves and adapts to the changing aspects in the social as well as biophysical environment. For instance, natural resource management stems from local knowledge about biophysical surroundings enacted through various socially sanctioned practices. As such natural resource management often works as a 'binding force' linking the biophysical surroundings with a social identity (Olupona, 2003; Salm and Falola, 2002). In that sense, local experience-based knowledge functions as an integrating construction that generates as well as adds meaning to the particular local environment to which it is linked. However, this grounding within a particular locality can make the local knowledge somewhat limited (Agrawal, 2008) and its validity might be challenged if it were to cover new elements at a local scale, such as, for example, climate variability. For instance, local knowledge that guides farming practices get validity and support from the community only as long as they work. But when the surrounding biophysical environment changes the knowledge might get flawed:

> [T]rees, wind and birds have been subjects of attentive scrutiny by local farmers who rely on them to predict seasonal rainfall. But where climate change is eroding the reliability of such indicators, public attention may shift from them to different, external sources of information, such as radio and television weather forecasts.
>
> (Roncoli et al., 2009: 91)

Local communities, under changing conditions caused by, for instance, climate variability, might, in other words, turn towards Western scientific knowledge when local experience-based knowledge becomes insufficient. This often leads to a juxtaposition of Western scientific knowledge and local experience-based knowledge. The actual outcome of such an encountering process depends on the (often unequal) abilities among individual community members to make use of and combine the two knowledge modes (Peet and Watts, 2004). It also requires actors who understand and have ability to draw on both Western style knowledge and the local mechanisms at play. Roncoli et al. argue, for example, that an adaptation strategy to climate variability often involves:

> balancing risk and uncertainties in one area with those in other areas, (...) [and hence], people constantly juggle different kinds of risk, not only related to climate variation but also to livestock disease, price fluctuations, violent attacks, legal prosecution, and social marginalisation.
>
> (Roncoli et al., 2009: 100)

The analysis of this encountering process requires an understanding of the differences and similarities between the two knowledge modes, because local people often combine, or juxtapose, the modes when facing new conditions. The scientific and the experience-based knowledge modes are dissimilar when it comes to 'knowledge potential or actual application, the level of codification, the individual or collective form of possession, and legal status' (Lefale, 2010: 319). Scientific knowledge is largely based on scientifically established understandings, concepts and methods within a relatively small and well-defined field. It includes therefore the history of the studied only to a small extent, as focus is on how a constituent is perceived in the here and now by a 'neutral' scientist (Fairhead and Leach, 1996). In contrast and in line with the argument of Hountondji (1995), the local knowledge mode functions as a point of connection between past, present and future contextual relations that rely on a constant (re)negotiation in order for the mode to be upheld.

One consequence of its dependence on contextual relations is that the local knowledge mode is understandable primarily to the insiders making it difficult to convey its concepts and values to an 'outsider'. Furthermore, it is often functional only inside certain geographical boundaries, making the scope of the mode limited and potentially relatively inflexible in relation to larger external influences, such as climate variability and change. This does not imply that local knowledge is useless, but merely that the holders, be they 'insiders' or 'outsiders', of scientific knowledge can relatively easily come to disregard it as being too limited in scope. In contrast, scientific knowledge, even though it might also be seen as contextual, both in terms of its place of production and creation of data (Latour, 1993), is legitimised through its ability to be generalised. Thus, a potential to reach across the scales, such as local and global, is inherent in scientific knowledge and the institutions based largely upon it, such as, for example, development organisations, government and higher educational institutions (Agrawal, 2008).

These distinctions have implications for analysis of the juxtaposition of the knowledge modes or the way in which scientific knowledge becomes contextualised. When development organisations, for example and as we shall see in the next section, enter the local scene with scientific knowledge and/or scientific methods, the effect might be that a new standard for knowledge validity and production is set. This new standard is often difficult to embrace by the people mostly grounded by the local experience-based knowledge. In contrast, resourceful and often educated people are better positioned to understand, acquire and use new knowledge modes, in other words, the hybrid (or indeed replacement) of localised experience and scientific knowledge is often reared by the people having a Western educational background (Venema and van den Breemer, 1999).

The case

The case that a Western educational background can matter in cultural spaces of knowledge negotiation in Sub-Saharan Africa is reflected in the ethnographic data presented in this section. Based upon fieldwork carried out in the village of Biidi 2 in Oudalan, the northernmost province of Burkina Faso, it is illustrated how education makes a difference when a climatic situation requiring new livelihood strategies emerges.[1]

Biidi 2

After an initial population boom in the early 1900s, the village developed into its present shape in the mid-1900s, with four separate quarters (*debeere*), organised according to patrilineal descent and ethnicity (see also Matlon, 1994; Riesman, 1977). Three ethnic groups, Rimaiibe, Fulbe and Wahilbe, are living in the village. Of these, 44 per cent are under the age of 15 years. The village is located upon a dune and surrounded by fields cultivated with millet, sorghum and

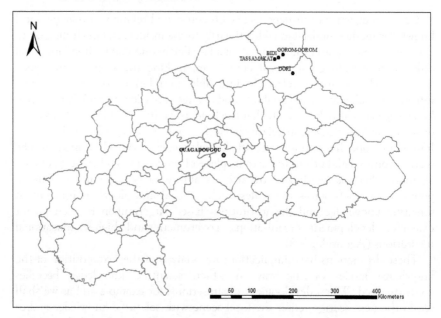

Figure 6.1 The location of Biidi 2 in Burkina Faso

Source: adapted by Sarah D'haen on basis of data from Institut National de la Geographie, Burkina Faso.

cowpeas, and savannah on which most of the cattle graze. The presence of gardens makes possible the cultivation of several vegetables and fruits such as sweet potatoes, tomatoes, aubergines, mangos and banana. These, together with livestock and straw mats, are the only products that are marketed in Gorom-Gorom and Tasamakat. There is, however, no strong market potential as population density in the region is low, poverty is widespread and both markets are relatively far away. Hence money is earned mainly via migration to Abidjan, Ivory Coast, and working for development projects, both are becoming increasingly important activities (e.g. Nielsen, 2009; Nielsen and Reenberg, 2010b; Nielsen et al., 2012).

Climate variability

A major reason why off-farm livelihood strategies have become so important is the climate variability experienced in the region since the early 1950s. This variability has in general made rain fed agricultural production very difficult.

The 1950s and 1960s were relatively wet decades compared to the previous five decades. The extreme drought that hit the region in the early 1970s heralded a two-decade long period of below average rainfall (Le Barbé et al., 2002; Lebel and Ali, 2009). The dry periods of 1970s and 1980s have been replaced by a more complex rainfall pattern after 1990s to present. Dry conditions still prevail over the Western Sahel, whereas it is wetter in the Eastern and Central Sahel wherein Biidi 2 is located (Lebel and Ali, 2009; Mertz et al., 2012). The role of the current wetter trend in signifying a climatic shift remains highly contested (Christensen et al., 2007). Yet, rainfall in Sahel continues to display a high degree of variability across the region 'leaving some areas in some years well supplied, yet other regions and other years dry and parched' (Hulme, 2001: 19). This variability is likely to increase in African drylands, and both prolonged droughts and extreme rainfall events may become more frequent (Adger et al., 2007; Kurukulasuriya et al., 2006).

Despite these general scientific predictions of more rain, the villagers in Biidi 2 emphasise that the rainy season is worse and less predictable now than it used to be 40 years ago and that it has a larger number of 'false starts' (making it extremely difficult to know when to sow). The wind is also perceived to have become stronger (compared to 2007/2008), causing more pronounced movements of sand, filling up river beds and destroying crops. Furthermore, the villagers mention soil degradation, the disappearance of plants, trees, wild fauna and watering holes, and growing problems with pests as consequences of climate variability.

Off-farm livelihood diversification

Prior to the dry 1970s and 1980s, the village was self-sufficient in food. Since the dry decades, the harvests have only provided food for about seven to nine months, the latter being the case only in the best of years for the largest and most efficient households. The increasing rain after the mid-2000s has not changed this. The rain often falls too hard causing significant run-off with very little soil saturation and crop damage. It also tends to fall within short time periods with long breaks in between the two falls; this can cause the millet to wither. The rain is also often accompanied by heavy winds, which makes 'the millet dance' and results in crop damage. Therefore all households in Biidi 2 have to buy food in order to cover their subsistence needs. Over the last 35 years mainly Rimaiibe and Wahilbe (Nielsen and Reenberg, 2010b) have diversified their livelihoods in the response of continuously unreliable outcomes of rain-fed agriculture.

A large number of livelihood strategies are present in the village. The two most important ones are labour migration and development work. This is due to the income that these strategies generate compared to others like gardening, small-scale commerce, fishing, brick making, fire-wood collection and even selling of cattle. Moreover, the perceived stability and dependence on these strategies are important factors. Most households in general seem to earn enough money to buy food to last the whole year. The growing importance of livelihood diversification over the last 30 years is supported by comparison with a study done in Biidi 2 in 1995 by Reenberg and Fog (1995), who note that in the early 1990s, off-farm strategies only rarely supplemented agricultural production, whereas today, they are common in the village (Nielsen and Reenberg, 2010a). Consequently, off-farm livelihood strategies today represent the mainstay of income and food security.

Off-farm livelihood strategies and education

The importance of development work and migration for food security has resulted in an emphasis on knowledge, skills and technologies that facilitate successful participation in off-farm strategies. The most important of these are the ability to understand and speak French, read and write Fulfulde, do basic arithmetic and negotiate with and organise work related to development projects.

Like most other villages in Burkina Faso a group 'Comité Villageous de Dévelopment' has been in place since the mid-1990s. Dealing with all matters regarding development projects, this group is influential regarding the presence and management of development projects. Besides running established projects, they spend a great deal of time in convincing managers of not yet present projects to establish in Biidi 2. This task requires that the members have a wide network, language skills, a mobile phone and the ability to meet and negotiate with representatives of the projects. After launching a project, its execution requires literacy, basic accounting, the ability to organise labour according to a time schedule and a working knowledge of French as many project extension officers speak very little Fulfulde. The development extension workers also deemed the educational level of the committee members important for maintaining their relationship with the village: '[F]or a project to be successful', a representative of a Dutch funded project explained, 'the members of the *Comité Villageous de Dévelopment* need to have an educational level making it possible for us to communicate regarding their needs and our abilities.' Moreover, he continued: '[W]e need to be able to trust that the project is left in capable hands as the villagers themselves are to manage it once we are gone.'

Figure 6.2 Sign just off the main road indicating some of the international development agencies present in the village

Photo: J.Ø. Nielsen.

Having an educational background is also deemed important for the second most important livelihood strategy: migration. Again the ability to speak French as well as Jula is considered important when migrating, as these are the working languages in Abidjan. Navigating the urban sprawl of Abidjan and increasingly Ouagadougou (Nielsen, in press), finding employment, a place to rent, negotiate wages and labour conditions, and paying bills also require a network, literacy and basic mathematical skills.

It was also noted in almost all interviews that working with urban employers in Abidjan requires 'civilisation'. Besides a general level of schooling, a 'civilised' person possesses the ability to grasp political and economic information as well as knowledge about places such as France (Nielsen, 2009; Nielsen and Reenberg, 2010b). Something 'the young people going to school in Gorom-Gorom learn how to do' an older couple explained in an interview.

Livelihood diversifications, the relegation of old people's knowledge and education

All of the above attributes are found, in the village, mainly among the men less than 45 years of age. It is hence also, to a very large extent, them who migrate and work for the development projects.[2] The members of the *Comité Villageous de Dévelopment* are, for example, all under the age of 45 years. Every year, after the end of the agricultural activities in November and December, a large proportion of men migrate. In December 2007, for example, a total of 39 per cent of men in the age group 25–40 years left, and among the men older than 40 years only 7 per cent left (Nielsen and Reenberg, 2010b). The age distribution of men working for development projects is very similar to that found for migration. Almost all the young men not on migration participate to a large extent in development project work. For men older than 40 years this is not the case.

The low participation of men over 40 years of age in migration and development work was by both young and older men linked to their lack of what was termed in the village 'important knowledge'. None of the men in the group older than 40 years had ever been to school, none were literate, spoke French, knew even simple arithmetic, had any network outside the immediate area and only one owned a motorbike and a mobile phone. One effect of this was, as Hamadou, a 60-year-old Wahilbe put it, that 'young people are therefore not interested in what we have to say'. This state of affairs was in contrast with the stories from the old people, who were young prior to the major droughts, when the elders were consulted on various occasions and particularly in connection with agricultural activities. Their fathers and uncles were portrayed in the interviews with older men and women as possessing the crucial knowledge of when to sow, for example. Now this is impossible to guess and agricultural knowledge is simply no longer valued as much due to the ever-diminishing harvests.

Figure 6.3 A young man just back from migration proudly showing off his newly acquired motor bike

Photo: J.Ø. Nielsen.

Another old man said:

> Who would want to know about how it used to be. Agricultural and pastoral knowledge needs to be applicable. I used to know when to take the cattle and where, when to plant millet and all that. The rain has changed so much I no longer know this. So why ask me?

The marginalisation of the knowledge held by old people was echoed by men in the age group 18–40 years. The elders were acknowledged as wise regarding issues such as religious traditions and illnesses, but not in relation to how to feed the village. Layya, a young Fulbe man, expressed it like this: 'The old have no "jambaade" [answer(s)] on how to get by. They don't know how things are done today.'

The rise to power of the 'Gol-Kokko-Tinndinooje'

The nexus of climate change, livelihood diversification strategies and education was personified by the rise to power of Mamadou, or, as he was locally known, the 'Gol-Kokko-Tinndinooje', meaning the one who gives advice. Mamadou was only a young Rimaiibe man of 23 years when the early Non-Governmental

Organisations (NGOs) began to enter Oudalan including Biidi 2 in the beginning of the 1990s, largely due to the food crisis caused by diminishing rain. Due to need of establishing local partners in order to carry out the various projects a *Comité Villageous de Dévelopment* was established on decree from the government. The purpose of the committee was to ensure that development projects comply with good governance including local participation in and control over the projects once implemented.

In Biidi 2 the *Comité Villageous de Dévelopment* presented the first public challenge to the established power and knowledge regimes within living memory in the village. One representative of the local municipality and two of the potential projects (an Italian and a Dutch) made their appearance in the village in 1994. Getting the whole village together in front of a mosque the three explained how the president of the *Comité Villageous de Dévelopment* should be elected. While explaining the roles and responsibilities of the president, it was emphasised by the three outsiders why this position requires someone able to read and write French and Fulfulde and have basic mathematical and organisational skills. Many of the old men, including the 'Jorro', or traditional chief, at the time, did not have these skills. They nonetheless realised that the position entailed real power as the projects were becoming increasingly important for village life (Nielsen et al., 2012), and they argued that although they did not

Figure 6.4 The president of the *Comité Villageous de Dévelopment*, Mamadou, indicating where a new community garden is to be established

Photo: J.Ø. Nielsen.

have the required educational skills they knew how to run and organise things. At the end, however, the village, including the old men led by the Jorro, decided to appoint Mamadou as president of the *Comité Villageous de Développement*.

This choice, according to the people interviewed about the event, was relatively simple. Mamadou was well liked, had his own fields and was considered a good hard-working farmer, but most importantly he was the best 'educated' person in the village. Mamadou graduated from secondary school at the age of 18 with a total combined schooling of 12 years. While not as such a high education, none else in the village had this level of education and he was the only person possessing the requirements of literacy and basic arithmetic skills put forward by the three visitors.

The election of Mamadou did not in itself bring about any shift in internal power relations in the village as the Jorro remained de facto in charge of the village affairs. But more and more projects arrived, and many villagers began to note that Mamadou was actually making their life better. Mamadou himself felt how his influence increased during the late 1990s and early 2000s: 'I was more frequently asked for my opinion and even the Jorro did not interrupt me in meetings if I was talking.' Mamadou linked this to the need for food: 'Project work means income. Income means food. And food is what we need.'

The power shift from the 'Jorro' towards Mamadou was institutionalised administratively in 2006. The local administration in Gorom-Gorom decided that the surrounding 81 villages needed to elect a 'Conseiller' to make administration easier. In Biidi 2, one of the men running for office was Mamadou, and the second, the Jorro. The Jorro wanted the position, as he saw himself as the rightful leader and representative of the village, while Mamadou drew on his ability to provide work and, in turn, food for the village. Mamadou won a comfortable victory. His proven ability to attract and administrate projects and, again, his better education and his knowledge of life outside the village were crucial explanatory factors for this. 'A Conseiller needs to be able to understand and get along with people from Dori and Ouagadougou and therefore he needs civilisation', a group of women stated in an interview. The Jorro, on the other hand, was perceived as having little civilisation and knowledge of value for contemporary life in which agriculture play a smaller and smaller role (see also Rasmussen and Reenberg, 2015) and as lacking the ability to actually get this as he was illiterate. 'How then is he to make life here better?' it was often put.

Because the Conseiller was considered to be a local mayor in the village, voting for Mamadou was moreover seen by many of the voters as a way to extend his power into other domains. Soon after the election, Mamadou appropriated this perceived mandate. Land rights, for example, were still largely administrated by the Jorro at the time, but Mamadou quickly began adjudicating in matters related to land. It was also him that attended all meetings in Gorom-Gorom, who negotiated with all projects and that most people needing advice on various matters went too. While the older men often noted how this state of affairs was somewhat regrettable, they unanimously acknowledged that it was for the better: 'For in a time of wrong rain he knows how to feed the village', a couple of men in their late 50s explained.

Discussion and concluding remarks

The purpose of this chapter was to contribute to the discussion about changing conditions related to the 'crisis of knowledge' debate based on a case study from Northern Burkina Faso. The central idea in the 'crisis of knowledge' literature, as articulated by Dei et al. (2002), is viewing external changes as causing a deterioration of local knowledge conditions. Such deterioration occurs due to a diverse and often mutually related array of external factors, primarily globalisation and commodification, which change the contextual conditions within which local experience-based knowledge was created and maintained. In this chapter we added to these external factors climate change and internationalisation in the form of development projects.

In line with the arguments put forward by Roncoli et al. (2009), the case showed how climate change and variability can create a situation in which localised experience-based knowledge on agricultural production no longer matches with the biophysical environment wherein it was articulated (Olupona, 2003; Salm and Falola, 2003). The erosion of the reliability of this knowledge mode resulted in – by the villagers – shifting of the attention to different and external sources of knowledge. This illustrates the point made in the literature (e.g. Agrawal, 2008) that experience-based knowledge might be somewhat limited when facing fundamental changes like climate variability as these often transcend scales such as the local and the global. Geographically bounded and articulated in often close connection to a particular local biophysical setting, this limitation is not surprising (Olupona, 2003; Salm and Falola, 2003), but this does not necessarily mean that turning towards a different kind of knowledge represents a 'knowledge crisis'. Rather, the nexus of climate change, diminishing agricultural production, the need for new livelihood strategies and the presence of development projects provided a situation in which new knowledge was negotiated and put into practice.

Following the rise of Mamadou's influence, it was shown how his skills, such as literacy, basic arithmetic and civilisation, or Western/scientific styled knowledge made him able to take advantage of this new situation. Free from a close embedding in a particular geographical context, the generalisability of Western style knowledge is often argued to be an inherent property of this knowledge mode (Agrawal, 2008). This was also the case in Biidi 2. Making it possible to actually keep living in the village despite very dramatic local climatic changes, the legitimacy of this knowledge mode was based upon its transferability from one context to another. In research on local knowledge, the ability to embrace different types of knowledge is argued to constitute a central element of this mode (e.g. Lefale, 2010; Salm and Falola, 2002; Zimmerman, 2005). The knowledge context in villages like Biidi 2 is hence not a given but rather generated through a negotiated field of different knowledge modes and inter-personal relations influenced by authorities within local or endogenous institutions (Zimmerman, 2005). Local authorities in Sub-Saharan Africa are often chiefs and elders but might also, if the context changes, include people like Mamadou together with more officially sanctioned systems of governance like development projects (Mbiti, 1996). Local knowledge is, in other words, founded upon its ability to manage economic, social, global and environmental resources and administrative and more traditional forms of power (Lefale, 2010; Salm and Falola, 2002; Zimmerman, 2005). Embedded often in these counterpoised power and knowledge regimes, local knowledge constantly evolves and adapts to changing aspects within these regimes. Understanding knowledge under changing conditions is not just a matter of documenting such social and biophysical regimes and their impacts on local lives and established knowledge, but also, or rather, a matter of exploring how such conditions are dealt with locally through the process of knowledge contextualisation.

This insight adds to the literature (e.g. Lefale, 2010; Peet and Watts, 2004; Roncoli et al., 2009; Salm and Falola, 2002) arguing that local knowledge cannot be seen as one homogenous and temporal stable system but rather as an outcome of cumulative and contextual negotiations often rooted in particular social positions and biophysical settings. If this is so, and the case presented in this chapter indicates this, the understanding of what is contextual or local experienced-based knowledge in the literature needs to include how Western modes of knowledge become contextualised in local settings such as Biidi 2. Mamadou's Western style education (his schooling and his abilities to read, write and do arithmetic) was not interesting per se rather it was his ability to use it in a particular local context dominated by climate variability, food shortage and the need to diversify livelihood strategies that made it relevant. As such, his Western style education was turned into local experience-based knowledge. Local experience-based knowledge hence can be understood best as an integrating construction that generates meaning from as well as adding meaning to the context in which it is to be utilised; it is not only a 'stable' entity handed down through the generations (Lefale, 2010; Salm and Falola, 2002).

The flexibility and multi-dimensionality in terms of what is contextualised and utilised make local experience-based knowledge potentially apt in light of the three main causes of 'crisis of knowledge' – globalisation, commodification and climate change – because such externalities are de-scaled locally, so to speak, by way of contextualisation. The fact that this process of de-scaling was best done by a person with a Western style education is an important insight when discussing the importance, direction and state of education in Africa. It also highlights how the understanding of local experience-based knowledge as something that is claimed to be in 'danger' fails to appreciate how knowledge is never static but always contextualised – something the chapters in this book so eloquently illustrate.

Notes

1 The fieldwork took place in 2007–2008 and 2010 (for detailed methodological information see Nielsen and Reenberg, 2010a; Nielsen and Vigh, 2012).
2 Biidi 2, like other villages in this region (Riesman, 1977), is a patriarchal society where to a large extend only the boys and often only one within a household is given a secondary education as this is a costly affair. Due to this and to a general expectation on behalf of older household members of them migrating to make money for food it is always young men that migrate.

References

Adger, N.W., Agrawala, S., Mirza, M.M.Q., Conde, C., O'Brien, K., Pulhin, J., Pulwarty, R., Smit, B. and Takahashi, K. (2007) 'Assessment of adaptation practices, options, constraints and capacity'. In Parry, M.L. et al. (eds) *Climate Change 2007: Impacts, Adaptation and Vulnerability. Contribution of Working Group II to the Fourth Assessment Report of the Intergovernmental Panel on Climate Change*. Cambridge: Cambridge University Press, pp. 719–743.

Agrawal, A. (2008) *The Role of Local Institutions in Adaptation to Climate Change*. Paper prepared for the Social Dimensions of Climate Change, Social Development Department, Washington DC: The World Bank.

Ahlborg, H. and Nightingale, A.J. (2012) 'Mismatch between scales of knowledge in Nepalese forestry: epistemology, power, and policy implications', *Ecology and Society*, 17 (4), 16.

Christensen, J.H., Hewitson, B., Busuioc, A., Chen, A., Held, I., Jones, R., Kolli, R.K., Kwon, W.T., Laprise, R., Magana Rueda, V., Mearns, L., Menendez, C.G., Raisanen, J., Rinke, A., Sarr, A. and Whetton, P. (2007) 'Regional climate projections'. In Solomon, S. et al. (eds) *Climate Change 2007: The Physical Science Basis. Contribution of Working Group I to the Fourth Assessment Report of the Intergovernmental Panel on Climate Change*. Cambridge: Cambridge University Press, pp. 847–940.

Cruikshank, J. (2005) *Do Glaciers Listen? Local Knowledge, Colonial Encounters & Social Imagination*. Vancouver: UBCPress.

Dei, G., Hall, B. and Rosenberg, D.G. (2002) *Indigenous Knowledge in Global Contexts: Multiple Readings of Our World*. Toronto: The University of Toronto Press.

Fairhead, J. and Leach, M. (1996) *Misreading the African Landscape: Society and Ecology in a Forest-Savanna Mosaic*. Cambridge: Cambridge University Press.

Ford, J.D. and Furgal, C. (2009) 'Foreword to the special issue: climate change impacts, adaptation and vulnerability in the Arctic', *Polar Research*, 28 (1), 1–9.

Green, D. and Raygorodetsky, G. (2010) 'Indigenous knowledge of a changing climate', *Climatic Change*, 100 (2), 239–242.

Hountondji, P. (1995) 'Producing knowledge in Africa today', *African Studies Review*, 38 (3), 1–10.

Hulme, M. (2001) 'Climatic perspectives on Sahelian desiccation: 1973–1998', *Global Environmental Change*, 11 (1), 19–29.

Kurukulasuriya, P., Mendelsohn, R., Hassan, R., Benhin, J., Deressa, T., Diop, M., Eid, H., Fosu, K.Y., Gbetibouo, G., Jain, S., Mahamdou, A., Mano, R., Kabubo-Maiara, J., El Masafawa, S., Molua, E., Ouda, S., Ouedraogo, M., Sene, I., Maddison, D., Seo, SN. and Dinar, A. (2006) 'Will African agriculture survive climate change?' *World Bank Economic Review*, 20 (3), 367–388.

Latour, B. (1993) *We Have Never Been Modern*. Cambridge: Harvard University Press.

Le Barbé, L., Lebel, T. and Tapsoba, D. (2002) 'Rainfall variability in West Africa during the years 1950–90', *Journal of Climate*, 15 (2), 187–202.

Lebel, T. and Ali, A. (2009) 'Recent trends in the Central and Western Sahel rainfall regime (1990–2007)', *Journal of Hydrology*, 375 (1–2), 52–64.

Lefale, P.F. (2010) 'Ua 'afa le Aso stormy weather today: traditional ecological knowledge of weather and climate. The Samoa experience', *Climatic Change*, 100 (2), 317–335.

Livingstone, D.N. (2003) *Putting Science in Its Place: Geographies of Scientific Knowledge*. USA: University of Chicago Press.

Livingstone, D.N. (2012) 'Reflections on the cultural spaces of climate', *Climatic Change*, 113 (1), 91–93.

Matlon, P. (1994) 'Indigenous land use systems and investments in soil fertility in Burkina Faso'. In Bruce, J.W. and Migot-Adholla, S. (eds) *Searching for Land Tenure Security in Africa*. Washington DC: World Bank, pp. 41–69.

Mbiti, J.S. (1996) 'African views of the universe'. In Gottlieb, R. (ed.) *This Sacred Earth: Religion, Nature and Environment*. London: Routledge, pp. 174–180.

Mertz, O., D'haen, S., Maiga, A., Moussa, I.B., Barbier, B., Diouf, A., Diallo, D., Da, D. and Dabi, D. (2012) 'Climate variability and environmental stress in the Sudan-Sahel zone of West Africa', *Ambio*, 41 (4), 380–392.

Nielsen, J.Ø. (2009) 'Drought and marriage: exploring the interconnection between climate variability and social change through a livelihood perspective'. In Hastrup, K. (ed.) *The Question of Resilience: Social Responses to Climate Change*. Copenhagen: The Royal Danish Academy of Science and Letters, pp. 159–177.

Nielsen, J.Ø. (in press) 'I'm staying. Climate variability and circular labour migration in Burkina Faso'. In Dietz, T. et al. (eds) *Climate and Culture. Environmental Change and African Societies*. Leiden: Brill Publisher.

Nielsen, J.Ø. and Reenberg, A. (2010a) 'Temporality and the problem with singling out climate as a current driver of change in a small West African village', *Journal of Arid Environment*, 74 (4), 464–474.

Nielsen, J.Ø. and Reenberg, A. (2010b) 'Cultural barriers to climate change adaptation: a case study from Northern Burkina Faso', *Global Environmental Change*, 20 (1), 142–152.

Nielsen, J.Ø., D'haen, S. and Reenberg, A. (2012) 'Adaptation to climate change as a development project: a case study from Northern Burkina Faso', *Climate and Development*, 4 (1), 16–25.

Nielsen, J.Ø. and Vigh, H. (2012) 'Adaptive lives. Navigating the global food crisis in a changing climate', *Global Environmental Change*, 22 (3), 659–669.

Olupona, J.K. (2003) 'Introduction'. In Olupona, J.K. (ed.) *Beyond Primitivism: Indigenous Religious Traditions and Modernity*. New York and London: Routledge, pp. 1–20.

Peet, R. and Watts, M. (2004) 'Liberating political ecology'. In Peet, R. and Watts, M. (eds) *Liberation Ecologies: Environment, Development, Social Movements*. London: Routledge, pp. 3–42.

Rasmussen, L.V. and Reenberg, A. (2015) 'Multiple outcomes of cultivation in the Sahel: a call for a multifunctional view of farmers' incentives', *International Journal of Agricultural Sustainability*, 13 (1), 1–22.

Reenberg, A. and Fog, B. (1995) 'The spatial pattern and dynamics of a Sahelian agro-ecosystem', *GeoJournal*, 37 (4), 489–499.

Riesman, P. (1977) *Freedom in Fulani Social Life: An Introspective Ethnography*. Chicago: University of Chicago Press.

Roncoli, C., Crane T. and Orlove, B. (2009) 'Fielding climate change in cultural anthropology'. In Crate, S. and Nuttall, M. (eds) *Anthropology and Climate Change, From Encounters to Actions*. California: Left Coast Press, pp. 87–115.

Salick, J. (2009) 'Traditional peoples and climate change', *Global Environmental Change*, 19 (2), 137–139.

Salm, S.J. and Falola, T. (2002) *Culture and Customs in Ghana*. Westport, CT: Greenwood Publishing Group.

Venema, B. and van den Breemer, H. (1999) 'Natural resources management in Africa: approaches, constraints and opportunities'. In Venema, B. and van den Breemer, H. (eds) *Towards Negotiated Co-management of Natural Resources in Africa*. Münster: LIT Verlag, pp. 1–18.

Zimmerman, E. (2005) 'Valuing traditional knowledge: incorporating the experiences of indigenous people into global climate change policies', *New York University Environmental Law Journal*, 13 (3), 803–847.

7 Producing scientific knowledge in Africa today

Auto-ethnographic insights from a climate change researcher

Hanne Kirstine Adriansen, Muhammad Mehmood-Ul-Hassan and Cheikh Mbow

Introduction

This chapter analyses a life-history interview with an African climate change researcher to explore the conditions for scientific knowledge production in Africa. We are inspired by the North Irish geographer David Livingstone and his 2012 article 'Reflections on the cultural spaces of climate' in which he calls for attention to the spatial, the geographical and the location-specific in climate change research. We explore how these issues manifest themselves in the life-history of an African climate change researcher. Thus, we follow Livingstone's recommendation to inquire into the particular, the specific and spatially located knowledge, through which we hope to be able to show something more general about conditions for scientific knowledge production in Africa today. In doing so, we touch upon both the universality and particularity of knowledge. We are also inspired by Beninese philosopher Paulin Hountondji and have partly borrowed our title from his 1995 article 'Producing knowledge in Africa today'. Hountondji applied classic concepts, arguments and theories from development research such as dependency, centre-periphery and world-system to argue that research in Africa was 'extroverted' and 'dependent'. By this he meant that research was dependent on the Global North in a number of ways and not related to the local situation in Africa. This was similar to the industrial economies in Africa that were oriented towards the Global North, dependent on the capitalist markets there instead of being oriented towards the African continent and national and regional needs and economies (Hountondji, 1990). In our discussion, we follow Hountondji's line of thought and look into ways to make African research more 'introvert' and directed towards society. As the chapter is based on the life history of an African researcher who has been actively involved in a number of Danida's research capacity-building projects, we also touch upon the role of donor aid in African higher education. As we will see, such programmes can be important for the career trajectories of African researchers. We use an auto-ethnographic approach (see e.g. Ellis, 2004; Maréchal, 2010) in analysing Cheikh Mbow's life history, which can be defined as: 'A form or method of research that involves self-observation and reflexive investigation in the context of ethnographic field work and writing' (Maréchal, 2010: 43). However, we also reflect upon the auto-ethnography of the other two authors in order to be able to compare and contrast the African experience with experiences from Asia and Europe. The other two authors also have knowledge of and practical experience with capacity development efforts taking place in Africa and have conducted research here.

Before providing a brief account of Mbow's life history, we outline the life-history approach. Mbow's history points to three important and intertwined issues that played out differently through the different phases of his life: an inherited or colonial curriculum; universality of knowledge, namely the transfer of methods and theories from the Global North; and the cultural production of African researchers. Although intertwined, these three issues are analysed separately. In the discussion, we draw on these analyses in order to discuss issues related to producing climate change research in Africa today. Finally, we conclude the chapter by arguing for more place-based approaches to both climate change teaching and climate change research.

A life history approach to understanding African research

In this chapter, it is not the life history *per se* that interests us; instead, we use the life history approach as a novel way of entering the analysis of problems inherent in scientific knowledge production among African academics.

In research from Africa, life history research is linked to oral history projects aiming to explore the culture and history of certain places through the memories and recollections of its people – in their language, using their vocabulary (e.g. Cross and Barker, 1994). In particular, perceptions of change have been subject to study by human geographers and anthropologists alike. The method used in this chapter was developed by one of the authors for studying Senegalese pastoralists and their mobility, taking their oral history tradition into account (Adriansen, 2002). It is a narrative approach that has been subsequently used for understanding shaping of identity of African scholars (see Chapter 8 as well as Møller-Jensen and Madsen, 2015). Cheikh Mbow's narrative was constructed on the basis of informal conversations between the authors and through a time line interview conducted by the second author, Muhammad Mehmood-Ul-Hassan, using a method developed by the first author, Hanne Kirstine Adriansen. First Hassan and Mbow read the article about timeline interviews (Adriansen, 2012) and agreed that it was an appropriate approach. Then they conducted and taped the interview, which was then analysed by all three authors.

In life history research, the intention is to understand how the patterns of different life stories can be related to their wider historical, social, environmental and political contexts. In particular in sociology, the life history interview has been taught as a method for capturing people's own perceptions of their lives (Goodson and Sikes, 2001). It is, however, rare to use the life history approach to academics even though academic knowledge production has come under closer scrutiny, for instance through sociology of scientific knowledge (SSK) and in science and technology studies (STS). We find, however, that life stories can be a good supplement to SSK and STS because the narrative approach can enhance the geographies and power of knowledge production from a personal perspective, and thereby the narrative can be used for pointing to the dilemmas of knowledge production experienced by an academic within her/his context. In the following analysis, we use Goodson and Sikes' (2001) life history approach in a slightly different fashion. Instead of analysing how Mbow's life history can be situated in the wider historical, social, environmental and political context, we use his narrative to point to a range of quite different issues of importance for understanding the conditions for producing scientific knowledge in Africa today.

The life history of an African climate change researcher

Cheikh Mbow was born in Senegal in 1969. As our main interest was Mbow's academic life, we have focused on the educational and professional life history.

The first schooling was a Quran School that Mbow attended from when he was three to six years old. Subsequently, he began primary school where the medium of instruction was French; speaking his local language *Wolof* was forbidden and punished. Mbow enjoyed going to school; he was good at it and won many prizes. After secondary school, he went straight to high school, where he also excelled and expected to win a scholarship to go to France to study physical geography. However, Mbow did not get the scholarship as the Senegalese government wanted students to register to a new university in Saint Louis in the north of Senegal. For various reasons, he ended up studying physical geography at Université de Cheikh Anta Diop in Dakar.[1] Reflecting over the curriculum, Mbow points out that primary and secondary school, as well as high school, were French inherited programmes with a curriculum that was basically inspired from France. From first to third year of geography at university, all maps and fundamental books were from France and concerned European realities. Many of Mbow's lecturers were French researchers who had relocated to Senegal under technical cooperation or were members of research organisations such as Institut de Recherche pour le Development (IRD), formerly known as ORSTOM. Only after the third year at university did knowledge about Africa and Senegal feature as part of the course and Mbow could study climate, hydrology, geology, vegetation and geomorphology of Africa. The information was mostly based on rare sources such as doctoral theses and limited publications written by local academic staff either inspired by or based on French theories and methods.

When doing his MSc and PhD, Mbow was supported by Danida's ENRECA (Enhancement of Research Capacity) programme. For his master's degree, Mbow worked on detecting fires using satellite data. Fieldwork for his PhD research was carried out in a national park in Senegal where he studied the impacts of bushfires on biodiversity in collaboration with geographers from the University of Copenhagen, Denmark. For his MSc and PhD research, Mbow was working on topics relevant to his own country, but using methods designed in the Global

North, in particular from France. Some peculiar situations arose in relation to non-adapted approaches; for example, phytosociology was taught using a mechanistic application of plant community assessment using minimum quadrat techniques (see next section). There were many other examples e.g. soil science and climate analysis where particular methods and theories from the Global North were used as if these were universal. However, the transfer and applicability of these theories and methods in an African context was only debated on rare occasions.

After his PhD, Mbow obtained a Post Doc position for two years at Sherbrook University in Quebec, Canada, where he was working on the development of a fire-behaviour model and using remote sensing for fire risk assessment. As required by the French system, Mbow decided to work towards his second doctoral thesis, the habilitation (Doctorat d'Etat), with the Université de Cheikh Anta Diop de Dakar. After acquiring it, he became professor at the Institute of Environmental Science. After some years of research, Mbow began to challenge some of the received knowledge and managed to specify what was particular to Africa (see example 1). He labels this: 'New knowledge made for Africa by an African'.[2] It turned out that this expertise was in high demand internationally. Part of this demand was related to network development and the need to find the critical mass necessary for international initiatives. Then most of Mbow's work became validation of global or regional analyses. While there were positive aspects of being involved in large consortia for project development, the African team was involved mostly in data collection; when it came to analysis and publication, the Northern partners took over. In 2012, Mbow decided to pursue his career outside the Senegalese university system and became employed as a senior scientist at the International Centre for Research in Agroforestry (ICRAF) in Kenya, while also serving as an adjunct associate professor at the University of Michigan in the US. As a prominent climate change researcher, Mbow is concerned about how to unlock the potential of African universities to support and inform societal efforts on climate change. Despite being trained in satellite remote sensing, issues of legitimacy and ownership of climate change research are very important for Mbow. Through this interest, Mbow has also seen a need to supplement satellite remote sensing with local knowledge. He argues that the scientific community and decision makers should increase their recognition of local experience-based knowledges. For centuries, this knowledge – which is transmitted and translated from one generation to another – has been used and adapted to respond to climate change. Applied science is at the heart of Mbow's work; he argues that researchers should listen more to local people who are used to finding solutions to their everyday problems. He wants to change things, which is also reflected in his career choices; Africa is his preferred continent. He would also like to move back to Senegal, if he can get a job where he can make changes to the system. The changes he wants to make are to some extent inspired by his academic travels, as will become clear.

In the following, we use Mbow's history as an entry point for analysing three intertwined issues that can be distilled from Mbow's account. In the analyses, we draw on literature and debates from quite different fields ranging from biology, to pedagogy, to post-colonial critique. The first issue is an inherited curriculum and its Africanisation; the second issue is the geography of knowledge production; the third issue is the cultural production of African researchers. In the discussion, we address a pertinent issue for Mbow: how climate change research can have more impact on the ground.

An inherited colonial curriculum and Africanisation

When looking back at his experiences in the first years at university, Mbow notes: 'I knew all about the geography and biology of France but nothing about that of Senegal.' This is quite typical of education programmes in Africa after independence. The present day school systems in Africa were introduced by the colonial regimes and are largely dependent on imported Eurocentric systems (Shizha, 2014). This means they inherited the curriculum and way of thinking from Western epistemology out of which the whole idea of mass-schooling grew (Anderson-Levitt, 2003). Breidlid (2013) has shown how the modernist, Western epistemology became hegemonic in Africa during and after colonialism and the spread of capitalist market economy. Through a series of case studies, Breidlid illustrates how this hegemonic discourse has shaped the educational architecture across Africa. This architecture of formal schooling had different purposes: over and above teaching children to read and write, formal schooling also entailed the production of modern citizens and was thus related to the whole concept of nation building (Anderson-Levitt, 2003). This means that after colonialism, the newly independent nation states kept the formal schooling systems because now they served national interests – shaping national citizens in the post-colonial era (Woolman, 2001). In that respect, the new independent elite took over the hegemonic discourse of modernisation inherited from the colonial powers – a discourse within which they had been trained (Shizha, 2014). An important part of the inherited school system was the curriculum, as pointed out in Mbow's quote above.

However, since the 1990s, there has been a new desire to Africanise or indigenise the curriculum (Semali, 1999). The Africanisation of curriculum debate has been most pronounced in South Africa, where it was used as a vehicle for building African identity in the period following democratic elections in 1994 (Crossman, 2004). While some refer to the indigenisation of the curriculum, we find the word Africanisation more appropriate. However, by applying the word Africanisation we do not wish to imply that only one type of African knowledge or knowledge system exists; instead, we want to emphasise the spatially situatedness of knowledge.

During the interview with Mbow, the colonial heritage is evident at a number of different levels. When talking about his education and professional life, Mbow sees the issue of language and curriculum in different ways. With regard to his own life and intellectual development, Mbow identifies four distinct phases, as seen in Box 7.1.

Box 7.1 Phases of Mbow's intellectual development

Dependence: I went to primary, secondary and high school in Louga, Senegal. All public schools had French inherited programmes and the curriculum was inspired from France. The university was no different; from first to third year of geography, all maps and fundamental books were from France and many of my lecturers were French.

Transition: After my 3rd year at university (*license* in French), knowledge about Africa and Senegal became part of our training. We studied the climate, hydrology, geology, vegetation and geomorphology of Africa. This literature was not textbook based, but often doctoral thesis and other publications written by local academic staff.

Production: For my MSc and PhD research, I worked on topics relevant to my own country, namely about how Niokolo Koba national park was affected by recurrent bush fires. However, I used methods designed from the Global North, in particular from France, and benefitted from a capacity-building programme in Denmark.

Emancipation: After several years of research, I began challenging some of the received knowledge and managed to specify what is particular to Africa. After being able to contextualise knowledge, I was able to create knowledge that concerned and responded to societal needs and local realities in Africa. As this expertise is in demand internationally, I try to negotiate strong roles in partnership with researchers from the Global North.

While some Africanisation of curriculum has taken place after independence, this is most common within the liberal arts (African history, literature and philosophy). Natural science was and is more marked by the ideas of universality of knowledge; consequently, little Africanisation has taken place within this part of the curriculum (Shizha, 2014; Woolman, 2001). Even though there has been some Africanisation of curriculum, we would argue that Mbow's experiences are by no means resigned to history. Moreover, the selection of curriculum is not objective and innocent; curriculum is in fact a very powerful area: 'The curriculum is power-saturated and involves the power to construct, validate, and legitimize knowledge, and what is acceptable and not' (Dei, 2014: 171). Thus, the selection of curriculum is based on the values of the powerful and reproduces their values. A large part of the knowledge that is validated in African schools by being presented as curriculum is a cultural reproduction of the Global North, structured in ways that may alienate African students (Shizha, 2014; Woolman, 2001). Curriculum concerns the decisions about what is taught in schools, making it highly embedded in the politics of knowledge. By choosing a certain curriculum, we also decide on questions such as: 'What is valid knowledge? Whose knowledge?

What is the purpose of that knowledge?' (Shizha, 2014: 114). Therefore, we should pay attention to school curricula, the way teaching takes place in schools, and notice who decides on curriculum knowledge. Recent research within climate change research and environmental education focus on the importance of paying attention to the location specific (e.g. Engel-Di Mauro and Carroll, 2014; Livingstone, 2012). Livingstone argues that climate knowledge is not stable, secure or self-evident and therefore we need to 'problematise climatic knowledge [...] particularise climatic experience [...and] pluralise climatic meaning' (Livingstone, 2012: 92–93). Furthermore, he calls for the need to attend to human experiences of climate through inquiring into the particular, the specific and the spatially located. This is because:

> What climate means to people is conditioned by the places people occupy, the histories they share, the cultural values they absorb. Presumptions about what the idea of climate change must – or should – mean to people fall foul of precisely this careful interrogation of particularity.
>
> (Livingstone, 2012: 92–93)

Finally, Livingstone emphasises that climate is not limited by any single meaning. Climate and climate change are contested concepts, located in different worlds. Thus Livingstone's arguments are relevant in regard to the discussion of Africanisation of the curriculum even though they are not made with particular reference to Africa. With respect to environmental education, Engel-Di Mauro and Carroll call for a 'place-based' approach, this entails calling into question 'received views about how people relate to land and environments, and, more specifically, raise awareness and sensitivity to colonial relationships underlying people/environment relations' (Engel-Di Mauro and Carroll, 2014: 70). Thus their approach is very similar to Livingstone's geographical approach.

Climate change research and its policy implementation is a multi-disciplinary field encompassing social science. As shown in Chapter 2 in this book, social scientists (e.g. Connell, 2007; Smith, 2012) have also pointed to the issues of a Eurocentric curriculum and raised a post-colonial critique of research that does not take the spatial context of people into consideration. As argued by Engel-Di Mauro and Carroll (2014), 'conventional' environmental education approaches have often neglected lived experiences in society, the diversity of environments and the ways in which environments are also products of social processes. When Mbow started teaching students about climate change in Senegal, he had to make his own curriculum due to the lack of Senegalese-based case studies in the books being taught: 'Climate change is particularly interesting because this curriculum has to be place specific.' There were no references on what to teach at various levels. He used his own research and some existing information on nascent African knowledge in that field to design the structure and content of the course. Even today, Mbow explains, there are only few examples of a specific African curriculum on climate change, despite efforts of the START[3] international, WASCAL/SASCAL[4] in West and Southern Africa, differentially targeted at degree seeking students as well as at various societal stakeholder groups outside academia. Moreover, there is limited faculty development for excellence in teaching climate change issues, despite many existing resources and emerging efforts in integrating climate change issues into the curriculum (e.g. by African Forest Forum, ANAFE). In Mbow's experience, when climate change curriculum is place-based, it is more likely that it will have impact on the ground. However, it is difficult to obtain an African curriculum because the educational systems of Africa still rely on a colonial structure, and the scientific knowledge systems are embedded in those of the Global North. While indigenous or local experience-based knowledge is given more attention, it is important to bear in mind that 'not all knowledges are given the same amount of capital in the academy', to use the words of Emeagwali and Dei (2014: xi). Therefore, it is difficult to exchange the inherited colonial curriculum in African schools.

The geography of knowledge production

For Mbow, his PhD project entailed knowledge production about Africa 'but using methods designed in the Global North, in particular from France'. This is related to the fact that hegemonic knowledge is sometimes presented as universal knowledge, as we will show in this section. Some 20–25 years ago, the Beninese philosopher Paulin Hountondji wrote about the conditions for scientific knowledge production in Africa. In his articles 'Scientific dependence in Africa today' (1990) and 'Producing knowledge in Africa today' (1995), Hountondji pointed out that theories and methods developed in the Global North were transferred to Africa as if they were universally applicable. Hountondji introduced his argument about scientific dependence of African universities by quoting the French biologist De Certaines, who was enrolled at Université Cheikh Anta Diop in Dakar, Senegal, some years after independence.[5] Based on these experiences, De Certaines wrote:

> In the African universities where I was trained, there was a scientific teaching quite valid in the subject matters I had to learn, but it taught dependence rather than real science. I mean that, for three years I was told how biology had developed through experiments that necessitated the use of facilities unavailable on the spot. Therefore in order to do biology, students had to go abroad. Such and such scientific results were published in such and such journals, but these journals were European or American, and one had to read them abroad [...] I learned that, in the end, all I could do as a biologist in the future would have to be done under the control of American centers, American periodicals, with European facilities, and that all I could ever do at the University of Dakar was to duplicate European experiments, or to conduct minor experiments that would have to be submitted, for publication, to European journals [...] I was told, in a sense: here you are

working on the margins of science; if you really want to reach the heart of the matter, you will have to leave.

(De Certaines, 1978, quoted in Hountondji, 1990: 5–6)

In order to understand De Certaines' experiences, it should be noted that Université Cheikh Anta Diop was the largest and most prestigious university in French West Africa. The university grew out of several French institutions set up by the colonial administration, until 1957 when it became the 18th French public university, attached to the University of Paris and the University of Bordeaux.

Using De Certaines' account as an entry point, Hountondji shows the geography and power of scientific knowledge production in Africa some 25 years ago. However, the uneven geographies are also evident in Mbow's narrative. When he had studied satellite remote sensing in Senegal, it had been purely theoretical: 'One of the shocks when I joined the PhD program in Denmark was to put in practice the theoretical knowledge. I had to learn how to put in practice the theories I had learned.' It is worth noticing that contrary to De Certaines' account about longing for facilities in the Global North that were not available in Africa, Mbow did not come to Denmark to get hands-on-experience. 'You cannot want something you don't know exists,' he says. Uneven geographies are not simply a matter of Global North vs. Global South. Two years before Mbow came to Denmark in relation to his Master's degree, the Danish co-author of this chapter, Hanne Kirstine Adriansen, went to Australia to study for a Master's in satellite remote sensing. For Adriansen, the University of New South Wales in Australia appeared as the best place for these studies and therefore she went there at her own expense – longing for the facilities and opportunities available in Australia. This is an example of mobility within the Global North, a type of mobility that has become even more typical over the past 20 years through the increased internationalisation and commodification of higher education. The main winners of these mobilities are the Anglo-Saxon countries (Brooks and Waters, 2011; Rizvi, 2005). Thus, we find it important to add this dimension to the uneven geographies of higher education described by De Certaines and Hountondji.

Hountondji's main concern in regard to scientific knowledge production is that the Global South remains a data mining site, while theorising takes place in the Global North. The central aspect of scientific activity is theorising, which is why this division of labour is so detrimental to African universities, leaving them in a dependency relationship with universities and research institutions in the Global North. Mbow recognises this situation and considers it as the new knowledge subordination that follows the geopolitics of other sorts of North–South relationships. In the life history interview, Mbow also mentions this uneven division of labour where African researchers are used for data validation of new models – not for developing them. Sometimes this work is not even recognised through co-authorship. Mbow's and Hountondji's experiences are not the only ones pointing to the unequal geographies of knowledge production. A number of researchers from the social sciences and humanities have analysed how particular Western concepts and theories get labelled as universal (e.g. Chen, 2010; Connell, 2007; Smith, 2012). In the following, we provide two examples of how methods (example 1) and theories (example 2) that were developed under and for particular circumstances in the Global North have been transferred to Africa as if they were universal. These examples are taken from experiences we have had as researchers interested in environment, ecosystems, and climate in Africa.

Example 1: a new method for plant community assessment in African ecosystems

Josias Braun-Blanquet is one of the most influential French phytosociologists and botanists of the twentieth century. Braun-Blanquet developed tools and methods for phytosociology (plant sociology) analysis of the natural vegetation – an approach that has been labelled the Braun-Blanquet approach (Westhoff and Van Der Maarel, 1978). He defined and set methods for many important concepts such as plant community taxonomy, characteristic species, plant associations, etc. Braun-Blanquet's studies spread rapidly over Europe and further afield as his approach was seen as robust and highly repeatable. The method is based on a combination of transect and sampling design that uses quadrats to measure density, frequency, cover and biomass of vegetation (Westhoff and Van Der Maarel, 1978). Mbow and his colleagues at the Institute of Environment Sciences found out, however, that the application of the method in a savannah ecosystem was problematic because different vegetation types require different sample sizes. Furthermore, defining the size of the quadrats in highly sparse vegetation, such as in the African Sahel region, can results in quadrats with an unmanageable size. Given the high spatial variability in vegetation composition in woodland savannah, the Braun-Blanquet method was simply inappropriate. It turned out that it was a method developed under particular conditions, but which had gained a reputation as a universally applicable method. Mbow and his colleagues developed a more suitable approach for plant community assessment of highly mosaicked vegetation types (Sambou et al., 2008). This was an approach that was designed by combining botany with satellite remote sensing methods (not available at Braun-Blanquet's time). This methodological contention came after the direct application of a well-established method to the African context, which is quite different from the European context where the method was originally developed.

Example 2: theories of the relationship between climate and grazing

In this example, we show how a particular theory (about the relationship between grazing and climate) developed in the US was transferred to Africa as if it was universal. This example is derived from Adriansen's research on pastoral mobility in Senegal (see Adriansen, 2002). For decades, the basis for studying ecosystems in Africa – as well as in Europe and the US – was Clements' model of vegetation succession (Clements, 1916), the idea of equilibrium ecosystems and livestock density dependent limitations of primary production. The American plant ecologist Frederic Edward Clements argued that vegetation changes are deterministic series of vegetation types that end with a vegetation climax community. The climax community may fluctuate in composition, but it will remain relatively unchanged over long periods. Grazing pressure produces vegetation changes in a direction opposite to the succession tendency. Therefore, vegetation equilibrium can be produced by setting the stocking rate, and thus grazing pressure, at a level equal to the natural vegetation succession tendency. Implicit in the model is the idea of equilibrium ecosystems; from an equilibrium grazing ecosystem, a relatively constant production of livestock can be expected. In equilibrium ecosystems, livestock density is generally limited by a relatively stable primary production, which – in turn – is controlled by the grazing pressure or livestock density. Hence, equilibrium between primary production and livestock density will occur. In the 1970s, a shift in ecological thinking began. The applicability of Clements' model of vegetation succession for drylands was questioned: it was suggested that drylands such as the Sahel were under density independent control in relation to rainfall; and more than one ecological equilibrium was seen as possible in these ecosystems. However, a new model based on these findings was not proposed until the late 1980s. According to this new model, dryland ecosystems are considered disequilibrium, changing from one state to another, due to strong external controls e.g. droughts, fires or insect attacks (Ellis and Swift, 1988). Productivity of dryland ecosystems is controlled mainly by the highly variable rainfall: because livestock seldom reaches densities high enough to influence vegetation productivity, rainfall is the principal factor controlling inter annual vegetation dynamics. This shift in thinking had important implications for the perception of pastoralists and agro-pastoralists' livelihood strategies in Africa. These people were now seen as rational managers of the natural resources instead of destructive and irrational (Adriansen, 1999).

The spatiality of knowledge production

The two examples above show the localness of knowledge – ecologists from the Global North thought their theories of ecosystem functioning and methods for measuring vegetation were universal, but they were not. Hence, the examples illustrate the importance of paying attention to spatiality of scientific culture and knowledge production. All too often, localised methods and theories from the Global North are portrayed as universal methods and theories, resulting in transference to other contexts without recognising their particularity. Mbow explains the difficulties in conducting valuable climate change research when scientific knowledge production is based on particular theories and methods that are presented as universal rather than context specific. Yet, Mbow also points out that the whole framing of research as dependent or independent may be futile:

In reality, we are all interconnected and interdependent. No one can do science in isolation. I am influenced and I influence others' thinking. In the context of inter-disciplinary requirements to addressing complex environmental issues, my independence in research is the possibility I have to probe and accept or probe and reject ideas or arguments received.

While we prefer the concept of subordination instead of dependence, we argue that Hountondji's work is still relevant in its recognition of the spatial aspects of scientific knowledge production. In emphasising the particularity of theories and methods, we do not want to advocate complete relativity of scientific knowledge or deny universality of certain parts of (natural) science. Rather, we want to emphasise that scientific knowledge is produced by humans in places. After having shown the importance of place in scientific knowledge production, we will turn our attention to the cultural production of the researcher who actually produces knowledge.

The cultural production of African academics

As was shown in Box 7.1, Mbow sees his intellectual development in four stages, moving from dependence to emancipation. This development is closely linked to the wider geographies and power of knowledge production:

> I was also lucky to be offered opportunities such as the DANIDA scholarship, the post doc scholarship, the position at Université Cheikh Anta Diop, and the position at ICRAF. I learned to maintain a high level of commitment and hard work, dosed with moderation. I did my best to build a good reputation through diligence, discipline and rigor.

For Mbow, the Global North represented both the imposed curriculum through colonial heritage and the possibility to acquire the skills to become an emancipated academic capable of creating new knowledge. This experience of a 'double bind' is not unique to Mbow. Even though Africanised curricula have been introduced across the continent after independence, schooling in general, and academia in particular, is still marked by the hegemonic discourse of enlightenment and modernity derived from European intellectual history (Breidlid, 2013). This is a way of thinking that is not always aligned with the languages, discourses and belief systems of the majority of Africans. Assié-Lumumba (2006) even finds the European roots of African universities one of the major obstacles for African countries trying to use universities for their national development. While the previous sections have discussed the conditions for higher education teaching and knowledge production in Africa, this section will dig deeper into the lives of African researchers. Using Levinson and Holland's (1986) notion of 'the cultural production of the educated person', we will analyse the cultural production of African academics and how they are affected by the capacity-building projects funded by the Global North.

Levinson and Holland (1986) use the idea of the cultural production of the educated person as a way of understanding the dynamics of power and identity formation underlying different forms of education. The authors argue that the 'educated person' is a culture-specific construct that can be used for studying how conflicts and connections between cultural practices and knowledges are produced within and outside schools. In the present context, we are interested in the cultural production of academics in Africa, which takes place both within and outside the African continent. As analysed in Chapter 8, some African academics become socialised into academia through scholarships and capacity-building projects in/from the Global North. Through these projects, the academics are exposed to different ideals and values about what constitutes an academic person. Cheikh Mbow is a case in point. His academic learning journey began at the Université de Cheikh Anta Diop in Dakar, where questioning the knowledge and methods of older professors was perceived as misbehaviour. When he arrived at the University of Copenhagen in Denmark, he realised that the system there was different. The cultural production of an academic was closely related to issues of academic freedom, questioning what was taken for granted even when it entailed questioning older professors. While Mbow appreciated a system where freedom of thought was highly valued, it was a challenge to learn how to question colleagues and professors using a new working language (English) while simultaneously learning new methods of using satellite imagery for doing geographical science. When asked what he brought back home, Mbow replies: '[G]ood collaboration and continuity in work efforts, organizational skills and humility. Good planning and ambition are central.' The main thing, however, was the ability to produce new knowledge. Too much of the learning Mbow had been brought up with was reproduction of knowledge, rather than creation of new knowledge. Critical thinking and questioning what is taken for granted are important for constructing new knowledge. The questioning of the Braun-Blanquet method mentioned earlier was a result of this ability to challenge existing knowledge.

When trained in the Global North, researchers naturally become accustomed to the working conditions (e.g. academic freedom), infrastructure, working styles and organisational cultures abroad (Møller-Jensen and Madsen, 2015). Returning to their home universities, where conditions for teaching and research are difficult and politics is common in reward and promotion, many such researchers end up being pessimistic about their future career growth. While university academics all over the world have obligations in terms of research, teaching and outreach, the typical demands on the African researcher are extraordinary. In *African Higher Education: An International Reference Handbook* (Teferra and Altbach, 2003) the authors take stock of the situation in the different countries of the continent; despite the differences, Teferra and Altbach (in a later publication) argue that there are a number of similarities:

> In virtually all cases, researchers observe the constant decline of the direct and indirect resources allocated for higher education by governments. The

impact of this trend and how this over time has eroded the quality of teaching and research, the moral and physical well-being of the academic profession, and the general state of the universities as a whole remains a subject for more discussion and analysis.

(Teferra and Altbach, 2004: 29)

More specifically, massification of higher education in Africa has not been followed with funding of extra teaching and research activities. This means that the student/teacher ratio is very high. Lecturing for 500–1000 students is not uncommon and faculty members have very many students to supervise; thus, student obligations can take up all the time for faculty members. Lack of funding also means lack of e.g. laboratories and up-to-date libraries. Research is largely funded by donor agencies, which has implications for the type of research conducted – for instance, focus on applied rather than basic research. Moreover, poor governance of universities means that the bureaucracy in African universities is disproportionately large, with an excessive number of non-academic staff. An African academic, especially a university employee, is perceived to be in a privileged position and thus has many family obligations (Møller-Jensen and Madsen, 2015). Salaries (especially at public universities), however, are often low and sometimes delayed. With a growing number of private universities, an increasing number of academic staff hold part-time positions at these new institutions (Teferra and Altbach, 2004). How these conditions affect African academics can also be seen in the narrative presented in Chapter 9.

When African academics are trained abroad through scholarship and capacity-building programmes, they are not only exposed to more privileged working conditions, but are also trained in different ways of thinking and behaving that may not always be applicable when they return home. Therefore, some researchers start looking for careers either in the country where they studied or with foreign-funded projects and research organisations that entail some of the characteristics experienced during their oversees study. Many of the researchers trained abroad choose to work for foreign agencies and not for their governments or academic institutions. This tendency can be interpreted as brain drain[6] from the perspective of the public universities, especially if African academics trained abroad choose to stay abroad altogether. Emigration from Africa is skill-intensive (Ndulu, 2004): there are more African scientists and engineers working in the US than there are in Africa (IOM, 2000). Those who choose to stay in Africa and work at public universities are faced with severe difficulties in terms of finding time and resources for research and securing an income. Therefore, many researchers conduct consultancies for private or international companies, which can both contribute in terms of income as well as provide empirical material for research (as shown in Chapter 3). Mbow explains that while many consultancy reports contain valuable research-based information, this type of publication does not count in terms of academic merit. He further argues that many African researchers find themselves caught between a rock and a hard place: they conduct consultancies in order to survive, which in turn means they do not have time to gain the necessary merits in the academic system. He describes knowledge production of African university climate change researchers as follows: 'Science for donors', which can be with the attitude of 'let them hear what they want to hear' to secure their money; 'science for researchers', which takes the form of peer-reviewed articles that are not accessible to the majority of African scientists and do not operationalise the knowledge generated but satisfy the criteria for excellent research; and 'science for local communities', which through co-design and co-implementation include local stakeholders whose problems science is supposed to help alleviate. Mbow has seen all these during his career in African academia and has mostly made 'science for researchers' himself, which has been good for his academic career opportunities. The multiple and conflicting demands on African academics means that there are multiple cultural productions of African academics. Some return from the Global North with excellence and high ranking journal publications as the main ideal; others maintain a belief in making science for communities, emphasising the importance of outreach; however, the encounter with different notions of the educated person may lead some to leave African universities because they no longer feel they fit in.

Some of these issues are not unique to Africa. One of the co-authors, Muhammad Mehmood-Ul-Hassan, currently based at ICRAF's headquarters as Head of Capacity Development, has been working in international organisations since 1995, prior to which he worked for the Government of Pakistan. Mehmood-Ul-Hassan provides this narrative about his reasons for leaving the Pakistani civil service:

> Completing my MS in 1989, I started my civil services career in Pakistan as a rural economist with the human resources department in 1990. The civil services career for an average Pakistani professional is a coveted one, as only 4 per cent of those who apply get selected. Part of my initial job was to head the recently established state of the art computerised data processing centre. My research and coordination work was much appreciated by my superiors. A six-month overseas training period in the Netherlands in 1994 exposed me to the working styles of Dutch institutions. Returning in early 1995, and in pursuit of enhancing the work efficiency of my centre, I tried to introduce new work standards and ethics in my data centre, part of which was prohibiting entertaining visitors in the computer room of the centre. During a confrontation involving a very direct Dutch style of argument, I inadvertently annoyed some of my assistants' politically important visitors, who were using the computer room to hold political meetings. The problem was not with the argument, but the way in which I presented it – I was perceived as rude because I did not employ the more diplomatic style expected in a Pakistani context. However, in the Netherlands, I had experienced that this diplomatic style meant that the meaning and message of the argument could be lost. The union representing research assistants went on strike in protest against me, demanding my removal from the centre.

My superiors insisted that I should apologise for my rudeness. I felt that instead of protecting work ethics, my superiors took politically motivated decisions by aligning themselves with those who were in the wrong rather than protecting me. As a result of my dissatisfaction with the governmental system, I applied for a job at the International Water Management Institute (IWMI) office in Pakistan, and was selected. Since I did not want to quit my civil service job for good, I had to mobilise political influence through one of my influential cousins within the bureaucracy to secure a long-term leave of absence for joining IWMI. Since then, however, I was always able to find jobs in international organisations and thus resigned from my governmental post in 2001. When I visit Pakistani institutions and discuss professional issues, I feel I could no longer survive in the Pakistani system.

The similarity between African and Asian experiences outlined here appears to be the lack of motivating environments to retain excellence within the academic systems. The structural problems in the higher education and policy making systems mentioned previously make some researchers choose a career in international research organisations instead of within the national universities.

Based on nine narrative interviews with former Ghanaian PhD students funded by the ENRECA capacity-building programme, Møller-Jensen and Madsen (2015) analysed becoming and being an African scholar. While the article shows the different experiences of the nine scholars, it also highlights the similarities. People who have been socialised into academia though a capacity-building programme in the Global North have to negotiate the various cultural productions of an academic and the multitude of positions they have. Many of the PhD students became empowered both personally and professionally during the course of the studies; this empowerment sometimes led to contradicting positions, for instance when they had better equipment or IT competencies than their professors in Ghana. Yet, this empowerment was not always welcomed locally as it disrupted the established power relations. For PhD students who treasured belonging to an academic community, it could be difficult to be empowered, and it could be difficult for the pursuit of an academic career within the department. Interestingly, the authors show that academic life came at a cost; it was the change from rural life to an urban 'Westernised' lifestyle, however, which represented the major change, not the ENRECA programme and studies in the Global North. Like Møller-Jensen and Madsen, we find it meaningless to provide one single description of the educated person. Moreover, with these descriptions of the different cultural production of academics, we do not mean to imply that one is better than the other, merely to point at some of the consequences of academic mobility and internationalisation of higher education. The consequences can be both positive and negative. We see it as positive when African researchers return with the capacity to challenge what is taken for granted and with a wish to protect academic freedom. If, on the other hand, African researchers become socialised into the neoliberal competition fetish (Naidoo, 2008) where researchers are more engaged in publishing in high ranking journals than with engaging with local stakeholders, it could be detrimental for climate change researchers desirous to make impact on the ground.

Producing climate change research in Africa today

Mbow perceives climate change as a pertinent problem in large parts of the African continent; at the same time, climate change research is a good example of some of the problems inherent in constructing knowledge of relevance for various audiences and translating this knowledge in order for it to have authority and impact in African societies. Rapid and sustained action to build more resilient and adaptive development pathways is needed for Africa to effectively address challenges emerging from climate change and associated drivers of change. A well-informed citizenry, responsive institutions and a problem-focused knowledge generation are imperative to achieving a more sustainable future. Universities in Africa clearly have a vital role to play in helping to realise this vision. However, the potential of African universities to be active participants in fostering transformative change is not being fully realised (START, 2011). Moreover, as argued by Okolie, it is important that African universities study:

> The extent to which the idea of development promoted by development agencies and governments is informed by the wishes and thoughts of local communities. It ought to examine the source of the knowledge that informs what is imposed on or prescribed for Africa, and how scholars are implicated in the universalization of the European experience. It should ask which ways of knowing scholars validate and promote and which ones they ignore, invalidate, and why. In short, it can help to construct new development knowledges that will be African-centred.
>
> (Okolie, 2003: 244)

As climate research is largely funded and carried out by external funding and organisations, many African governments do not own it. The general perception among African researchers and politicians is that external donors fund research that is in their own interest rather than in the interest of the recipient countries and their local communities (Mehmood-Ul-Hassan and De Leeuw, 2015).

In regard to climate change research, Mbow notes the difficulties in reconciling scientific knowledge and local knowledge. These can be seen as different modes of knowledge as explained in Chapter 2. For instance, there are no common concepts translating science into local knowledge: what is carbon in the languages *Dioula*, *Wolof* or *Swahili*? Moreover, the scientific community ignores or neglects to assess the quality of local knowledge. Mbow ponders:

> My challenge was to select from local knowledge or identify the best sources of knowledge. There are methodologies that underpin the best way to retrieve local knowledge, and from which target group. Additionally, these

local knowledges are sometimes, or most of the time, culturally enigmatic. The role of symbols and sense in interpretation through images, which are important parts of the knowledge system, will vary from one society to another. Although I recognise the importance of local knowledge, I have to admit that it is not easy to systematically refer to it in combination with formal scientific knowledge. My quantitative background in assessing scientific evidence contrasts strongly with the qualitative and interpretative nature of local knowledge substances.

Mbow's interest in local knowledge has grown in recent years as he has become increasingly concerned with how to conduct climate change research that has impact on the ground in Africa. Hence, he can see the benefit of including local knowledge, but he has not been trained in how to do so. In this respect, the proponents of the Africanisation of curriculum discourse are right; when the hegemonic knowledge is masqueraded as universal it is difficult to deconstruct it, and African schools do not provide students with the tools for validating their own knowledge systems (Dei, 2014). Yet, Mbow is careful not to dismiss the universal aspect of academia. Large parts of the natural sciences are based on the laws of physics, which are universal although challenged as all knowledge is. Moreover, historically, the university as an institution was premised on the idea that academics learned a shared language that enabled them to travel and engage in intellectual debate. Mbow's life history shows how he has benefitted from this. While he sees the benefits from an increased Africanisation of curriculum, the main emphasis should be on the curriculum used at primary and secondary school level. Universities should still retain a focus on the ideals of the universities and in that sense Mbow does not see much difference between the cultural production of an academic in Denmark and in Senegal:

> Reputation is based on the same values wherever you are: invariable sense of responsibility, delivery on the job description, good ethical behaviour, interpersonal skills and willing to progress while supporting your peers. I have not changed anything about my work style in my new job or in my international role despite my growing responsibilities.

This is no surprise, given that the curriculum is a social construction of what it means to be an educated person (Dei, 2014) and the curriculum, which Mbow has been exposed to, has indeed been a Western curriculum.

Nonetheless, Mbow agrees with Dei's argument:

> While excellence is considered to be a hallmark of the university, there is some concern as to whether this excellence is really making an impact on local communities […] With some exceptions, it is excellence defined in terms of a validation with Western intellectual codes, norms, and accreditation.
>
> (Dei, 2014: 165)

This is evident when working with climate change research. Therefore, climate change research should work with the dimensions mentioned by Livingstone, i.e. to problematise climatic knowledge, particularise climatic experience and pluralise climatic meaning. In an African context, this could be seen as similar to working towards an Africanisation of curriculum. Moreover, for climate change research to gain importance on the ground, more attention should be paid to the connection between mental structures of communities and adoption of science. However, working with local knowledge is not enough; dissemination, communication and outreach are also important. In this way, in the words of Hountondji (1990), research can be more introvert. As Mbow explains, research, education and communication are intrinsically interlinked, as he has illustrated in Figure 7.1. The ability to produce climate change research that matters to the local communities requires enabling conditions that catalyse the translation of knowledge into action.

In summing up, it can be noted that even though the conditions for producing climate change research in Africa today have changed over the past 25 years, African researchers are still embedded in the colonial power structures through the curriculum, the universalisation of particular knowledge and the cultural production of an academic person in Africa. In order for this to change, and in order for climate change research to have greater impact on and relevance for African communities, there is a need for: 1) Africanising the curriculum from primary school; 2) researchers to problematise climatic knowledge, particularise climatic experience and pluralise climatic meaning; 3) providing researchers with better tools for working with these different knowledges; and 4) working more with the communication and outreach to local communities. These are complementary points for action to improve the aspects of Figure 7.1.

Concluding remarks

With this chapter, we wanted to shed light upon the geography and power of (higher) education and scientific knowledge production in Africa, with a point of departure in the life history of an African climate change researcher. However, we did not use this history for a typical case analysis; rather, we used the narrative to point to some general conditions for knowledge production in Africa. Nonetheless, we are inspired by Lund's compelling question: 'Of what is this a case?' (Lund, 2014: 224). This case illustrates the conditions and struggles for knowledge production experienced by an African climate change researcher, while pointing to issues beyond any single narrative. By highlighting the geographies and power of knowledge through Mbow's schooling, we have illustrated the conditions for producing climate change research in Africa today. The question is whether there are contributions which are also relevant 'out of Africa'.

The issue of an inherited curriculum and school system is pertinent for many of the former colonies, which have not managed to adapt these to their local context. Moreover, the debate on what constitutes canonical literature and

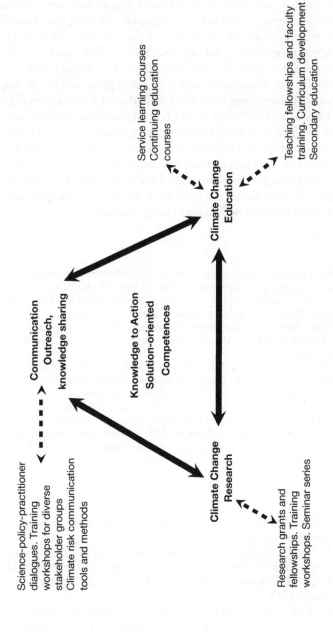

Figure 7.1 Model of solution oriented research on climate change. There is focus on the interaction of the three aspects: research, education and outreach. Each can be extended to further consideration with dotted arrow links

relevant curriculum becomes even more pertinent with the internationalisation of higher education. Increased globalisation and subsequent mobility of people and knowledge systems call for close attention to the various cultural productions of the educated person. This chapter has shown how it can be difficult for individuals to transfer the ideals of an educated person from one context to another. Likewise, paying attention to geographies of scientific knowledge production is important for all researchers living in the periphery of the hegemonic Anglo-American knowledge production. The examples of the transfer of a particular ecological theory from the US to dryland Africa shows how universalisation of Western research also takes place within the natural sciences. Previously, researchers from the humanities and social sciences (e.g. Chen, 2010; Connell, 2007; Smith, 2012) have shown how theories, concepts and methodologies from the Global North are being treated as universal when in fact they are particular to the Global North. Consequently, these authors have argued in favour of deimperialisation or decolonialisation of knowledge production by recognising its spatiality. We want to conclude by following this line of thought and pointing to the need for more place-based approaches to both climate change teaching and climate change research.

Notes

1 Until 1987 the university was known as Université de Dakar, then it changed its name to honour the Senegalese philosopher and anthropologist, Cheikh Anta Diop.
2 All the quotes without further reference are from the interviews with Cheikh Mbow.
3 START: Global Change System for Analysis, Research and Training.
4 WASCAL: West African Science Service Center on Climate Change and Adapted Land Use. SASCAL: Southern African Science Service Centre for Climate Change and Adaptive Land Use.
5 Jacques de Certaines, who holds a PhD in biology as well as one in sociology of science, was born in Lyon, France, in 1946. Besides his studies in Dakar, he attended universities in Paris, Nantes, Rennes, and has later been affiliated with Harvard.
6 Rizvi (2005) has argued that in an era of globalisation, brain drain is a complex phenomenon; he uses concepts such as brain drain, brain gain and brain circulation to denote the composite character of flows of skilled labour and remittances. While accepting Rizvi's argument about the composite nature of migration, we would also like to address the issues involved when academics return with new skills.

References

Adriansen, H.K. (1999) 'Pastoral mobility as a response to climate variability in African drylands', *Geografisk Tidsskrift*, 1 (99), 1–10.
Adriansen, H.K. (2002) *A Fulani Without Cattle is Like a Woman Without Jewellery: A Study Of Pastoralists in Ferlo, Senegal*. Copenhagen: Geographica Hafniensia A11.
Adriansen, H.K. (2012) 'Timeline interviews: a tool for conducting life history research', *Qualitative Studies*, 3 (1), 40–55.
Anderson-Levitt, K.M. (2003) 'A World Culture of Schooling?' In Anderson-Levitt, K.M. (ed.) *Local Meanings, Global Schooling. Anthropology and World Culture Theory*. New York: Palgrave Macmillan, pp. 1–26.

Assié-Lumumba, N'dri T. (2006) *Higher Education in Africa – Crises, Reforms and Transition.* Imprimerie Saint Paus, Dakar, Senegal: CODESRIA Working Paper Series. Available at: www.codesria.org/IMG/pdf/Ndri_lumumba.pdf (accessed 14 April 2015).

Breidlid, A. (2013) *Education, Indigenous Knowledges, and Development in the Global South: Contesting Knowledges for a Sustainable Future.* Sabon: Routledge.

Brooks, R. and Waters, J. (2011) *Student Mobilities, Migration and the Internationalization of Higher Education.* New York: Palgrave Macmillan.

Chen, K.H. (2010) *Asia as Method: Toward Deimperialization.* Durham: Duke University Press.

Clements, F. (1916) *Plant Succession: An Analysis of the Development of Vegetation.* Washington: Carnegie Institute.

Connell, R. (2007) *Southern Theory: The Global Dynamics of Knowledge in Social Science.* Cambridge: Polity.

Cross, N. and Barker, R. (1994) *At the Desert's Edge: Oral Histories from the Sahel.* Glasgow: Panos/SOS Sahel.

Crossman, P. (2004) 'Perceptions of "Africanisation" or "endogenisation" at African universities: issues and recommendations'. In Zeleza, P.T. and Olukoshi, A. (eds) *African Universities in the Twenty-first Century: Vol. 2.* South Africa: CODESRIA, pp. 319–340.

Dei, G.J.S. (2014) 'Indigenizing the school curriculum'. In Emeagwali, G. and Dei, G.J.S. (eds) *African Indigenous Knowledge and the Disciplines.* Rotterdam: SensePublishers, pp. 165–180.

Ellis, C. (2004) *The Ethnographic I: A Methodological Novel about Autoethnography.* Walnut Creek: AltaMira Press.

Ellis, J.E. and Swift, D.M. (1988). 'Stability of African pastoral ecosystems: alternate paradigms and implications for development', *Journal of Range Management Archives,* 41 (6), 450–459.

Emeagwali, G. and Dei, G.J.S. (2014) *African Indigenous Knowledge and the Disciplines.* Rotterdam: SensePublishers.

Engel-Di Mauro, S. and Carroll, K.K. (2014) 'An African-centred approach to land education', *Environmental Education Research,* 20 (1), 70–81.

Goodson, I. and Sikes, P. (2001) *Life History Research in Educational Settings: Learning from Lives.* Buckingham: Open University Press.

Hountondji, P. (1990) 'Scientific dependence in Africa today', *Research in African Literatures,* 21 (3), 5–15.

Hountondji, P.J. (1995) 'Producing knowledge in Africa today. The Second Bashorun MKO Abiola Distinguished Lecture', *African Studies Review,* 38 (3), 1–10.

International Organization for Migration (IOM) (2000) *Migration in Africa: Globalization and Prospects for Regional Mechanisms. A Statement by Brunson McKinley, Director General.* Addis Ababa, Ethiopia: IOM.

Levinson, B.A. and Holland, D. (1996) 'The cultural production of the educated person: an introduction'. In Levinson, B.A., Foley, D.E. and Holland, D. (eds) *The Cultural Production of the Educated Person: Critical Ethnographies of Schooling and Local Practice.* New York: SUNY Press, pp. 1–54.

Livingstone, D.N. (2012) 'Reflections on the cultural spaces of climate', *Climatic Change,* 113 (1), 91–93.

Lund, C. (2014) 'Of what is this a case? Analytical movements in qualitative social science research', *Human Organization,* 73 (3), 224–234.

Maréchal, G. (2010) 'Autoethnography'. In Mills, A. J., Durepos, G. and Wiebe, E. (eds) *Encyclopedia of Case Study Research: Vol. 2*. Thousand Oaks, CA: Sage Publications, pp. 43–45.

Mehmood-Ul-Hassan, M. and De Leeuw, J. (2015) 'Enhancing the quality of African climate change science by investing in peer review'. Brief for Global Sustainable Development Report 2015. Available at: https://sustainabledevelopment.un.org/content/documents/623065-Muhammed_Enhancing%20the%20quality%20of%20African%20climate%20change%20science.pdf (accessed 14 April 2015).

Møller-Jensen, L. and Madsen, L.M. (2015) 'Becoming and being an African scholar: a 15 year perspective on capacity building projects in Ghana', *Forum for Development Studies*, 42 (2), 245–264.

Naidoo, R. (2008) 'The competitive state and the mobilised market: higher education policy reform in the United Kingdom (1980–2007)', *Critique Internationale*, 39, 47–65.

Ndulu, B.J. (2004) *Human Capital Flight: Stratification, Globalization, and the Challenges to Tertiary Education in Africa*. Washington, DC: World Bank.

Okolie, A.C. (2003) 'Producing knowledge for sustainable development in Africa: implications for higher education', *Higher Education*, 46 (2), 235–260.

Rizvi, F. (2005) 'Rethinking "brain drain" in the era of globalisation', *Asia Pacific Journal of Education*, 25 (2), 175–192.

Sambou, B., Ba, A.T., Mbow, C. and Goudiaby, A. (2008) 'Studies of the woody vegetation of the Welor Forest Reserve (Senegal) for sustainable use', *West African Journal of Applied Ecology*, 13 (1), 67–76.

Semali, L.M. (1999) 'Community as classroom: (re)valuing indigenous literacy'. In Semali, L.M. and Joe, L.K. (eds) *What Is Indigenous Knowledge? Voices from the Academy*. New York: Garland Publishing, pp. 95–118.

Shizha, E. (2014) 'Indigenous knowledge systems and the curriculum'. In Emeagwali, G. and Dei, S.G.J. (eds) *African Indigenous Knowledge and the Disciplines*. Rotterdam: SensePublishers, pp. 113–129.

Smith, L.T. (2012) *Decolonizing Methodologies: Research and Indigenous Peoples*. London: Zed Books.

START (2011) *The African Climate Change Fellowship Program: Final Technical Report For the period 1 August 2007–31 December 2010*. Washington, DC: START. Available at: http://start.org/download/2011/technical-report-accfp-8.2007-12.2010.pdf (accessed 29 May 2015).

Teferra, D. and Altbach, P.G. (2003) *African Higher Education: An International Reference Handbook*. Bloomington: Indiana University Press.

Teferra, D. and Altbach, P.G. (2004) 'African higher education: challenges for the 21st century', *Higher Education*, 47 (1), 21–50.

Westhoff, V. and Van Der Maarel, E. (1978) 'The Braun-Blanquet approach'. In Whittaker, R.H. (ed.) *Classification of Plant Communities*. The Netherlands: Springer Netherlands, pp. 287–399.

Woolman, D.C. (2001) 'Educational reconstruction and post-colonial curriculum development: a comparative study of four African countries', *International Education Journal*, 2 (5), 27–46.

8 Negotiating scientific knowledge about climate change

Enhancing research capacity through PhD students

Lene Møller Madsen and Thomas Theis Nielsen

Introduction

This chapter focuses on two main issues: production of scientific knowledge and capacity building at African research universities and how these two subjects are interwoven. The global production of scientific knowledge has been contested by authors like Connell (2007), who describes how social science theory has formed itself not only on Western ethnocentric assumptions but also from a position of privilege claiming universal knowledge and universal values. Taking a somewhat broader perspective, Linda Tuhiwai Smith describes this as 'research through imperial eyes' (Smith, 2012: 44), giving a wide range of examples of its implications for our understanding of, for example, conceptions of the individual and society, as well as space and time. Research outside the Global North (e.g. Africa) has often been perceived as a place for collecting empirical data, while research in the Global North has been seen as a place for theory development (Hountondji, 1995). Against this background, this chapter also sees scientific knowledge as situated as described in Chapter 2 of this book.

It can be argued that the concept of capacity building with donors from the Global North supporting research capacity building in the Global South is encapsulated in this hegemonic discourse of how and where knowledge is legitimately produced and consumed. In this chapter we wish to explore this argument by providing insights into the negotiations and production of scientific knowledge in a specific research capacity-building project (AREPRO).[1] This project concerns climate change impacts on land use and water resources using satellite remote sensing and GIS techniques. It is based on long-standing professional and personal relations between Global North and Global South partners and was initiated as a South–South research network.

This chapter is structured as follows. First we attend to the issue of positionality and situate ourselves within the analysis. Secondly, we give a brief outline of the AREPRO project, situating it within the Nordic capacity-building tradition. Thirdly, we discuss how scientific knowledge production in capacity-building projects can be interpreted as being situated within a Western hegemony of knowledge production. Subsequently we outline and analyse AREPRO in relation to the negotiation of scientific knowledge production in the different stages of the project, and by the PhD students. Finally, we take a step back and analyse the AREPRO project within a broader framework of post-colonial critique of Western hegemonic knowledge production.

Positioning ourselves – looking out from the Global North

To provide a context for how the AREPRO project is described, perceived and conceptualised, we as authors need to outline and engage in positionality. Originating from feminist studies, the issue of positionality has been addressed with different focuses in geography, anthropology and educational studies (Edwards, 2002; Neal and Gordon, 2001; Rose, 1997), the main argument being that one's position as a researcher interacts with and constitutes one's field of study. Further, it acknowledges that this is the case both when the researcher is an outsider and an insider, for example when the researcher is a friend (Browne, 2003) or colleague (DeLyser, 2001; Madsen and Winsløw, 2009). In the case of being an insider in one's own research field, Adriansen and Madsen state: 'When doing insider research it is necessary to address the insider relationships explicitly in order to reveal the complexity of research relations' (Adriansen and Madsen, 2009: 146). They further discuss the issue of being insiders in different ways, for instance in relation to one's research matter and in relation to one's interviewees. Being an insider presents a number of challenges, such as putting one's own role as a researcher and colleague at stake – something that we have also experienced and needed to negotiate in writing this chapter.

From the onset of AREPRO we, the authors, were part of the planning and the subsequent implementation. We therefore approach this study from within the project, and as such are privileged with knowledge not only of the project, but also of the intentions behind some of the project initiatives, the negotiations between partners during the process and the different positions of interest taken in the project. Like most projects, AREPRO did not start in a vacuum. We were already part of the research fields and engaged with the people involved in different ways, and as such we were insiders in different aspects. Box 8.1 shows reflective narratives by the authors using Webster and Mertova's inquiry approach (2007). Hopefully the process of formulating and sharing our history with the project as reflective narratives has made us more aware of our own role and given us what Smith describes as a 'critical understanding of the underlying assumptions, motivations and values which inform research practices' (Smith, 2012: 21).

Finally, we feel a need to stress that we are also approaching this investigation with considerable caution, as we are discussing the processes and results of former and present co-operations with colleagues and PhD students within the research field. We have strived to make confidentiality arrangements as far as possible, and followed the code of conduct for the Association of American Geographers (AAG, 2009). That said, the views and perceptions expressed in this chapter are solely those of the authors.

Box 8.1 Reflective narratives by the authors

Lene Møller Madsen

I studied human geography and earned my PhD degree from the geography department where the project was based, and currently work in a science education department. So in terms of research fields I belong partly to the field of geography, and partly to the field of science education. Within geography my research lies in a different field from climate change research; however, I was trained in the ideas and methods used in the project during my studies. My role in AREPRO was an educational one. I was invited to join the project at a time when the project description needed a stronger educational focus and the project's educational elements needed to be outlined. My task was to describe and make research-based arguments for the educational setup. At the same time I situated myself in an unclear double position: 1) organising parts of the PhD programme within the project, participating in the meetings, workshops and interviewing the PhD students to understand their situations and communicate this to the others in the project; and 2) being a researcher who was interested in the PhD programme in AREPRO and other capacity-building projects in the region (e.g. Møller-Jensen and Madsen, 2015). In relation to the participants in AREPRO, all of the North partners and one of the South partners are former colleagues of mine whom I have worked with professionally in various ways and shared the ups and downs of academic life.

Thomas Theis Nielsen

I gained a master's degree in human geography in the 1990s and continued my studies as a PhD student and later as a postdoc in the field of satellite remote sensing and geographical information systems (GIS) in geography, specifically using satellite remote sensing in surveillance of environmental issues in West Africa. As such, I was one of the original members of the group that conceptualized AREPRO and later applied for funding. I participated in the meetings and negotiations right from the start and saw AREPRO as a continuation of much of the scientific work and collaboration I was already part of due to my position at the geography department that led the project. However, when AREPRO began I was employed at a different university that placed much less emphasis on technical matters such as satellite remote sensing. Hence, my role in AREPRO gradually changed from a purely technical-scientific role – teaching courses on satellite remote sensing techniques, time series analyses and statistics – to a much broader role involving student progression interviews and other educational measures. As with the first author, many of the research members of AREPRO were colleagues, former colleagues and personal friends of mine.

The AREPRO project

In the Nordic countries there has been a relatively long tradition of involvement in higher education in Africa, often based on personal relations among faculty members within specific disciplines, but also in the form of institutional partnerships. This involvement has often been linked with and supported by the different Nordic Development Agencies, based on an overall goal of strengthening research capacity in the Global South, albeit with somewhat different focuses (Møller-Jensen and Madsen, 2015).

Within this framework, the ENRECA programmes (ENhancement of REsearch Capacity), funded by the Danish International Development Assistance (Danida), supported higher education academic institutions in a number of African countries from 1989 to 2009. The specific goals of ENRECA were to facilitate the education of Masters and PhD students, to establish advanced research facilities and laboratories, and to promote joint research activities between universities in the Global South and Danish university staff (Danida, 2000). A substantial part of this capacity building has taken the form of educating PhD students. Initially the students were hosted at universities in Denmark, but in later years universities in the Global South tended to host and educate the PhD students, supported by the donor funding and in collaboration with a Danish partner institution. As outlined in Hjortsø and Meilby (2013), a twinning and partnership approach focusing on genuine commitment, long-term projects and equitable relations gained currency during the 1990s and 2000s in these types of research capacity-building projects.

AREPRO was an ENRECA project initiated in the early 2000s. From the onset it was framed specifically as a South–South network of four West African universities which would be involved in joint research and research capacity-building activities in collaboration with two universities from the Global North. It focused on studies of ecological and environmental change, including climate change impacts on land use and water resources, using contemporary satellite remote sensing and GIS techniques. All of the partner universities had previous experience with these topics within the framework of other capacity-building projects and research relations in general. AREPRO aimed at building on these past experiences to build a network of institutions in Africa with the expressed aim of strengthening the capacity within each institution in the field of satellite remote sensing and GIS. Further, it aimed to facilitate stronger South–South interaction, ensuring that the specialised competences were developed and shared. Three of the partner universities in the Global South had previously received funding for capacity building or research in collaboration with the geography department hosting the project. Hence, both personal and professional relations between partners in the Global North and Global South existed prior to the project.

The AREPRO project sought new ways to build research capacity in higher education. It was intended to focus on South–South collaboration and more South-driven knowledge production, as opposed to the previous more indirect support via Northern universities (described in Chapter 2). In the rest of this chapter we want to address the influence of this approach on the negotiations of legitimate scientific knowledge production in the project. However, first we need to provide a brief outline on how scientific knowledge production in capacity-building projects can be interpreted as being situated within a Western hegemony of knowledge production.

Scientific knowledge production within a Western epistemology

In his book *Education, Indigenous Knowledges, and Development in the Global South* Breidlid (2013) discusses how the hegemonic Eurocentric knowledge system originated in sixteenth-century Europe together with industrial capitalism, producing a specific understanding of knowledge. He argues that this understanding is embodied in the practice and perception of today's modern science and describes it as the foundation of the hegemonic role of Western epistemology. He further shows how this hegemonic epistemology has been seen as the only means by which to achieve progress and development in different Global South settings (Breidlid, 2013).

The hegemonic role of Western epistemology has resulted in the exclusion and othering of other epistemologies, as described for example in the seminal book *Orientalism: Western Conceptions of the Orient* by Edward Said (1995 [1978]). But it has also has a crucial influence on knowledge production in higher education across the globe, not least in universities in the Global South. As David Livingstone describes it: 'Scientific knowledge has been, and continues to be, promoted as a universal undertaking untouched by the vicissitudes of the local' (Livingstone, 2003: 134).

In line with these approaches, many post-colonial texts see scientific knowledge production as both a field where power is exercised and a field that is embedded in a hegemonic perception of western knowledge as universal. Kuan-Hsing Chen writes: 'Knowledge production is one of the major sites in which imperialism operates and exercises its power' (Chen, 2010: 211), and Raewyn Connell argues that within social theory 'there is a strong and repeated claim to universal relevance [...] the very idea of theory involves talking in universals. It is assumed that all societies are knowable, and they are knowable in the same way and from the same point of view' (Connell, 2007: 44). Connell's main argument is that the Global North has made itself into a place of theorising while turning the Global South into a place of data-mining. Throughout her book she provides numerous examples of how sociological theory developed in the Global North is happily applied in the Global South under the (implicit) assumption that these theories possess universal qualities despite being derived in a European context: '[O]n close examination, mainstream sociology turns out to be an ethno-sociology of metropolitan society. This is concealed by its language, especially the framing of its theories as universal propositions or universal tools' (Connell, 2007: 226). Connell further argues that theories developed in the Global South are generally overlooked, and when they are addressed by other researchers, they are perceived as local rather than as having universal qualities. Importantly, Connell also suggests that this universality is not only implicit but also has to remain tacit, because otherwise it has to be questioned. As a consequence, research in the periphery cannot claim universality, but must stay local, creating a notion of centre and periphery that has many dimensions, including in this book and this chapter. For example, we as authors of this chapter are situated in the Global North and can be perceived as being in the centre of the capacity-building project we are part of in the Global South. However, just as our partners in the Global South can be interpreted as being in the periphery of the Global North, we as Scandinavians are situated in the periphery of Anglo-American research (Madsen and Adriansen, 2006). As such we are all intertwined in a global set of relations with our partners both in the Global South and Global North.

A number of post-colonial authors have taken a stand against the western hegemonic epistemology and offered new views on how to create platforms for acting, for example Chen (2010) in *Asia as Method: Toward Deimperialization*, Connell (2007) in *Southern Theory: The Global Dynamics of Knowledge in Social Science* and Smith (2012) in *Decolonizing Methodologies*. This struggle to establish non-hegemonic scientific knowledge systems is unfolded in different ways, for example by Chen as follows:

> [U]sing the idea of Asia as an imaginary anchoring point, societies in Asia can become each other's points of reference, so that the understanding of the self may be transformed, and subjectivity rebuilt. On this basis, the diverse historical experiences and rich social practices of Asia may be mobilized to provide alternative horizons and perspectives.
>
> (Chen, 2010: 212)

The idea is that by taking history and geography into account a deimperialisation of knowledge can occur – a call that has been taken up in the field of educational studies in the volume edited by Zhang et al. (2015).

Based on a perception of scientific knowledge production as situated within a Western hegemonic epistemology, we now turn to the specific capacity-building project of AREPRO, with the aim of exploring whose reality counts and how this is negotiated in the specific interrelations within the concrete capacity-building project. First, we focus on scientific knowledge as outlined in the project application, and discuss how this was negotiated in the joint inception workshop. Secondly, we look at the negotiation of the scientific knowledge in relation to the PhD programme. This section is divided into three parts: the negotiations of knowledge in the PhD courses, the PhD students' negotiation of scientific knowledge during the project period and finally the PhD students' scientific knowledge production in their theses.

Negotiating the scientific knowledge production in AREPRO

To carry out the following analysis, we have drawn on a wide range of empirical material, including project documents, interviews with the PhD students and chapters written by the PhD students describing their results. However, the analysis is also derived from our reflections on writing the application, attending the meetings, being responsible for some of the PhD courses and discussions with our South partners.

As part of the first authors' involvement in addressing educational issues in AREPRO, it was decided to follow the PhD students and their way through their PhD programme by interviewing them. What we did not know at this time was that this would give us unique insights into the processes of the PhD students' scientific knowledge production. We interviewed the students three times – most often in connection with PhD courses where all the students were gathered. Seven PhD students were financed by AREPRO and enrolled in universities in the Global South, and we were able to follow six of these more or less throughout the project. The interview approach was not designed to evaluate their work or discuss scientific content or methods, but to get a feeling for the needs and concerns of the PhD students. We preferred interviewing to informal talks; the topics discussed required mutual trust as they concerned supervision, access to resources, etc., often involving partners in the project who were our research and project colleagues. This trust would have been difficult to gain in situations such as coffee breaks with other partners around. During the interviews we used different methodologies, such as motivational charts and drawings, and were inspired by the timeline approach, letting the PhD students draw and explore their educational pathways (Adriansen, 2012; Adriansen and Madsen, 2014). The timeline approach gave access to knowledge about the PhD students' considerations and aspirations when it came to choosing an academic career, and by encouraging the PhD students to draw up motivational charts of the progress of their PhD projects, we became aware of power relations often related to supervision and access to and understanding of technical issues.

In regard to the development of this chapter, we sent an earlier version of it to all the partners involved in the project: Global North and Global South academics and PhD students. Based on comments and reviews from this process, we reworked parts of the chapter and included some of the comments on our initial analysis in the chapter in the form of quotes.

The application: scientific knowledge at play within the project

We start by looking into the project application as one of the places where legitimate scientific knowledge production can be identified. The project derives from a long-standing research interest in using satellite remote sensing and GIS in studies of land use and land-use changes to understand ecological systems in different countries in the Global South. Prior to the application, four scientific research areas were agreed on based on previous relations and negotiations in the initial phase of the project:

1   Satellite remote sensing of changes in rural land use/cover and vegetation productivity

2   GIS-based studies of urban and peri-urban land-use dynamics
3   Satellite remote sensing of changes in water resource availability
4   Satellite remote sensing of savanna fires and GIS-based analysis of their causes and effects.

The expected output from AREPRO can be summarised in four points: first, well-performing and well-equipped research units at four African universities; secondly, a strengthening of North–South and particularly South–South collaborative links; thirdly, production of scientific papers with joint authorship; and finally a number of completed PhD programmes funded by the project. To achieve this, the following activities were begun: joint research projects within the four research areas stated above; PhD courses and workshops related to these research areas; and an upgrading of the facilities for satellite images analysis and GIS (Application, 2008).

Thus the project can be interpreted as a wish to relocate scientific knowledge production from the centre (Global North) to the periphery (the Global South) and further situate the Global South in the centre of studies of ecological systems located in the African partners' region by integrating remote sensing and GIS into the academic development of young scientists of the future.

At least two of the project's research areas (1 and 4) are part of wider topics that are debated and contested both in the scientific literature and in the political arena. In relation to the theme of rural land-use change (research area 1), the application states: '[L]and degradation is seen by many governments across the region as a major problem and an obstacle to economic development. However, recent research has challenged this traditional perception' (Application, 2008: Annex A: 8). Recent studies of long-term trends in vegetation productivity estimated from satellite remote-sensing techniques indicate a persistent and significant positive trend in vegetation productivity across much of the region (e.g. Fensholt et al., 2012; Olsson et al., 2005). These studies are based on analyses of more than 30 years of satellite data and have caused considerable debate in the scientific community, not only in the satellite remote-sensing community (see Mbow et al. 2015 for a recent update), but also in other fields (e.g. Sop and Oldeland, 2013). The basis of the debate is that a significant increase in vegetation productivity is in stark contrast to the generally accepted and almost hegemonic narrative that the region is severely degraded and that desertification is manifest in the drier parts of the region (Cleaver, 1992; Geist and Lambin, 2004; UNCCD (2008–2018).[2] This degradation narrative has also been contested from a local knowledge point of view (Fairhead and Leach, 1996; Leach and Mearns, 1996).

The other research area that is debated in the wider community is savanna fires (research area 4). Savanna fires have been studied for many years, with different points of departure and different methods. The application states that:

> Savannah fires are a controversial subject; they are often indiscriminately labelled a harmful and hazardous phenomenon, a point of view adopted by

colonial administrators and which may still be encountered in … [West Africa]. Gradually this perception is changing, and in certain areas fires are increasingly considered a rational element in natural resource management. This reflects the practices of cultivators, pastoralists, forestry agents and national park administrators who use fire as a tool. While fires may serve rational purposes, they also have harmful effects, and what may constitute a positive outcome at one scale may be considered negative at another.

(Application, 2008: Annex B)

Ecologist, botanists, agronomists and geographers have all studied the spatial and temporal distribution of savanna fires as well as the impacts of these fires across the region. Much scientific evidence has been accumulated to support the proposition that bush fires can be understood as a management tool – often the only tool available to small-scale farmers in the region – and that the use of fires in the agricultural sector is not necessarily as environmentally damaging as previously suggested (Mbow et al., 2000). However, these findings have not been widely accepted in the African context, where both the scientific community and decision-making institutions view bush fires differently. Here, fires are seen as ecologically damaging and hazardous to the populace at large (e.g. Laris and Wardell, 2006). The general perception of fires as harmful and something to be combated, and land degradation as the result of inappropriate land utilisation, is at its core a colonial argument. Wardell et al. (2004) discuss how these views can be traced back to influential colonial administrators in West Africa more than a century ago, and how they can be identified in contemporary policies in the region. This is nowhere as clearly illustrated as in the 'three struggles' campaign launched by the former president of Burkina Faso, Thomas Sankara, which singled out bush fires, wood cutting and inappropriate livestock production as major areas of intervention (Wardell et al., 2004).

Today the scientific and political debate is still ongoing as to whether bush fires are harmful to the environment and its surroundings, whether West Africa is undergoing a general greening as a result of large-scale changes in the climate, or indeed whether land degradation is widespread and a direct threat to human sustenance. All of these positions exist at university level to various degrees and in various research communities, both in the Global North and in Africa, and certainly the position of land degradation is a position widely accepted and promulgated by many universities and research institutions in the West African region.

To interpret the influence of these different positions in relation to the negotiations of scientific knowledge within AREPRO, it is important to be clear that the research approach of using remote sensing and GIS was not part of a negotiation. In fact, it was a prerequisite based on research interest in the Global North and a strong interest in building up expertise and facilities in the Global South. Using this methodological approach acknowledges the position that the region is in fact getting greener. Hence the different positions outlined above were not explicitly negotiated during the project, but were implicit during the production of scientific knowledge.

The use of remote sensing and GIS in AREPRO can be interpreted as an opportunity for African partners to gain access to powerful knowledge and technical skills that can enable them to engage in the scientific and political debate about land degradation and bush fires; in other words, that can empower them. This interpretation contrasts with the interpretation of the approach as a methodological hegemony, which will be discussed below.

Joint inception workshop: negotiating the scientific content

The scientific knowledge was explicitly discussed at the joint inception workshop. It was held early on in the project period and was attended by all the main participating academics from North and South, as well as a number of PhD students who had already been enrolled.

While the overall objective of AREPRO was clearly situated in the scientific approach of remote sensing and GIS and the research discourses associated with these, the specific content and components of the collaboration were established in a common inclusion process: each of the participants was asked to provide a number of relevant topics and methods that could be studied under the umbrella of climatic and environmental change in the region. Each participant would then write the topic on a sticky note and attach the note on the wall. However, the participants were asked to take the relative position of their topics into consideration, ensuring that sticky notes with compatible topics and methods would be clustered and each of these topics would be separated out. Following this initial expression of interests, clusters were identified and partners tried to label each cluster in a meaningful and overarching manner. As topics began to materialise, partners were asked to sign up to the topics they felt confident they would be able to contribute to, both as individual institutions and as institutions in a larger network.

At the same time, all partners present at the inception workshop were very aware that none of this could happen without the presence and initiative of a number of PhD students who would undertake the research in collaboration with the researchers in AREPRO. Therefore, negotiations concerning possible candidates and research themes were a constant feature of the discussions and negotiations concerning the research areas' content and methods. Among other things, this led to a common understanding that the research area involving GIS-based studies of urban and peri-urban land-use dynamics could not be fully studied within the AREPRO project (research area 2 earlier). As a comment to the above description of the process of negotiating scientific knowledge in the project at the inception workshop, one of our African partners wrote:

> Generally inception workshops are meant to harmonise the understanding of the project and define tasks, roles and responsibilities. Internally, the African scientists do not play the same role or have the same strength in this

initial negotiation phase. Without imposing anything, Northern scientists use what we can call 'soft power' which usually implies: 'We brought the money; this is our tax payers' money, guys ... so comply or perish'. No choice or only one choice is suggested. Usually there is no assessment of what the African scientists would like to do or what is a priority for them. It is about what the project wants, which reflects what the donor wants.

It is our impression that, based on the intentions of the AREPRO project to initiate and support South-driven knowledge production, the inception workshop deliberately tried to address the exact power relations mentioned in the quote above. This was done in connection with the negotiations of the topics and methods. However, on reflection, the fact that the scientific approach based on remote sensing and GIS was not negotiable could be termed a methodological hegemony. This is echoed in another comment from one of our African partners reflecting on an earlier version of this chapter: 'It appears to me, that [...] the hegemony comes from the various tools used in generating knowledge, not the knowledge. When it comes to training using existing sources of information, Africa is still dominated by Europe in most instances.'

This methodological hegemony of satellite remote sensing and GIS can enforce and dictate a specific way of conceptualising and implementing the work done in the project, whereby the Northern partners maintain what Linda Tuhiwai Smith (following Edward Said) has termed a: 'Flexible positional superiority' (Smith, 2012: 63). In this context, this means that the individual AREPRO partners can question each of the research areas, the content of the PhD courses and even the composition of the project itself, but the fact remains that the scientific knowledge production is carried out within the framework of a methodological hegemony. Thus the position is flexible but still characterised by superiority as regards the use of remote sensing and GIS as methods.

Also, it must be noted that discussions of the possible relations of the agreed research questions and findings to the broader society in the region were lacking at the inception workshop. This was left as an overarching issue framing AREPRO in the project application, but was not a guiding factor in the specific parts of the project. This may suggest an unconscious perception of AREPRO's role as a capacity-building project at university level and hence a perception that as long as scientific knowledge is produced it will trickle down into society to the benefit of the broader society in the region. This is a view that is much contested (Dei, 2014) despite often being implicit in ideas about capacity building.

The PhD courses: transferring scientific knowledge?

During AREPRO a number of PhD courses were held. These courses were both methodological (research practice) and more skill-oriented (learning to use a specific software). In the following, the content and tasks of the PhD courses are analysed in order to identify the perceptions of scientific knowledge and knowledge transfer that are at stake.

The first course offered as part of AREPRO was conducted by two Global South and two Global North lecturers in one of the African partner universities soon after the project initiation. The aims of the course, as decided at the joint inception workshop, were to address general academic qualifications, philosophy of science and methods, such as how to find relevant scientific literature, how to build strong arguments, how to read academic articles, etc. In the course, the PhD students were challenged to engage in critical debates and reflection on their own situations and philosophical stances. These are classical virtues of the Humboldtian model of the university. However, as discussed in Chapter 7 in the narrative by a West African climate change researcher, it is not necessarily part of university education in an African setting. From this perspective, this PhD course can be interpreted as being a way to enable the PhD students to engage critically with both the research and political discourses of climate change based on research methodologies. Another way to interpret the course is to see it as being embedded in a perception of knowledge transfer from the Global North to the Global South: the PhD students need to be able to act within the scientific field regardless of what education they brought with them, so it is just a matter of giving them the existing research methodologies that have already been developed in the Global North.

The next PhD course that was offered was hastily established by one of the universities in the Global South as a result of the experiences of the first course, with no direct involvement by the Global North. Although AREPRO focused on highly technical skills, none or at least very few of the PhD students, when asked directly during our interviews, felt confident that they had the necessary skills to tackle the research questions it involved. This second course was thus established as a technical crash course in order to bring the capabilities of the PhD students up to a technical level where the completion of their programmes was realistic. Accordingly, this second PhD course can be interpreted within a knowledge transfer perspective: the PhD students need to possess the skills and competences needed to engage in basic analyses of satellite images, so let's teach them.[3] As one of our African partners wrote:

> The design of the training courses was oriented by project expectation, not necessary gaps in knowledge and priority in relevant science. Also, there was no training needs assessment prior to these training workshops. I have seen these courses as 'this is how good we [the Global North] are and let us show you'. If you evaluate the impact of the many PhD courses few end up using the many tools taught.

We agree with the comment that the PhD courses in capacity-building projects are often not related to the local and specific knowledge and needs. However, we feel that the second PhD course in AREPRO can also be interpreted as a response to expressed local needs and as such shows the flexibility within AREPRO. Further, we want to stress that negotiations of the content of the PhD courses are embedded in different positions held not only between the Global North and

Global South but also between the Global South partners themselves. And in AREPRO, for example, the crash course held by one of the African partners acted as centre to the periphery of the other South partners.

As we will see in the following, the third and fourth PhD courses clearly showed the power relations regarding knowledge production in the project. The third course focused on highly technical issues and data analysis and was held in the Global North, whereas the final PhD course on field methodology was held in the Global South – clearly illustrating the point made by Hountondji (1995) that the Global South has mainly been perceived as a place for collecting empirical data and the Global North as a place for developing theories. However, these two courses raise a range of other issues which we will reflect upon below.

The third PhD course was a course in advanced remote sensing and time-series analysis. From the onset of AREPRO, this course had been singled out as somewhat of a pinnacle for the PhD students to take part in. The course, in principle, would bring the students to a level from which they could participate in the analysis of the core research outcome of AREPRO: the analysis of long-term satellite image data archives would yield new and interesting insights into issues such as bush fires and desertification. This course was the only one to be held in one of the Northern universities and the only one to only have lecturers from the Northern universities. As with the previous courses, the students' attendance levels were high, but it was obvious that, with a few exceptions, they were struggling – not necessarily struggling to come to terms with the underlying concepts, but rather to orient themselves within data structures, software interfaces and spatial statistics. The approach taken in this PhD course very much reflects the earlier quote by our African partner and is also reflected in the impact of this course on the students' scientific production. Many of the students were frustrated by the difficult situation they found themselves in: on the one hand challenged by requirements to adopt scientific methods of great technical complexity, and on the other hand finding themselves working within a broad conceptual framework, so that much of the work they had so far been part of was somehow invalidated, or at least questioned, by these new methods and probably by the teaching as well. It is our interpretation that the PhD students were experiencing some of the power relations between the different partners in the project and the contested scientific field – namely the contradictory approaches of advanced remote sensing as opposed to more traditional fieldwork to understand land use and land-use changes.

The fourth and final PhD course concerned field methods. This course was held at one of the African universities and mainly consisted of contributions from lecturers and research partners from the Southern universities, even though some technical assistance was provided from one of the Northern universities. This course in field methods included questionnaire techniques, interviews, etc., but there was also an attempt to incorporate high tech in the form of GPS-assisted field measurements and in-situ radiometer techniques.

The PhD students' negotiation of scientific knowledge over time

In the following we will point out and discuss three issues which on reflection we see as important to the PhD students' negotiations of their scientific knowledge production during the project period: their paths to becoming PhD students, their motivation over time and finally their engagement in the local knowledge.

Regarding the first issue, the PhD students had quite different approaches for wanting to become PhD students. Some saw it as a step up the social ladder, some had a strong urge to give something back to the societies they came from and others were pursuing an academic career as one of different careers to choose from. As it turns out, these aspirations are important to understanding how the PhD students engaged with the scientific knowledge and choices made during their PhD programme. For example, one student's strong sense of social empathy combined with an educational path of hardship were related to constant considerations on how to make conditions better for the local community the student was studying. Hence in this case, gaining local knowledge was a priority of the scientific knowledge production. This approach required negotiations during the scientific knowledge-production process, despite having been spelt out as a central component in the original application: that the education of a new generation of academics would strengthen local decision-making on issues of climate change and its impact. In hindsight we interpret this need for negotiations of the legitimacy of using local knowledge as a result of AREPRO's satellite remote-sensing approach, which, as mentioned earlier, was non-negotiable.

One aspect of the students' path to becoming PhD students that also later influenced the negotiations regarding scientific knowledge was the qualification process. Different ways of qualifying for being accepted as a PhD student were available to the different PhD students: some had to pass exams, some applied and some had been apprentices to qualify. These different ways of qualifying shaped their approaches to both their role of being a PhD student and interacted with their views of scientific knowledge production, for example their views on whether the knowledge production should serve personal or institutional purposes.

The second issue of importance was the PhD students' motivation during the project. Their motivation was expressed in relation to power struggles, often to do with supervision and access to and understanding of technical issues. It became clear that the students' motivation to use the different methodologies (e.g. remote sensing and fieldwork) was related to their different approaches for engaging in the PhD programme. The ways in which these challenges were approached and became meaningful in the individual PhD project were related to whether the student saw the PhD as, for example, a way to help the community, gain a position at the university or in general be respected in society. In other words, the motivation and negotiations regarding the scientific knowledge production were related to the PhD students' aspirations for the future.

The third issue of importance – the students' engagement in local knowledge – became clear when we met the students for the last interview. In their reflections on their theses and their future scholarly work, the issue of fieldwork and its status is important for understanding this. All the students perceived fieldwork as a fundamental and for some an implicit aspect of doing research that was necessary to obtain local knowledge in their fields. They used fieldwork to varying degrees; what is important is that their engagement in bringing in local knowledge was closely related to their negotiations of the scientific content in their theses. AREPRO's methodological approach involving the use of remote sensing and GIS to study climate change is very far from approaches to studying the climate from a much more local perspective, for example as described by Livingstone (2012). The PhD students drew on their aspirations and reasons for engaging in their PhD programme when negotiating the methodological approach of AREPRO with their interest in the local knowledge in their study areas. This is reflected in their resulting scientific work, which we now turn to.

The PhD students' scientific knowledge production: a matter of academic navigation

In this section we outline and discuss the scientific work produced by the PhD students in the form of individual book chapters presented at the final meeting of AREPRO. We will focus on the kind of scientific knowledge that was produced and how the PhD students navigated within this production.

Of the six PhD students included in this analysis, five submitted book chapters for publication. While the five chapters appear very different at first read, it is also clear that they are bound together by methodological issues reflecting the overall aim of the project. First of all, it is clear that all of the chapters share a focus on the application of contemporary satellite remote sensing and GIS techniques in the study of ecological and climatic change at various spatial levels, even though the students have taken very different approaches. Equally clear in the chapters is the deeply felt commitment to studying climate change, disseminating knowledge and making a difference in the local communities studied. However, the five students have adopted very different positions in their alignment with AREPRO and the ambitions of the project on the one hand, and their home universities on the other.

The majority of the PhD students submitted chapters which were based on solid, proven methodologies involving the analysis of a certain and limited number of high resolution satellite images and substantial fieldwork in selected sites. This methodology has been used in numerous studies of ecological and environmental change and its applicability has been proven in many studies. This methodology has also been used in a number of former ENRECA projects and other capacity-building projects, and as such it is a solid and familiar position for both the Southern and Northern universities involved in AREPRO. Within this framework, the analysis of satellite images remains a source of highly localised information which optimally should be gathered at as detailed a spatial resolution as possible to allow for further in-field validation and application. Results from the analysis of satellite images are seen as another source of information, on a par with fieldwork, questionnaires, household interviews or large-scale climatic data. Meaning is ascribed to the analysis only after in-depth fieldwork, whereby abstract notions of, for example, satellite-derived indexes of vegetation or changes in albedo are converted into physical experience and observations. While the majority of the PhD students did indeed perform analyses along the lines already described, some of the students pursued different lines of inquiry, conducting analyses on large amounts of frequent, but less spatially detailed data. In these studies of long time series of coarse satellite data, a focus on fieldwork and validation of results from field data was maintained. As earlier, this is well in line with proven methods and almost paradigmatic for the satellite remote-sensing community.

The above analysis of the book chapters could leave the reader with an impression that, given that AREPRO was a development project, not much was achieved when it came to using the methods imparted in the third PhD course (which were a cornerstone of the project). The PhD students can be said to have experienced what could be termed epistemological friction: they were educated within a tradition that they are continuing while at the same time trying to meet the demands of AREPRO and new approaches to their scientific work. Another way to analyse this is by seeing the individual PhD students as negotiating their ways towards becoming academics (Madsen, 2014; McAlpine and Åkerlind, 2010). To understand the process of becoming we can use the descriptions of social navigation of urban youth in Guinea-Bissau by Vigh (2010) where the becoming is conceptualised as a navigation process. In our case the PhD students' scientific knowledge production can thus be interpreted as a result of what could be termed academic navigation: they navigate between what they bring with them in terms of ontological and epistemological knowledge and social and academic practice, and what they encounter in the project in terms of training and expectations.

This academic navigation can be seen in the chapters, where the PhD students inscribe themselves into a specific rhetoric when it comes to explaining and contextualising their work and their thoughts on the root causes of ecological and climatic change. There are many references to linkages between unsustainable cultivation practices, the harmful effects of bush fires, farmers' insufficient knowledge, and so on. This is perhaps shown most strongly by the following quote from one of the book's chapters, which explains climate change as follows: '[C]oupled with human activities such as population pressure, annual bushfires, over-harvesting of wood coupled with unsustainable cultivation practices and soil nutrient depletion without replenishment are responsible for the accelerated land degradation.'

As outlined earlier, the project employed a methodological hegemony that was somewhat distant from both the PhD students' former education and the often used rhetoric of climate and ecological change in Africa. The resulting scientific knowledge production as outlined in the chapters shows how the PhD students in their academic navigation balance and negotiate their epistemological foundation, their everyday scientific knowledge production and empirical context within the project.

Discussing the case: the notion of the universalism of scientific knowledge production

In this chapter we have focused on the negotiation of scientific knowledge in selected documents and points in time, both in connection with the project as a whole and specifically in connection with the PhD students' knowledge production. In the following we want to take a step back and look at the case of AREPRO within a broader framework of the post-colonial critique of Western hegemonic knowledge production.

The idea of knowledge transfer

Capacity building can be seen as a matter of knowledge transfer from the Global North to the Global South – an approach implicitly based on a perception of scientific knowledge as universal, as described by Connell (2007). As Smith (2012) puts it: 'The globalisation of knowledge and Western culture constantly reaffirms the West's view of itself as the centre of legitimate knowledge generally referred to as "universal" knowledge' (Smith, 2012: 66). The project of AREPRO could be interpreted as a matter of facilitating knowledge transfer from the metropole to the periphery and enabling the Southern partners to do research like the Northern partners. Capacity building thus becomes a question of knowledge transfer. However, we found it much more complex when exploring the scientific knowledge production in the project.

At the heart of AREPRO was a deep-rooted aim to help African universities educate young scientists who could later partake in the international scientific debate and facilitate an enlightened national debate and decision-making process. Hence, the use of remote sensing and GIS can be interpreted as an opportunity for African partners to gain access to powerful knowledge and technical skills that can empower them. On the other hand the methodological hegemony of remote sensing and GIS applied in the project can also be interpreted as legitimising a certain flexible positional superiority: the participants can question each of the research areas and the content of the PhD courses, even the project itself, but it cannot be questioned that the project is being carried out under a methodological hegemony based on using remote sensing and GIS. As Smith (2012) argues, this flexible positional superiority means that even if the foundations of the science are questioned, this can be contained within the science and transformed in such a way as to maintain superiority. In our case, the Global South stays in the periphery of scientific knowledge production in the Global North despite the fact that extraordinary measures are undertaken to avoid it: for example South–South collaboration, PhD students graduating from

Global South universities, Global South supervisors, most PhD courses being held in the Global South.

Educating the Global South PhD students: mirroring the Global North

Is the PhD programme in capacity-building projects just a matter of mirroring PhD programmes in the Global North? Hountondji (1995) discusses what he terms 'scientific dependence' and argues that 'scientific and technological activity, as practiced in Africa today, is […] "extroverted", or externally oriented' (Hountondji, 1995: 2). He further lists the consequences of this scientific dependence in terms of research equipment, institutional nomadism and mastering foreign languages. Smith (2012) explicitly points to the field of education as the major agency for imposing this Western hegemony.

Using Hountondji's approach to interpret the education of PhD students within the AREPRO project shows that the setup of the programme and the type and content of the PhD courses can all be interpreted as a mirror of our own Northern PhD educational system. An implicit notion of the project's knowledge production being universal may have been the reason for this. It should be mentioned that, to our knowledge, this issue was never raised either by the Global South or Global North partners. Bringing in another analysis by Hountondji (1990) can shed light on this. He argues that being trained in an African university makes African students and academics feel that 'whatever their special fields might be, everything that matters for them is located or taking pace elsewhere [outside Africa]' (Hountondji, 1990: 6). More recently, this issue has been raised in more general terms by Shizha (2014), who describes how the African independent elite took over the hegemonic discourse of modernisation inherited from the colonial powers. Hence, it is not questioned that research and education is superior in the Global North or that an African setting is not attractive. To give an example from AREPRO; in the first PhD course on methodological issues, we had a discussion on the differences between the requirements for a paper-based thesis in an Nordic setting (us) and a monograph in a French setting that applied to the PhD students in the AREPRO project who were from former French colonies where the French educational system is still in use. None of us or the participants pondered on what might be the appropriate format for a PhD dissertation in an African context.

Unavoidable scientific knowledge dependence

It can be argued that the project of AREPRO goes beyond the divide of the Global South as a place for the collection of empirical material and the Global North as a place for theory development. The PhD students involved in AREPRO produced both theoretical and applied knowledge in the local context, and this was reinforced by the South–South collaboration. Also, as further discussed by Hountondji (1990), in some sectors the end of colonialism has meant that data processing now occurs in African countries due to their well-equipped laboratories and research institutes. Nonetheless, he argues that: 'Scientific activity remains basically extraverted, alienated, dependent on an international division of labour that tends to make scientific invention a monopoly of the north, while confining southern countries to the importing and application of these inventions' (Hountondji 1990: 9).

Based on our case we must agree with this, and it is exemplified by that fact that satellite remote sensing of environmental issues is a very technical issue, which is not only dependent on a number of educated scientists, but also an array of technical tools for acquiring and interpreting the vast amounts of data needed to undertake many of the necessary analyses, as discussed in detail by Mbow et al. (2014). It can be argued that the import and application of these technical tools make knowledge dependence unavoidable in the case of AREPRO.

Concluding remarks

We introduced this chapter by saying that we wanted to look at new ways of carrying out capacity-building projects with a focus on South–South collaboration. We must end by concluding that even though new paths have been paved, the negotiations of scientific knowledge production are, on the one hand, still situated within what could be termed a Western methodological hegemony and, on the other hand, that the very access to this methodological hegemony can be an opportunity for African partners to obtain access to powerful knowledge and hence empower them.

The case clearly shows that the issue of scientific knowledge production in capacity-building projects is much more complex than simply a question of getting away from the idea of knowledge transfer and the 'tradition' of data collecting in the Global South and theorising in the Global North (Connell, 2007; Hountondji, 1995). This is a case of a specific capacity-building project where effort has been put into focusing on South–South collaboration, PhD education in the South (graduation from Southern universities), assigning supervisors in South, and facilitating negotiations on scientific knowledge based on many years of cooperation between the involved partners. These can all be seen as issues in line with post-colonial authors' call for creating new platforms for acting (Chen, 2010; Crossman, 2004; Zhang et al., 2015). However, despite these efforts our analysis shows that the scientific knowledge production in the project is still situated within a Western position of superiority, however flexible (Smith 2012). We have found that the post-colonial education of PhD students in the Global South is inextricably related to scientific knowledge production in the Global North. Therefore, we need new ways to think about and act on this relation. Nonetheless, being situated in the Global North the question we are left with is: can a capacity-building project ever be situated outside this positional superiority?

Involving oneself in capacity-building projects in higher education is about trying to make a difference as well as building personal relationships that you would not wish to be without. However, writing this chapter as insiders has also made us question our roles as researchers and our involvement in capacity building, which has sometimes taken unforeseen turns. This chapter has been written of engagement with the field and a wish to look for new ways forward. It has also been one of the most difficult academic texts for us to write, as we have had to reflect on our own roles and work as academics.

Notes

1 We have chosen to give this project an anonymous acronym: AREPRO (A REsearch PROject).
2 Established in 1994, UNCCD (United Nations Convention to Combat Desertification) is the sole legally binding international agreement linking environment and development to sustainable land management. In the 10-Year Strategy of the UNCCD (2008–2018) that was adopted in 2007, Parties to the Convention further specified their goals: 'To forge a global partnership to reverse and prevent desertification/land degradation and to mitigate the effects of drought in affected areas in order to support poverty reduction and environmental sustainability' (UNCCD, 2008–2018).
3 Using the term 'basic analysis' in this context is to be understood in its technical context. That is, the students clearly exhibit their abilities to manipulate single images or even numbers of images, but have not fully embraced the idea of regular time series analysis.

References

AAG (2009) *Statement on Professional Ethics*. Endorsed by the Council of the Association of American Geographers. Available at: www.aag.org/cs/about_aag/governance/statement_of_professional_ethics (accessed 21 October 2014).

Adriansen, H.K. (2012) 'Timeline interviews: a tool for conducting life history research', *Qualitative Studies*, 3 (1), 40–55.

Adriansen, H. and Madsen, L.M. (2014) 'Using student interviews for becoming a reflective geographer', *Journal of Geography in Higher Education*, 38 (4), pp. 595–605.

Adriansen, H.K. and Madsen, L.M. (2009) 'Implications of doing insider interviews: studying geography and geographers', *Norwegian Journal of Geography*, 93 (3), 145–153.

Breidlid, A. (2013) *Education, Indigenous Knowledges, and Development in the Global South: Contesting Knowledges for a Sustainable Future*. New York: Routledge.

Browne, K. (2003) 'Negotiations and fieldworkings: friendship and feminist research', *ACME: An International E-Journal for Critical Geographies* 2 (2), 132–146.

Chen, K.H. (2010) *Asia as Method: Toward Deimperialization*. Durham: Duke University Press.

Cleaver, K. (1992) 'Deforestation in the western and central African forest: The agricultural and demographic causes and some solutions'. In Cleaver, K et al. (eds) *Conservation of West and Central African Rainforests*, World Bank Environment paper no. 1, Washington D.C.: World Bank, pp. 65–78.

Connell, R. (2007) *Southern Theory, The Global Dynamics of Knowledge in Social Science*. Cambridge: Polity Press.

Crossman, P. (2004) 'Perceptions of "Africanisation" or "endogenisation" at African universities: issues and recommendations'. In Zeleza, P.T. and Olukoshi, A. (eds) *African Universities in the Twenty-first Century*, Vol. 2, South Africa: CODESRIA, pp. 319–340.

Danida (2000) *Evaluation of Danida's Bilateral Programme. Danida's Bilateral Programme for Enhancement of Research Capacity in Developing Countries (ENRECA)*, Phase 3 report. Copenhagen: Danish Ministry of Foreign Affairs.

Dei, G.J.S. (2014) 'Indigenizing the school curriculum'. In Emeagwali, G.and Dei, G.J.S. (eds) *African Indigenous Knowledge and the Disciplines*. Rotterdam: SensePublishers, pp. 165–180.

DeLyser, D. (2001) 'Do you really live here? Thoughts on insider research', *Geographical Review* 91 (1-2), 441–453.

Edwards, B. (2002) 'Deep insider research', *Qualitative Research Journal*, 2 (1), 71–84.

Fairhead, J. and Leach, M. (1996) *Misreading the African Landscape: Society and Ecology in a Forest-savanna Mosaic* (Vol. 90). Cambridge University Press.

Fensholt, R., Langanke, T., Rasmussen, K., Reenberg, A., Prince, S.D., Tucker, C., Scholes, R.J., Le, Q.B., Bondeau, A. and Eastman, R. (2012) 'Greenness in semi-arid areas across the globe 1981-2007 – an Earth Observing Satellite based analysis of trends and drivers', *Remote Sensing of Environment*, 121, 144–158

Geist, H.J. and Lambin, E.F. (2004) 'Dynamic causal patterns of desertification', *Bioscience*, 54 (9), 817–829.

Hjortsø, C.N. and Meilby, H. (2013) 'Balancing research and organizational capacity building in front-end project design: experiences from Danida's ENRECA programme', *Public Administration and Development*, 33 (3), 205–220.

Hountondji, P.J. (1990) 'Scientific dependence in Africa today', *Research in African Literatures*, 21 (3), 5–15.

Hountondji, P.J. (1995) 'Producing knowledge in Africa today. The second Bashorun M.K.O. Abiola distinguished lecture', *African Studies Review*, 38 (3), 1–10.

Laris, P. and Wardell, D.A. (2006) 'Good, bad or "necessary evil"? Reinterpreting the colonial burning experiments in the savanna landscapes of West Africa', *The Geographical Journal*, 172 (4), 271–290.

Leach, M. and Mearns, R. (1996) 'Environmental change and policy'. In Leach, M. and Mearns, R. (eds) *The Lie of the Land: Challenging Received Wisdom on the African Environment*. Oxford: James Currey Press, pp. 1–33.

Livingstone, D.N. (2003) *Putting Science in Its Place: Geographies of Scientific Knowledge*. USA: University of Chicago Press.

Livingstone, D.N. (2012) 'Reflections on the cultural spaces of climate', *Climatic Change*, 113 (1), 91–93.

McAlpine, L. and Åkerlind, G. (2010) *Becoming an Academic*. Chippenham and Eastbourne: Palgrave Macmillan.

Madsen, L.M. (2014) *Multiple African Academic Identities*. Paper presented at the Academic Identities Conference, Durham University, July 2014.

Madsen, L.M. and Adriansen, H.K. (2006) 'Knowledge constructions in research communities: the example of agri-rural researchers in Denmark', *Journal of Rural Studies* 22 (4), 456–468.

Madsen L.M. and Winsløw C. (2009) 'Relations between teaching and research in physical geography and mathematics at research-intensive universities', *International Journal of Science and Mathematics Education* 7 (4), 741–763.

Mbow, C., Brandt, M., Ouedraogo, I., De Leeuw, J. and Marshall, M. (2015) 'What four decades of earth observation tell us about land degradation in the Sahel', *Remote Sensing*, 7 (4), 4048–4067.

Mbow, C., Fensholt, R., Nielsen, T.T. and Rasmussen, K. (2014) 'Advances in monitoring vegetation and land use dynamics in the Sahel', *Danish Journal of Geography*, 114 (1), 84–91.

Mbow, C., Nielsen, T.T. and Rasmussen, K. (2000) 'Savanna fires in east-central Senegal: distribution patterns, resource management and perceptions', *Human Ecology*, 28 (4), 561–583.

Møller-Jensen, L. and Madsen, L.M. (2015) 'Becoming and being an African scholar: a 15 year perspective on capacity building projects in Ghana', *Forum for Development Studies*, 42 (2), 245–264.

Neal, R. and Gordon, J. (2001) 'Fieldwork among friends', *Resources for Feminist Research*, 28 (3-4), 99–113.

Olsson, L., Eklundh, L. and Ardö, J. (2005) 'A recent greening of the Sahel – trends, patterns and potential causes', *Journal of Arid Environments*, 63 (3), 556–566.

Rose, G. (1997) 'Situating knowledges: positionality, reflexivities and other tactics', *Progress in Human Geography*, 21 (3), 305–320.

Said, E.W. (1995 [1978]) *Orientalism: Western Conceptions of the Orient*. Harmondsworth: Penguin.

Shizha, E. (2014) 'Indigenous knowledge systems and the curriculum'. In Emeagwali, G. and Dei, G.J.S. (eds) *African Indigenous Knowledge and the Disciplines*. Rotterdam: SensePublishers, pp. 113–129.

Smith, L.T. (2012) *Decolonizing Methodologies, Research and Indigenous People*. Croydon: Zed books.

Sop, T.K. and Oldeland, J. (2013) 'Local perceptions of woody vegetation dynamics in the context of a "greening Sahel": a case study from Burkina Faso', *Land Degradation & Development*, 24 (6), 511–527.

UNCCD (2008–2018) *United Nations Convention to Combat Desertification, 10-Year Strategy*. Available at: www.unccd.int/en/about-the-convention/Pages/About-the-Convention.aspx (accessed 17 May 2015).

Vigh, H. (2010) 'Youth mobilisation as social navigation. Reflections on the concept of dubriagem', *Cadernos de Estudos Africanos*, (18/19), 140–164.

Wardell, D.A., Nielsen, T.T. and Rasmussen, K. (2004) 'Fire history, fire regimes and fire management in West Africa: an overview'. In Goldammer, J.G. and de Ronde, C. (eds) *Wildland Fire Management Handbook for Sub-Sahara Africa*. Freiburg: Oneworldbooks, pp. 350–381.

Webster, L. and Mertova, P. (2007) *Using Narrative Inquiry as a Research Method, An Introduction to Using Critical Event Narrative Analysis in Research on Learning and Teaching*, London and New York: Routledge.

Zhang, H., Chan, P.W.K. and Kenway, J. (eds) (2015) *Asia as Method in Education Studies: A Defiant Research Imagination*. New York: Routledge.

Creating and using academic knowledge in Africa

Decolonising research?

Part III

9   My knowledge, your knowledge, whose knowledge is it?

Reflections from a researcher's journey through universities in North and South

Bevlyne Sithole

Introduction

This chapter presents a personal perspective on higher education. It is presented from a particular perspective that draws on an experience of education situated in the time during the Unilateral Declaration of Independence (UDI) and post-independence Zimbabwe. It is written from the perspective of a black African woman whose journey in higher education was both constricted and privileged. It is written too from the perspective of a black scholar moving around in the diaspora sometimes melting into the Global North educational landscape and other times standing out as a marker of what is different between the Global South and Global North but also finding myself in the in-between places where my own thoughts, positions and locations become blurred. The educational experience is conceptualised in this chapter through episodic events, encounters and experiences that have been narrated to stimulate and inform discussions and ideas about higher education. Throughout the chapter the importance of understanding power and politics over knowledge is obvious and underlined.

Reading Kagwanja's comment on the Africa's knowledge class as: 'A small, beleaguered group with an extremely weak intellectual infrastructure and is the sick man of the new knowledge based world order' (Kagwanja, 2000: 24) is quite confronting in many ways, as I reflect on my personal experience of higher education. He warns against what he calls the re-colonisation of the economic and intellectual space and observes that the weakened state of the knowledge class is evidence of further entrenchment of the dominance of the external scholars in policy making and policy implementation on the continent. I draw on my own history and experiences to reflect on intellectual and knowledge spaces that I have encountered. I show how culture and historical experience are intricately interwoven as subtext that can inform one's construction of interactive opportunities occurring in spaces for knowledge production. I use the terms Global South and Global North loosely in the chapter sometimes using Global South interchangeably with sub-Saharan Africa and use the term Global North interchangeably with the West to also include experiences derived from Europe and Australia.

Much is written about higher education and distributed knowledge producing spaces (Aarts and Greijn, 2010; Hountondji, 1990, 1995; Hwami and Kapoor, 2012; Kraak, 2000). Girvan (2007) finds that power imbalances in knowledge are expressed in Northern dominance in knowledge construction, reproduction and dissemination. He finds that there is a knowledge hierarchy between the Global South and Global North. The Global South lags behind in knowledge production (Sawyerr, 2004; Sithole, 2011). I explore some of the knowledge producing spaces I have encountered through telling stories from my own experiences both in a university context, in joint projects and in positions of employment. In order to do so, I begin with a brief story about my life journey in higher education. After that narrative, I reflect on some of the big influences that have shaped how I conceptualise my educational experience. In the subsequent analysis, I introduce each section with a small narrative – first I locate my own scholarship, then I consider some of the encounters in my scholarship with questions like which is my knowledge, which is your knowledge and whose knowledge is it. These have been crucial to me, as they have both challenged my notions about scholarship and galvanised my thinking about the form and character of the life journey I have travelled.

My life journey in higher education

I was born in 1965, a few months short of the Announcement of Unilateral Declaration of Independence (UDI), making me a child born to an education system primed to serve the white population in Zimbabwe. With Independence in 1980 came an opening up of opportunities for black children from townships to attend white schools. So I ended up sitting cheek by jowl with white kids in a previously white only government school because of a partial scholarship provided by a multi-national company that my father worked for. I and other black children thought of ourselves as the quota children put in the school to meet the quotas set by government for racial integration. By comparison, this school was well resourced and staffed by trained teachers and therefore provided a higher standard of education than in my previous schools. We sat for the British exams. Attendance in the school opened up possibilities to follow a new path to higher education. While the white children in our school had the pick of regional and overseas higher education institutions, for the majority of black kids the only option for higher education was the University of Zimbabwe. However, membership in a church could open up opportunities to study abroad on a Christian-based scholarship, but these opportunities were very limited in my church.

In 1984, I commenced higher education at the University of Zimbabwe on a partial grant and loan from the government to pursue a degree in geography. Hwami and Kapoor (2012) call students trained during this period the 'elite and vanguards' of the nation. In our villages and within the townships I and my fellow black students were celebrated as the future of post-independent Zimbabwe. The lecturers were highly respected in the region and were well-published scholars who spent time away at reputable universities in the Global North. Standards were said to be comparable with the Global North and within the region, there was great respect for the University of Zimbabwe. Ties and connections with universities and the British education system and the Commonwealth remained strong.

After my graduate studies, I found a job in a government research department alongside eight other new graduates. Each of us was designated a research officer for a province. Bilateral funding became available for capacity building within government that opened up new opportunities for further higher education and within a few years of employment, my colleagues and I found ourselves heading to different universities in the Global North for postgraduate training in Master programmes focusing on environmental studies. I saw my postgraduate experience as validation that standards of higher education in the Global South were still high and the international education system was opening up to Africans in a way that was both affirmative and complementary. I returned to Zimbabwe with new confidence and purpose to work alongside researchers from overseas governments who arrived in post-independence Zimbabwe to mentor the new government workers under various bi-lateral programs. Being mentored into the job by someone from another country with the same academic training and a little more workplace experience than yourself presented some challenges in terms of defining the scope of north to south mentoring and created its own challenges as far as conceptualising the basis for mentoring relationships between us. My postgraduate training in the Global North evened out the academic credentials yet here we were, my superior local knowledge against their workplace experience in the Global North. My own history and encounters with domination and discrimination made it acutely difficult to see every day relationships between my mentor and I through a clear lens. After some difficult encounters we resolved unofficially to be co-workers rather than mentor and mentee, but I still alternated between looking for evidence of domination and superiority while sometimes exploiting my special status of being mentored by someone from the Global North when I thought it useful. Because of this ambivalence towards the Global North, my attitude was alternatively submissive and rebellious.

When I got jobs at an international research institute in Sweden, was employed by an international research organisation in based Indonesia and had a job at a national research organisation in Australia, there was a certain excitement that jobs in a first world country or reputable international research organisations meant unequivocal recognition of my higher education experience and knowledge. There were no questions about sitting a test, getting assessed for competency or even an evaluation of my qualifications – I was a black woman from the Global South, recognised in the Global North. Now almost a decade later, I found that my previous comfort with my mixed education and the professional experience dissipating as more and more partners and employers in the Global North need validation of my qualifications and want to test my language skills. While working in Sweden, I applied for and got a scholarship from the Canadian International Development Research Centre to undertake doctoral research studies at the University of Zimbabwe as a part-time research fellow. Choosing the University of Zimbabwe was easy because of the reputation of the Centre for Applied Social Sciences (CASS) both regionally and internationally. It was a place that was pioneering research about community natural resources use and natural resources management and that was my main research interest. Now I am an adjunct fellow at Charles Darwin University and am sometimes invited to lecture at the Centre of African Studies at the University of Copenhagen. In between my commitments in Australia, and Denmark, I continue to look for and be involved when I get opportunities to work in Africa.

Conceptualising my educational experience

My lecturer and long-time mentor Professor Marshal Murphree delivered his valedictory address in 1997 and focused on strategic directions for enhancing scholarship at the University of Zimbabwe, where I was employed as a research fellow and lecturer. The speech was both timely and pivotal as it was made a few years before I completed my doctoral studies. Higher education was changing and in the speech Professor Murphree put forward his vision of what future scholarship should be:

> This scholarship should be dedicated to the generation, transmission and application of truth. It derives this dedication and achieves its function through an ethos of professional integrity, not through bureaucratic conformity, it stimulates excellence by coalescence of scholarship in disciplinary and transdisciplinary specialisms, located in departmental contexts. While holding service to its own society it is not content to be provincial. It seeks a place on the centre stage of international scholarship through focus on subject matter and fields where it has comparative advantage. And it achieves these through social contract with its environing society of reciprocal rights and responsibilities, and expectations.
>
> (Murphree, 1997: 3)

At the time, the University of Zimbabwe like other universities in the region was transforming and reconfiguring content foci at research and graduate levels and in certain fields to reflect issue sets which concern policy and practice (Murphree, 1997). He observed that to achieve this transformation would require a new coalition of multi-disciplinary scholarship. Kraak (2000) describes similar trends in South Africa where some universities are shifting to a transdisciplinary form of knowledge production. Transdisciplinary knowledge is described as knowledge that arises at the interstices of disciplines, and is generated in the context application (Gibbons, 2000). My postgraduate training in environmental science in the Global North had developed my interdisciplinary research skills and I started to get involved in projects with other departments at the University of Zimbabwe to develop my strength and competency in this area.

In 1990, I came across Ngũgĩ wa Thiong'o's *Decolonizing the Mind* a title that was both exciting and intriguing given my own euphoria in post-independent Zimbabwe. Zimbabwe had achieved political independence, so the title seemed to suggest that we needed to think about academic independence. This book made me consider my educational experience in the context of my historical and cultural experience. Wa Thiong'o (1987) explores the dominance of the Eurocentric theories and language in education. He also argues forcefully about use of language as a medium of power and writes about European languages as the authorising languages of knowledge. Ngũgĩ wa Thiong'o argues that knowledge is not really knowledge unless produced in a European language and thus he calls on African scholars to question this assumption. His arguments suggest a need to relook at the experience of education in the context of colonial history. One cannot fault wa Thiong'o's arguments, but they left me rather bewildered and uncomfortable with my higher education experience both in Zimbabwe and in England. Much later when I reached Australia in 2004, another book by Maori scholar, Linda Tuhiwai Smith on *Decolonising Methodologies*, brought me back to wa Thiong'o's arguments. Smith focuses on her own experiences as a Maori in New Zealand and explores the way colonial experience shapes and influences research and its representation. She quotes Bobbi Sykes who asks 'what, post-colonialism, have they left?' (Smith, 1999: 25) to suggest that colonialism persists. Smith finds that colonialism is far from 'finished' hence those with the colonised experience generally perceive a need to decolonise their minds, recover and claim a space within which they can develop a sense of authentic humanity. Thus, the real challenge at the beginning of my scholarship was to find ways to develop a sense of authentic African scholarship inspite of, and in some respects because of, my experience of being colonised.

Irele (1991) observes that despite individual achievements and reputations, African scholarship is at best marginal and at worst non-existent in the economy of intellectual and scientific endeavour. Similarly, Aarts and Greijn (2010) observe that the contribution of researchers in the developing world to global knowledge production has been relatively small. Irele (1991) laments what she calls the dark ages of scholarship that have descended on Africa when she had expected the emergence of Africa as an important if not autonomous area of scholarship. As a scholar I found the state of scholarship in the Global South a source of concern because of the frequent comparison with the Global North, sometimes spoken and other times unspoken. I found too that perceptions in the Global South, some which I shared, are not always informed by fact. More generally the primary reason was because as a scholar one wonders how one can be part of the shift that will see African scholarship move from the margins of scholarship to the centre. A lecture by Professor Al Mazrui in 2003 at the University of Nairobi, in Kenya was an important part of the discussion to think about African scholarship in a changing global knowledge economy. Mazrui's talk was called 'Towards a re-Africanisation of the African university: who killed intellectualism in the post-colonial era'. In the lecture, Mazrui highlights some of the factors affecting intellectualism in Africa and he describes the colonial legacy as uncompromisingly foreign that its impact has been alienating. He finds that:

> A whole generation of African graduates grew up despising their own ancestry, and scrambling to imitate the West. Those early African graduates who have later become university teachers themselves have on the whole remained intellectual imitators and disciples of the West. African historians have since begun to innovate methodologically as they have grappled with oral traditions, but most of the other disciplines are still condemned to paradigmatic dependency [...] What should be remembered is that by the time these African universities were being established, African intellectuals had already become so mentally dependent that they themselves insisted on considerable imitation of Western educational systems – including the importation of Western media of instruction for African schools and universities.
>
> (Mazrui, 2003: 143)

Thus I wondered whether, as Al Mazrui was intimating, (or) to what extent I had become an intellectual imitator?

Hountondji (1990) observes that most young scholars assume that education at home in the Global South means they start their careers on the margins of science. Because of this assumption most scholars accept the necessity of stepping up and moving from the margins to the centre. While accepting that intellectual imperialism remains alive and well and that African scholarship is at the periphery, Murphree (1997) suggests that African scholarship move to the international centre by engaging in scholarship that is robust enough to influence the modes of discourse that occur in disciplinary cognitive contexts, methodology and analysis. He cautions against what he calls 'autarkic scholarship' based on ethnocentric and nationalist sentiment and says this is not the answer. Hwami (2010) concurs and also finds that neo-liberalisation and radical nationalism of the type seen in Zimbabwe has affected the nature of and quality of higher education in Zimbabwe. Murphree (1997) argues that Africa has the intellectual talent required but it needs scholarship to be synergistically organised and applied to subject matter and fields where African scholars have a comparative advantage. In response, I found that community based natural resources management and indigenous peoples were areas where I felt I had competency, a comparative advantage and the necessary passion.

Locating my African scholarship

Some years ago, I attended an expert group meeting in Nairobi with an interdisciplinary group of experts drawn from different regions, different disciplines and organisations. Eminent scholars and professors were brought together to represent a group that would review and summarise key policy successes in Africa. Over coffee, the discussion turned to the African brain drain and its impact on

African scholarship. One of the uncomfortable questions raised then was whether African scholars in the diaspora could legitimately be called up to participate in panels such as these when they were living away from Africa and they were taking opportunities from scholars on the continent. My immediate reaction was of course indignation, that one's location could even be an issue. How dare they suggest that I had no legitimacy to be talking about Africa because of my location? Why was my location even important?

On another occasion I was invited to speak at a world conference as an African speaker and when I mentioned my attendance to a colleague, she asked me if that was because they could not find another speaker in Africa, was there no one else? she asked. Am I really the token African scholar? This was deeply upsetting, but this time as in the previous case in Nairobi, I began to think about this issue and realised that this question was a pertinent one. Clearly, there is an issue with one identifying as an African scholar located away from Africa. This repeated questioning raises important issues about location and scholarship, but also the more fundamental questions of identity, sources of knowledge and continuity of experience and understanding.

When I found an article by Karioki (1974) on 'African scholars versus Ali Mazrui' I got very excited because finally I had found someone who had addressed the very same questions I had started to ask myself. Karioki asks why do African intellectuals disown one another in relation to Professor Mazrui who was a respected scholar and an intellectual force throughout Africa. Here was Karioki looking into why other Africans were rejecting such a well-known scholar. Mazrui saw himself in his lifetime as a divisive individual straddling the Global North and the Global South higher education systems, but also frequently highlighting the triple identity that shaped his views and life experiences. Mazrui seems to have been aware of the attitudes towards him and wrote:

> In my own personal life I was respected more as an intellectual by Milton Obote in Uganda and Julius Nyerere in Tanzania than I was by either Mzee Kenyatta or Daniel Arap Moi in Kenya. Even Idi Amin, when he was in power in Uganda, wanted to send me to apartheid South Africa as living proof that Africans could think. Idi Amin wanted me to become Exhibit A of the Black Intellectual to convince racists in South Africa that Black people were human beings capable of rational thought. Fortunately, I was able to convince Idi Amin, not humour racists, with such a display.
>
> (Mazrui, 2003: 139)

Though Mazrui is writing here about intellectual recognition among his peers and alludes to colonial attitudes towards African scholars, Karioki considers his unpopularity by analysing Mazrui's work and concludes that:

> Africa wishes of its thinkers to be committed and relevant to the process of liberation from colonialism and neocolonialism and to play a significant role

in the reestablishment of its rightful place in the world, in short Africa
demands of its intellectuals to serve the communities from which they
spring.

(Karioki, 1974: 55)

Murphree (1997) finds that a scholar can be viewed in relation to where one
produces knowledge, or relative to those that support and fund research. Thus he
suggests that scholars do need to be careful and avoid the possibility of dangerous
alignment with whoever is paying for knowledge. Murphree further (1997)
argues that as long as scholarship is disciplined in its observations and responds
to methodological rather than client driven agendas, then there is need to relook at current definitions of research and research for development.

Aliet finds that the modern African scholar is more connected to the global,
but is often alienated from the local, only confronting a 'bit of his African side
when they visit rural Africa' (Aliet, 2007: 3). Pursuit of excellence forces African
scholars to move between or settle in the Global North (Hountondji, 1995).
Aliet (2007) concludes that the African intellectual is therefore a hybrid of
Western culture, courtesy of a colonial heritage, and traditional African culture.
Nyanchoga (2014) finds that the underpinning culture of African society is
Western and that makes the university the centre of Western cultural and
academic experience perpetuating scholarship that is judged on Western
standards. Irele (1991) presents a description of the African scholar and explores
what she calls the African's scholar's burden and the resulting scholarship.
Mazrui (2003) observes that over the last forty years East Africa has experienced
the rise and decline of African intellectuals while in Nigeria, Babalola (2013)
identifies a problem he calls the 'gradual de-intellectualization of the academia
and the intellectualization of indolence and mediocrity in some of our
institutions'. Sawyerr (2004) finds that more typical in Africa is the scholar who
is distracted by too many consultancies and project oriented research to devote
much time to mentoring and supervision. Consultancies and commissioned work
are not necessarily inconsistent with research, the core elements of data gathering
analysis and to some extend verification are common to both academic research
and good consultancy work (Murphree, 1997). Mkandawire (1995) identifies
three categories of African scholars. The first generation of scholars are well
educated to very high standards and most have an impressive record of scholarship.
They were educated in the 1960s. The second generation of scholars he argues
are scholars who were educated in the 1970s and 1980s. These scholars received
a good education and have local degrees supplemented by a degree awarded from
a Northern institution. They are called the brain drain generation because most
did not come back home after their education in the Global North or have since
left their home countries. The final category is the third generation scholars who
bore the brunt of the severe decline in higher education and in opportunities in
the Global South. This group constitutes the main group in the demography of
most universities as many of the first generation scholars retire leaving third
generation scholars in place. Based on Mkandawire's classification, I would be

classed as part of the 'brain drain generation'. Anti-diaspora sentiment is present in some countries, and certainly in Zimbabwe popular sentiment is that diaspora people desert the country and let the economy down. Kapungu describes the following situation:

> The nation has developed myopic behaviour and singular thinking. The main goal of each person leaving the educational system is to map out an exit strategy, to find whichever employment they can in other countries. Nationally, 0.6% of the population is estimated to migrate abroad in a year. The harsh economic environment is crowding out ambitions of career development, nation building and entrepreneurship development, and cultivating a thirst to make quick money.
>
> (Kapungu, 2007: 4)

Kapungu also observes that once people get to the Global North, it is very common to find individuals educated in a particular field that are working in a completely different field because of the limited availability of jobs within their area. For those that are able to engage with higher education in the Global North, Hountondji describes a phenomenon he calls scientific tourism. He explains the prevalence of this type of tourism is because 'no scholar from the third world can claim to be doing top level research in any field without travelling, without taking himself physically to the universities and research centres of industrial countries' (Hountondji, 1990: 10). Much has been written about brain drain from Africa (Nyanchoga, 2014; Teferra, 2000). Aarts and Greijn (2010) describe the periodic movement between the Global South and Global North as brain circulation where there is the temporary movement borne out of a necessity to develop and advance scholarship. The success of higher education will be seen through the ability of scholars to tap into the global knowledge economy and apply it to their situations. Teferra (2000) argues that greater efforts should be made by countries in Africa to create opportunities to engage with scholars in the diaspora for the benefit of Africa. Hountondji (1990) finds that African scholars are more involved in a vertical exchange and dialogue with scientists from the Global North than in any horizontal exchange with their fellow scholars from the Global South. This results in a lack of and/or poor development of internal scientific discussions and debates within and between our scientific communities, resulting in what Hountondji (1990) calls a general stampede of our scholars for individual acknowledgment by the Global North. Another scholar writing about scholarship in South Africa finds an individual who is challenged by his circumstance and position relative to a scholar in the Global North (Sithole, 2009). Sithole (2009) describes the environment in the Global North for the African scholar as hostile, it is made insecure because somehow the African scholar is assumed to need tutelage even of the most junior scholars from the Global North and that his facts must be checked. Sawyerr's (2004) vision of Africa is the sustained generation of world class research results and new knowledge that help our understanding of African conditions and contribute to development of its people. In this vision, Sawyerr envisages the research by: 'African researchers working primarily at African institutions, turning out first rate knowledge on locally relevant issues' (Sawyerr, 2004: 216). Sawyerr suggests that his insistence on Africans scholars in Africa as the scholars will ensure 'rootedness and the sustainability' of knowledge production.

Which is my knowledge?

When I arrived in Northern Australia, I worked on indigenous natural resources management issues among Aboriginal communities in Northern Australia. In my work I quickly realised that what I thought as my work or my research was not so, the question of ownership over knowledge took centre stage. My previous experience of doing research among communities in villages in Southern Africa were memorable and largely conflict free. Communities participated in research projects and were often satisfied when I made efforts to include, acknowledge or pass on knowledge gathered. But the situation was different in Australia. In Northern Australia, Aboriginal communities were in the fore front of questioning, negotiating and clearly defining the boundaries of proprietorship arrangements over the process of producing knowledge and control of knowledge that is produced from research through formalised and informal processes. On one occasion early in my time in the remote Aboriginal community, I was shocked when one of the Aboriginal elders wanted to know what guarantees I was giving that my research, which was in fact their intellectual property, would not end up in Africa. On seeing my expression and my surprise at the question, the elder explained gently that all I was doing was writing down what he was saying, but he was doing the talking and sharing his knowledge with me. I believed I was doing more than just noting what he said but I held my tongue. He explained that he knew about the poverty of my people in Africa and he did want to help Africa and would give permission if I asked, but it must be clear that they the Aboriginal people are acknowledged as the owners and holders of that knowledge. Compared to African communities, I found Aboriginal people more aware and cautious in their negotiations with outsiders about knowledge produced during research. This and many other discussions over knowledge underlined the importance of reconceptualising scholarship when one is working in community situations and or is using participatory methodologies. However, recognising communities as partners in knowledge generation requires that we develop new ways and new relations in new research arenas. Working with communities using participatory methods means I was now in a situation where I was co-producing knowledge. But what is knowledge and which of the knowledge produced in the research that I do is legitimately mine?

Koontz (2014) found that co-producing knowledge between scientists and non-scientists is done through a process in which scholars seek a connection with, rather than gain dominance over communities. Co-production of knowledge between scientists and communities is a prerequisite for research aiming at a more sustainable development path. In this type of co-production of knowledge, Koontz makes the following compelling argument:

> Instead of stabilizing the social identities that shape the boundaries between academic and non-academic communities, sustainability research aims to produce an agora in which the boundaries are provisionally blurred; the resulting 'messiness' of 'divided identities' is the necessary condition for engaging with 'others' and ultimately helping to reshape the involved groups' perceptions, behaviour and agendas that occur as a function of their interaction.
>
> (Koontz, 2014: 79)

Messiness and blurriness highlighted by Koontz is characteristic of some of the experiences described in Long and Long's (1992) *Battlefields of Knowledge*. Long and Long (1992) present an actor interface perspective to convey the idea that when one interacts with other actors, and in this case communities in Northern Australia, relations are formulated in contested arenas in which one's understandings, interests and values are pitched against those of the community and anyone else that is involved. They argue that the main advantage of adopting an actor interface perspective is its recognition of the central significance of human agency, self-organising processes and the mutual determination. Many indigenous communities have reason to be concerned about the appropriation of their knowledge by researchers, without permission or respect for customary law and with little benefit to them. According to Posey et al. (1995), the first concern for communities is about their right not to sell, commoditise or have expropriated from them certain domains of knowledge and sacred places, resources and objects be respected. Casimirri (2003) finds often researchers ask local and traditional knowledge holders to give their knowledge to outsiders who will then publish this knowledge and therefore often shifting the authority over knowledge from local people to outsiders. The issue of how one works with communities and makes public some of the knowledge gathered raises questions about how one views the use of that knowledge and future ownership of it. Other important questions are: Who can use this knowledge? What use will this knowledge be put to? Who will this knowledge benefit? Knowledge gathered or created with communities once public is free and non-excludable. Thus as Sibisi (2004) found out, intellectual property rights do not necessarily prevent infringements, and traditional practitioners or local communities commonly have no means for legal recourse. Posey et al. (1995) found that published knowledge can later be appropriated to the disadvantage of the communities we gather it from. So even when one makes agreements with communities and despite assurances and agreements between researchers and communities once published, knowledge can be appropriated from the public domain. The key challenge has been how to give real assurance of ownership to communities so that the knowledge that is produced remains their property.

Elisabetsky and Posey (1994) have taken the approach whereby they state in any work that they publish that the information was freely given and remind readers about their moral and ethical obligations to respect, acknowledge and share the benefits of the use of any of the knowledge they gain from reading the work. Gorjestani (2004) finds that developing innovative approaches to protect intellectual property associated with communities' knowledge is one of the key challenges facing the global development community since existing arrangements may not be applicable to the specific nature of the knowledge. At issue is what kind of knowledge should have exclusive ownership rights, and under what conditions? The proprietary view of knowledge could have a damaging effect on willingness by scientists to work with communities. Agrawal (1999) states that there is little consensus even today about issues of commensurability of different forms of knowledge, nature of ownership of specific indigenous practices, advisability of compensation and how to view cross cultural interactions.

Gaventa and Cornwall (2001) cite Chambers as saying professionals replicate hierarchies of knowledge and power that position them as knowing better. Gaventa and Cornwall (2001) see knowledge as power and in some cases asymmetrical control over knowledge create possibilities which can be imagined or acted upon. They give examples of the use of knowledge in situations where, for example, in public debates one body of knowledge is used to counter another. Agrawal (2002) finds the discourse about different knowledge systems ignores the prevailing power structures within which knowledge is embedded. He notes that holders of traditional knowledge have for most part remained in positions of resistance against domination of those who possess scientific knowledge. He concludes that one comes to distinguish between different systems of knowledge based on particular practices and institutions which are themselves products of different relations of power and its exercise. Sibisi (2004) is optimistic and observes that conflict and contradictions between the different knowledge worlds will vanish once the gap between traditional and modern scientists and practitioners can be closed through mutual acceptance of standards, continuous exchange, protection of rights, and recognition and reward for contributors. Please see Chapter 2 for a discussion of different modes of knowledge.

Which is your knowledge?

One of the defining moments in my interdisciplinary scholarship was my participation in a multi-disciplinary workshop hosted in Harare where experts were drawn from various disciplines to develop an integrated research framework for soil fertility management for small holder farmers. At the workshop the brief was simple, we were to work together across disciplines to come up with a simple integrated model or framework to use in soil fertility research. As the model started to take shape social scientists added more boxes, demanded that arrows change direction, become thicker, assume new meanings and change dimensions with the result that some scientists grew impatient with the process. Some scientists grew impatient with those from other disciplines and with the process itself. What started out as a big group of enthusiastic scientists disintegrated into disciplinary clusters and in some instances louder voices, and more experienced scientists were at times more dominant. During the meeting frustrations were apparent and on occasion scientists from some disciplines blurted out their irritation. At one point a biologist exclaimed in irritation – 'how many grandmothers per hectare does one need to know before making a soil fertility decision?' Amidst much laughter and indignation, this question represented a pivotal moment in the discussion and illuminated some of the challenges of working across disciplines. I was recognising that despite my interdisciplinary postgraduate training there were still deficiencies in my understanding of ideas and concepts from other disciplines and I was seeing that they too were lacking understanding of ideas from other disciplines. I was also looking at co-authored material and wondering how much of the co-produced knowledge incorporated my knowledge. I realise that co-producing knowledge and contributing to a process presented challenges when it came to determining one's contribution and owning the co-produced knowledge. The key question then becomes which is my knowledge and which is yours, is there enough integration to fully obliterate the boundaries between disciplines?

Working together in teams comprising of scholars drawn from other disciplines is not easy. Tress et al. (2005) define working in interdisciplinary situations as follows:

> We define interdisciplinary studies as projects that involve several unrelated academic disciplines in a way that forces them to cross subject boundaries to create new knowledge and theory and solve a common research goal. By unrelated, we mean that they have contrasting research paradigms. We might consider the differences between qualitative and quantitative approaches or between analytical and interpretative approaches that bring together disciplines from the humanities and the natural sciences.
>
> (Tress et al., 2005: 17)

Murphree (1997) suggests that scholars go back to school and strive to grasp concepts from other disciplines in order to conjoin scholarship with that of colleagues from other disciplines. He argues that reflexively one becomes a better scholar because of that conjunction. Murphree found that once achieved the interdisciplinary synergy can push interdisciplinary scholarship to the cutting edge. Integration in this context means that different knowledge cultures are bridged and their knowledge fused together when answering a research question. It also means that in a project the research question is defined jointly and answers derive from the integration. Wuchty et al. (2007) finds that research is increasingly done in teams across nearly all fields. Research over a five decade period shows two distinct trends. The first is a steady growth in knowledge that may have driven scholars towards more specialisation, prompting larger and more diverse teams. They also find that teams typically produce more frequently cited research than individuals, and this advantage has been increasing over time. Wuchty et al. (2007) also finds that while teams may bring greater collective knowledge and effort together, they sometimes experience social network and coordination problems that can cause them to underperform. Shifting authorship norms can influence co-authorship trends in fields with extremely large teams. Inclusivity rather than exclusivity over authorship and of knowledge is now an important feature of interdisciplinary scholarship.

In cases where knowledge is being produced in collaborations, relations over knowledge that is produced may be different. Gaillard (1994) in his review of collaborations in higher education finds that the Global North tends to be responsible for conception while the Global South is involved in execution of tasks (data collection and field experiments). Sithole (2011) observes that African scholars generally occupy positions of consumer, learner, research subject and research assistant in the relationship of knowledge production with the Global North and more worryingly some of our intellectuals may be merely extending Western theories to the African context in the name of innovation (see also Gaillard, 1994; Nyanchoga, 2014). Gaillard (1994) found that partners in the Global North publish twice as much as their Southern counterparts and present twice as many papers at conferences than their partners in the Global South. Advocacy for African scholarship to find itself and take ownership over knowledge that is created in Africa and facilitate and in some places accelerate a shift of the locations of the centres of knowledge to the Global South is growing (Aarts and Greijn, 2010; Kagwanja, 2000; Sawyerr, 2004). Kagwanja (2000) sees conditions in African universities as further weakening the African knowledge class and intellectual infrastructure thereby opening up floodgates for what he calls the domination of policy making and implementation in Africa by scholars from the Global North. In spite of all the collaborations between the Global North and Global South it would seem that Africa still remains at the bottom of the knowledge producing ladder (Nyanchoga, 2014; Sawyerr, 2004).

Whose knowledge is it?

> I attended a workshop in South Africa which brought together traditional healers, scientists and indigenous peoples from all over Africa to talk about health, but we spent a significant amount of time out of the workshop talking about ownership of knowledge. One of the important moments during the workshop was when participants described what knowledge systems they worked with and where they worked. The varieties of and sources of knowledge were quite staggering. Sometimes participants spoke about old knowledge handed down from generation to generation, other times they spoke of spiritually channelled knowledge, sacred knowledge or ancestral knowledge and in some cases experiential knowledge. As part of my own introduction, I recounted stories in my own youth of a grandfather who was known everywhere as a great healer, who was said to be able to talk to animals and use them as helpers in his healing feats and who had great knowledge. I also mentioned a great aunt who was taken by water sprites and disappeared under water in the village pool and came back some years later as a great healer using knowledge

gathered when she lived under water with the sprites. She is said to have used tornado like winds as part of her repertoire. Both were recognised holders of knowledge, but different kinds. In some accounts traditional healers spoke of work they were already doing which drew on traditional knowledge and science. An attempt to categorise knowledge was difficult. There were different sources of knowledge including spirit, ancestor or water sprites, elders and others that are connected to an individual or group. There were also individuals who we might term holders of knowledge or innovators who develop their knowledge and experience through hard work and then we had apprentices who worked alongside a holder of knowledge and acquire knowledge and the craft that way. Understanding sources of knowledge in collaborations is as important as knowing about the origins of knowledge, the spaces where it is created, ownership of that knowledge and conditions for accessing and using knowledge. How does one work with knowledge that is shared and widely distributed?

I found there is wide acknowledgement in the literature about the different types of knowledge and also the difficulties of classifying knowledge. For example, Mazzocchi (2006) observes that one of the difficulties in approaching knowledge from communities and indigenous cultures is already reflected in the variety of terminology used to describe it. Similarly, Muller (2013) states that traditional knowledge manifests itself in different forms and packages – sometimes as a body of knowledge, often too it is a process or it is a product. Generally, scholars assume they work with indigenous knowledge systems and that is a clearly defined category. Mazzocchi (2006) asks the questions who has rights, who consents to access and use of traditional knowledge, and how are benefits shared and between whom? Mazzocchi (2006) identifies some of the challenges of using classic intellectual property (IP) instruments. He finds that conventional instruments promote individual recognition in contrast to collective aspects of indigenous people's livelihoods and thus tend to grant monopoly and exclusionary rights which affect interests of other indigenous individuals and, especially, groups. Generally there is also a requirement for specific identification of a creator or innovator which may be difficult to achieve for indigenous knowledge. Further, IP instruments may also result in high transaction costs (i.e. administrative processes, negotiation of licences, legal fees, maintenance of right fees, etc.).

Turnbull (2009) argues for a need to reframe science in relation to other knowledge traditions. He describes scholars as undergoing a process of de-centring when they start to recognise that there are other ways of knowing in addition to conventional ones. He observes that all knowledge is both performative and representational. He adds that knowledge is historical, contingent and is co-produced with society. Turnbull sees a need to bring different knowledge systems together through the creation of what he calls a 'third space'. This means rethinking about knowledge as intersecting and overlapping in a knowledge space. Turnbull describes a knowledge space as follows:

That knowledge production process co-produces a knowledge space in which people, practices and places are linked. Such knowledge spaces have messy contingent and only partly acknowledged components: ontologies, systems of trust, technical devices and social strategies for moving and assembling the knowledge, narratives of spatiality and temporality. In addition to being profoundly narratological and spatial they are also performative, they are based in embodied practices, in the movement of human bodies in engagement with each other, with the physical environment, and with their own artefacts, in the movement along cognitive trails through conceptual space in making linkages and connections. In saying this I am producing my own narrative of commensurability in which knowledge spaces have common components that can be compared, shared and joined.

(Turnbull, 2009: 9)

Casimirri (2003) observes that traditional knowledge is often evaluated against 'expert' knowledge based on Western scientific paradigms before it is considered valid and useful. Agrawal (2002) calls this process 'scientization'. He cautions against processes that he argues can strip away all the detailed contextual and applied aspects that make knowledge useful. It is my experience that it is difficult for researchers and resource managers trained in the scientific tradition to integrate traditional knowledge. This is the source of tension between the indigenous knowledge and scientific knowledge. Communities are generally sceptical of science preferring to stay away from it especially after years of being dumped down on. Casimirri (2003) argues that rather than seeking ways to integrate this knowledge, there is a need to understand it as part of an entirely different worldview with its own associated values, institutions and management systems.

Watson and Huntington (2008) write in their article 'They are here – I can feel them: the epistemic spaces of indigenous and Western knowledges' an account of how different individuals are assembled in one space and together they become more than the authors' individual positions and selves. They find that knowledge production has an inherent spatial dimension to it and that an epistemic space is how these assemblages get recognised. Watson and Huntington (2008) argue that their experience is also ethnography about co-production of knowledge as much as it is about producing new knowledge together. Thus, they find that working in this way they were able to have cooperative control of the narrative, and were able to also integrate their theoretical and spiritual discourses so that they did not produce a discovery of indigenous knowledge, but a conversation. This type of attitude and handling of knowledge work to level out the asymmetries that may be present between the scholar and the communities and may also demonstrate who is contributing what knowledge.

Discussion

Sometimes a social scientist, an expert and most times a practitioner are all the different labels that are markers in my life journey spend with as many obstructions as it has had opportunities. My race, gender and history situate my interpretation of the journey within a cultural–political space where the discourse of domination and imperialism is inescapable. This is particularly true for an education experience located in what Hwami and Kapoor (2012) calls an Afro-radical and nativist paradigm that advocates for a 'Zimbabwe for Zimbabweans' doctrine. Wa Thiong'o's (1987) suggestions that the educational experience be analysed through lenses of the colonised experience is pertinent and challenges long-held views among African scholars that a superior education is only found in the Global North. Accordingly, the British education, the postgraduate education in the Global North, all underline an ongoing colonial experience. But Smith (1999: 14) then asks the questions does getting a colonial education precludes one from speaking with a real and authentic local voice? Is it possible that one can still find a real and authentic African voice? This seems very difficult given the nature of conditions prevalent for higher education in Zimbabwe and in Africa in general (Hwami, 2013; Hwami and Kapoor, 2012; Jansen, 2003).

Research on higher education in Africa points to the declining standards, the de-intellectualisation of scholars and declining opportunities and spaces to develop and advance one's scholarship. Leading scholars clearly point to a need to link in to the global economy and be able to tap the knowledge as a crucial step in advancing one's scholarship (Hountondji, 1995; Jansen, 2003; Murphree, 1997; Sawyerr, 2004). When Hountondji (1995) says no scholar can claim to be doing top level research without an interaction with the Global North, then my own location in the diaspora is an inevitable part of a trajectory created out of circumstance and the changes in the knowledge economy. If we accept Hountondji's argument about the inevitability of engagement with the Global North, then what do we make of the questioning of my periodic encounters with Africa as a scholar in the diaspora? We see an emergency of the hybrid scholars or what I could term third culture scholars who want to engage with the Global North without compromising the legitimacy and authenticity of their scholarship. Karioki (1974) concludes that Africa demands a lot from its scholars, only giving or accepting them and validating their knowledge and experience if they remain located and grounded in local realities. Nesbitt (2008) too explains that African scholars are characterised by the specificity of their intellectual concerns. By contrast the vision of most of the prominent scholars for Africa is to build the capacity of Africa as an autonomous area of scholarly endeavour and build a critical mass of scholars in Africa (Irele, 1991; Sawyerr, 2004). Such a vision runs counter to current global trends where the knowledge economy is global and boundaries between Global South and Global North are melting away. The nature of the global knowledge economy and the emergency of a global development research agenda makes the advocacy in Africa to decolonise knowledge or re-colonise intellectual space difficult but it is a message that scholars like me who have come out of a colonised experience easily relate to.

One of the ways higher education in Africa is transforming is the acceptance that knowledge and knowledge producers are socially distributed (Aarts and Greijn, 2010). The trend towards the involvement of communities and other actors in research has been part of a shift towards transdisciplinary scholarship and knowledge. Negotiating relationships over research and clarity over ownership and benefits from knowledge are important components of this scholarship. While researchers like Elisabetsky and Posey (1994) are working hard to safeguard interests and rights of communities in the work they publish, the reality is that once transdisciplinary work is public or is in the public domain, control over ownership of knowledge and how it is used becomes more difficult. It is also difficult to assure communities of the future benefit and recognition from the research. Within interdisciplinary groups ownership over knowledge is an issue. The conjoining of scholarship challenges conventional rules and protocols and defines new arenas of interaction. Turnbull (1997) finds that knowledge production is a social activity creating a particular type of space that is in turn defined by the interactions within it. In my experience the knowledge space that Turnbull describes is further complicated by contextual and political factors that may not always be visible or obvious.

Working with different knowledge systems, one engages not just with the difficulties of defining the type of knowledge but also difficulties of identifying the rightful holders of knowledge. Existing protocols for research do not provide adequate guidance about how one advances one's scholarship in this area and still be respectful, just and fair in sharing recognition and benefits deriving from working with indigenous knowledge. Ultimately, we must be concerned too about the role and responsibilities as scholars involved in what Agrawal (2002) terms 'scientisation' of knowledge. It is important that scholars heed the warning by Agrawal and are careful to ensure that their scholarship is not seen to strip away all the detailed contextual and applied aspects that make knowledge what it is.

Conclusion

My life journey in higher education frequently alternates between universities in the Global South and Global North where I encountered different knowledge systems and different spaces for producing knowledge. There are many contextual elements to the life journey, events and ideas that influenced the education experience and the direction it took. I still find tensions and ambiguities in how my persona as a scholar is constructed. In the Global South, I generally feel privileged both in the level of education achieved and also because I have had easy accessibility to the Global North. But in the Global North perceptions about my persona are constantly shifting, sometimes welcoming and other times repelling. At times in the Global North, I am simultaneously the 'token' African scholar in some fora and other times I am the expert whose knowledge now needs validation and verification.

My gender, race and historical experience situate my interpretation of the life journey within a cultural political space where the discourse of domination and imperialism is never far away. This narrative gives face to higher education experience that may be uniquely different from what the majority of scholars in

Global South have experienced, but is a case in point for looking at the nature of and purpose of higher education. Implicit in the narrative is the issue of ownership over knowledge and the imagined boundaries between education systems in the Global South and in the Global North and within that the tensions between science and traditional knowledge, which made me want to ask the following pertinent questions in an era of global knowledge production: Which is my knowledge? Which is your knowledge? Or/and/so whose knowledge is this? Power and ownership over knowledge challenge everyday conceptions of identity, scholarship and place. Encounters during my scholarship show that scholarship is now played out in new arenas where knowledge is more widely distributed and where the issue of who owns what must be carefully negotiated over.

Narrating one's life journey in higher education using episodes and encounters tends to be subsumed by subtexts related to one's views about domination and dependency, emerging at times in discussions about Africa and the rest of the world and at other times in stories about relationships in knowledge producing space. In the eyes of my compatriots in Africa, my nomadism has none of the romanticism associated with the old tribes of Africa, rather I am not seen beyond my bloated persona of privileged scholar and my easy proximity to the Global North while in the Global North, I struggle to find recognition and suitable employment. Ultimately, one must question the pervasive presence of the dominance/dependence discourse as the main and an inevitable lens through which I and most Africans use to reflect on life journeys. From my own experience, it has been very important to look back to where I have been in order to move forward as a scholar.

References

Aarts, H. and Greijn, H. (2010) 'Globalization, knowledge and learning: developing the capacities of higher education institutes'. In Teferra, D. and Greijn, H. (eds) *Higher Education and Globalisation – Challenges, Threats and Opportunities for Africa*. The Netherlands: Maastricht University Centre for International Cooperation in Academic Development (MUNDO), pp. 9–18.

Aliet, J. (2007) 'Convergence and globalisation – not counter penetration and domestication: a response to Prof Ali Mazrui', *Alternatives – Turkish Journal of International Relations*, 6 (1), 1–14.

Agrawal, A. (2002) 'Indigenous knowledge and the politics of classification', *International Social Science Journal*, 54 (173), 287–297.

Agrawal, A. (1999) 'Ethnoscience, TEK and conservation – power and indigenous knowledge'. In Posey, D.A. (ed.) *Cultural and Spiritual Values of Biodiversity*. Nairobi: United Nations Environment programme (UNEP), pp. 177–180.

Babalola, B.J. (2013) 'Reintellectualization of the deintellectualized academia in Africa: process product and pathway'. Available at: https://feathersproject.files.wordpress.com/2013/09/reintellectualizing_babalola-_obanya-paper-2013-final-final.pdf (accessed 12 December 2014).

Casimirri, G. (2003) 'Problems with integrating traditional ecological knowledge into contemporary resource management'. Available at: www.fao.org/docrep/ARTICLE/ WFC/XII/0887-A3.HTM (accessed 28 February 2015).

Elisabetsky, E. and Posey, D.A. (1994) 'Ethnopharmacological search for antiviral compounds: treatment of gastrointestinal disorders by Kayapo medical specialists'. In Chadwick, D.J. and Marsh, J. (eds) *Ethnobotany and the Search For New Drugs (Ciba Foundation Symposium 185)*. Chichester: John Wiley & Sons, pp. 77–94.

Gaillard, J.F. (1994) 'North and south research partnership: is collaboration possible between unequal partners?' *Knowledge and Policy*, 7 (2), 31–63.

Gaventa, J. and Cornwall, A. (2001) 'Power and knowledge'. In Reason, P. and Bradbury, H. (eds) *Handbook of Suction Research; Participative Inquiry and Practice*. London: Sage Publications, pp. 70–80.

Gibbons, M. (2000) 'Universities and the new production of knowledge. Some policy implications for government'. In Kraak, A. (ed.) *Changing Modes. New Knowledge Production and Its Implications for Higher Education in South Africa*. Pretoria: Human Science Research Council (HSRC), South Africa, pp. 34–44.

Girvan N. (2007) 'Power imbalances and development knowledge', *Strathmere Meeting and Wilton Park Conference: Southern Perspectives on Reform of the International Development Architecture*. Trinidad and Tobago: University of the West Indies, October 2006 and May 2007, pp. 1–52.

Gorjestani, N. (2004) *Indigenous Knowledge for Development: Opportunities and Challenge*. Washington: World Bank.

Jansen, J.D. (2003) 'On the state of South African Universities: guest editorial', *SAJHE/ SATHO*, 17(3), 9–12.

Hountondji, P.J. (1995) 'Producing knowledge in Africa today. The Second Bashorun M.K.O. Abiola Distinguished Lecture', *African Studies Review*, 38 (3), 1–10.

Hountondji, P.J. (1990) 'Scientific dependence in Africa today', *Research in African Literatures*, 21 (3), 5–15.

Hwami, M. (2013) '"The Nativist Turn" and the crisis in university education', *International Journal of Education*, (5) 4, 124–144.

Hwami, M. (2010) 'Neoliberal globalisation, ZANU PF Authoritarian nationalism and the creation of crises in higher education in Zimbabwe', *Journal of Alternative Perspectives in the Social Sciences*, 2 (1), 59–91.

Hwami, M. and Kapoor, D. (2012) 'Neocolonialism and higher education and student union activism in Zimbabwe', *Postcolonial Directions in Education*, 1 (1), 31–66.

Irele, A. (1991) 'The African scholar', *Transition*, 51, 56–69.

Kagwanja, P.M. (2000) 'Post industrialism and knowledge production: African intellectuals in the new international division of labour'. In Okoth G.P. (ed.) *Africa at the beginning of the 21st Century*. Nairobi: University of Nairobi Press, pp. 23–40.

Kapungu R.S. (2007) 'The pursuit of higher education in Zimbabwe: a futile effort?' A paper prepared for the Center for International Private Enterprise (CIPE) 2007 international essay competition on 'Educational reform and employment opportunities'. Available at: http://archive.kubatana.net/docs/chiyou/kapungu_cipe_essay_higher_ education_071002.pdf (accessed 28 May 2015).

Karioki, J. (1974) 'African scholars versus Mazrui', *Transition*, 45, 55–63.

Koontz, M.L. (2014) 'Co-producing knowledge: academics and non-academics partner to build synergistic teams to produce sustainable pathways to advance the emerging field of bamboo farming, manufacturing and processing in Alabama', *International Journal for Innovation Education and Research*, 2 (3), 72–83.

Kraak, A. (2000) *Changing Modes: New Knowledge Production and Its Implications for Higher Education in South Africa.* Cape Town: Human Sciences Research Council (HSRC), South Africa.

Long, N. and Long, A. (1992) *Battlefields of Knowledge: The Interlocking of Theory and Practice in Social Research and Development.* New York: Routledge.

Mazrui, A.A. (2003) 'Towards the re-Africanising African universities: who killed intellectualism in the post colonial era?', *Alternatives – Turkish Journal of International Relations*, 2 (3&4), 135–163.

Mazzocchi, F. (2006) 'Western science and traditional knowledge: despite their variations, different forms of knowledge can learn from each other', *EMBO Reports*, 7 (5), 463–466.

Mkandawire, T. (1995) 'Three generations of African academics: a note', *Transformation*, 28, 75–83.

Muller, M.R. (2013) 'Protecting shared and widely distributed traditional knowledge: issues, challenges and options', ICTSD Programme on Innovation, Technology and Intellectual Property, Geneva: International Centre for Trade and Sustainable Development (ICTSD), Issue paper 39.

Murphree, M.W. (1997) 'Strategic considerations for enhancing scholarship at the University of Zimbabwe', *Zambezia*, XXIV (i), 1–11.

Nesbitt, F.N. (2008) 'Post-colonial anxieties: (re) presenting African intellectuals', *African Affairs*, 107 (427), 273–282.

Nyanchoga, S.A. (2014) 'Politics of knowledge production in Africa: a critical reflection on the idea of an African university in sustainable development', *Developing Countries Studies*, 4 (18), 57–66.

Posey, D.A., Ditfield, G. and Plenderleith, K.A. (1995) 'Collaborative research and intellectual property rights', *Biodiversity and Conversation* , 4 (8), 892–902.

Sawyerr, A. (2004) 'African universities and the challenge of research capacity development', *JHEA/RESA*, 2 (1), 211–240.

Sibisi, S. (2004) 'Indigenous knowledge and science and technology: conflict, contradiction or concurrence?'. In World Bank (ed.) *Local Pathways to Global Development: Indigenous Knowledge.* Washington: World Bank, pp. 34–38.

Sithole, M.P. (2009) *Unequal Peers: The Politics of Discourse Management in the Social Sciences.* Pretoria: Africa Institute of South Africa.

Sithole, M.P. (2011) 'Wrestling with intellectual hegemony: the dwarfed status of knowledge production in SA'. In Kodhlo, K. and Ejiogu, C. (eds) *Governance in the 21st Century.* Cape Town: HSRC Press, pp. 81–89.

Smith, T.L. (1999) *Decolonising Methodologies. Research and Indigenous Peoples.* London: Zed Books.

Teferra, D. (2000) 'Revisiting the doctrine of human capital mobility in the information age', *Brain Drain and Capacity Building in Africa: Regional Conference.* Ethiopia, Addis Ababa, 22–24 February 2000. Ethiopia: Economic Commission for Africa, pp. 22–24.

Tress, B., Tress, G. and Fry, G. (2005) 'Defining concepts and process of knowledge production in integrative research'. In Tress, B., Tress, G., Fry, G. et al. (eds) *From Landscape Research to Landscape Planning: Aspects of Integration Education and Application.* Wageningen: Springer, pp. 13–21.

Turnbull, D. (1997) 'Reframing science and other local knowledge traditions', *Futures*, 29 (6), 551–562.

Turnbull, D. (2009) 'Working with incommensurable knowledge traditions, assemblage, diversity, emergent knowledge narratively and performativity', unpublished paper. Available at: http://thoughtmesh.net/publish/279.php (accessed: 12 December 2014).

Watson, A. and Huntington, O.H. (2008) 'They are here – I can feel them: the epistemic spaces of indigenous and western knowledge', *Social and Cultural Geography*, 9 (3), 257–281.

Wa Thiong'o, N. (1987) *Decolonising the Mind: The Politics of Language in African Literature*. London: Currey.

Wuchty, S., Jones, B.F. and Uzzi, B. (2007) 'The increasing dominance of teams in production of knowledge', *SCIENCE*, 316 (5827), 1036–1039.

10 Creating an African university
Struggling for a transformational curriculum in apartheid South Africa

Rajani Naidoo, Hanne Kirstine Adriansen and Lene Møller Madsen

Introduction

> One cannot expect positive results from an educational or political action
> program that fails to respect the particular view of the world held by the people.
> Such a program constitutes cultural invasion, good intentions notwithstanding.
>
> (Freire, [1970] 2000: 84)

Based on Paulo Freire's thoughts, this chapter will explore 'the particular view'
and how it can be taken into account in capacity building and other action
programmes in higher education. It uses Khanya College, a small South African
alternative tertiary access programme, as case study. Khanya College was
established in 1986 and had Neville Alexander among its founders. There were
two campuses, one in Cape Town, which had an agreement with the University
of Cape Town, and one in Johannesburg, which had an agreement with
University of the Witwatersrand. By participating in the one-year programme,
students classified as 'black' under apartheid legislation gained access to the
second year at these universities that were classified as 'white'. Khanya College
was based on Freirean pedagogy and embodied the idea of education for liberation
and it primarily targeted black youth, many of whom were activists involved in
the anti-apartheid struggle (Pape, 1997). Established during the time of unrest,
Khanya College worked to transform the university – and thereby also to
transform society – by assisting black students' access to universities. In this
chapter, we are primarily interested in the ways Khanya College faculty engaged
with 'the particular view' in this process; with (South) African history and
identity, while at the same time preparing students for the apartheid (white,
racial, Euro-centric) university system.

One of the lecturers involved in designing the programme and teaching up to
1991, Rajani Naidoo, tells the story about Khanya College during the last years
of apartheid. Rajani Naidoo is of Indian heritage (her ancestors came to South
Africa in 1860) and was classified as 'Indian' in the apartheid system. After
primary education in a school designated for Indian students, she attended
Waterford Kamhlaba United World College in Swaziland. Naidoo returned to
South Africa in the 1980s to finish her final year of school during a period of

political upheaval. She was one of the organisers of the academic boycott against apartheid in her school and was suspended for these activities before being reinstated (through legal action) just before the final year examinations. She became an anti-apartheid political activist at university and later became involved in Khanya College. Today, Rajani Naidoo is a professor in higher education management at the University of Bath, UK. She has written extensively on the development and policies of higher education (e.g. Naidoo, 2010, 2011). Rajani Naidoo has previously written about South African university admission policies (Naidoo, 2000, 2004), but this chapter is her first publication about her involvement in Khanya College. The other two authors Hanne Kirstine Adriansen and Lene Møller Madsen are both human geographers with a special interest in higher education. They have written about knowledge production (Madsen and Adriansen, 2006; Adriansen and Madsen, 2009) as well as teaching and pedagogy (Adriansen and Madsen, 2013a, 2014). Their interest in African higher education grew when they were involved in a higher education capacity building project in Tanzania (Adriansen and Madsen, 2013b).

Khanya College opened in 1986 and the Johannesburg campus still exists, although the purpose of the institution has changed after apartheid. As this chapter is based on Rajani Naidoo's narrative, we focus on the Cape Town Campus where she was involved during the period between 1985 and 1991. A few other authors have written about Khanya College. John Pape has applied a Freirian perspective in his analysis of the Johannesburg campus (Pape, 1997); Marie-Francoise Baker's PhD dissertation concerns both campuses in the period between 1981–1994 (Baker, 1995). Rassool and Witz (1990) analysed Khanya College's oral history project; this was put in the context of student participation and the development of the history curriculum in South Africa by Cornell and Witz (1994). Academic support programmes at the University of the Witswatersrand have been evaluated by Agar (1992). The analysis of Khanya College in this chapter departs from the existing literature as it analyses the Cape Town campus from its beginning to the end of apartheid, based on the narrative of one of the faculty members who was involved in designing the programme.

We begin with an outline of different approaches to the particular view. Afterwards, we situate Khanya College in the landscape of higher education within apartheid South Africa. Our analysis of Rajani Naidoo's story about Khanya College is then divided into four sections: finding alternative ways to assess competencies, increasing self-efficacy through teaching an Africanised curriculum, providing academic capital through teaching critical thinking, and transforming university and society. In the discussion and concluding remarks, we relate Khanya College to the wider debate about higher education and the particular view.

The particular view – analytical ideas

In the beginning of this chapter we introduced the often-cited words of Paulo Freire on the particular view. In this section we will briefly discuss Paulo Freire's educational philosophy, which was and still is the philosophy of Khanya College. Furthermore, we will situate Freire's thoughts in the on-going debate within educational research and research of knowledge production on how to address the situatedness of knowledge in educational programmes and research.

The work of the Brazilian educator and philosopher Paulo Freire has had seminal influence within education, most notably in Latin America. His books *Pedagogy of the Oppressed* ([1970] 2000) and *Education for Critical Consciousness* (1973) have been widely studied and used in the Global North where Freire has gained importance as one of the founders of the critical pedagogy movement. In particular, his notion of literacy as not only a means to be able to read, but also as a means of situating a text in its political, economic and social context has been influential. This way of situating a text is termed critical reading and it is outlined in Freire and Macedo (1987). As such, Freire's ideas about literacy correspond to one of the cornerstones of the university – namely the idea of the university as a place of critical thinking. In this chapter, however, we will not go further into detail with Freire's ideas about education for the oppressed. Instead we are interested in a specific part of Freire's work – namely what he has termed the particular view of the world held by the people. As cited in the beginning of this chapter, Freire argues that any educational or political action programme must respect this particular view. In this way, Freire's ideas have implications for capacity building projects in higher education and for development aid in education. But how can we understand the particular view in relation to African universities?

In his description of the particular view in *Pedagogy of the Oppressed*, Freire argues that the starting point for organising an educational programme 'must be the present, existential, and concrete situation, reflecting the aspirations of the people' (Freire, 2000: 95). He advocates the importance of entering into dialogue with the people about their views and ours. In his later work, Freire argues that studying culture can help us to specify and describe the particular view and he describes culture through examples like 'Cultural action and agrarian reforms' and 'Peasants and their reading texts' (Freire, 1985). In these examples culture is seen as the representation of lived experiences, material artefacts and practices within a given society at a particular point in historical time (Giroux, 1985). This suggests that we should:

> [be] taking seriously the cultural capital of the oppressed, developing critical and analytical tools to interrogate it, and staying in touch with dominant definitions of knowledge so we can analyze them for their usefulness and for the ways in which they bear the logic of domination.
>
> (Giroux, 1985: xxii)

While Freire argued that there is no such thing as a neutral education process, his arguments were to some extent based on European theories from Plato to Marx, as well as based on anti-colonialist thinkers. In fact, *Pedagogy of the Oppressed* can be seen as a reply to Frantz Fanon's *The Wretched of the Earth* ([1961] 1968).[1] In this book, Fanon argues that education for local populations should be both modern (instead of traditional) and anti-colonial (not necessarily adopting the views and culture of the coloniser).

In his research on education and development in the Global South, the Norwegian educationalist Anders Breidlid has been inspired by Paulo Freire. However, Breidlid (2013) focuses on epistemologies and argues that the modernist, Western epistemology became hegemonic during and after colonialism and the spread of the capitalist market economy. This epistemology originated in sixteenth-century Europe and is embodied in Cartesian-Newtonian science. It entails a mechanistic world view, universal laws of science and a logical-empirical methodological approach to knowledge production. Moreover, the epistemology is tied to notions of rationality, development and progress inherent in Enlightenment ideals. Through a series of case studies, Breidlid shows how this hegemonic discourse and especially the so-called Western epistemology have shaped the educational architecture across the world. The discourse of Western epistemology colonising the world has already been developed in Chapter 2, here we will focus on different approaches to the particular view.

While Freire and Breidlid are concerned with the particular view of people in relation to educational programmes and especially primary education, the Maori professor and educationalist Linda Tuhiwai Smith from New Zealand writes about knowledge production in academia, which makes her thoughts relevant for the Khanya case. Smith takes a special interest in the ways in which imperialism is embedded in academic research – that is, the way in which academia excludes and to some extent oppresses the particular view of indigenous people. With her book *Decolonizing Methodologies* ([1999] 2012), Smith wants to provoke revolutionary thinking about knowledge and how institutions, hierarchies and production of knowledge are involved in societal transformation. As we will argue later, there is a connection between Smith's ideas and the ideas about using knowledge for societal transformation applied at Khanya College. By decolonising methodologies Smith intends to critically examine research production: 'Whose research is it? Who owns it? Whose interests does it serve? Who will benefit from it? Who has designed its questions and framed its scope? Who will carry it out? Who will write it up? How will its results be disseminated?' (Smith 2012: 10). In her call for critical questioning and systemic change of knowledge production and its institutions, Smith is also inspired by Freire and his notions of praxis, theory, action and reflection as a means of retaining as much control over meaning as possible: 'By "naming the world" people name their realities' (Smith, 2012: 159). Like Breidlid, Smith relies on the concept of 'the West' and its hegemonic role, however, Smith is concerned with research and not primary education: 'This book identifies research as a significant site of struggle between the interests and ways of knowing of the West and the interests and ways of resisting of the Other' (Smith, 2012: 2). Smith does this by situating research in its historical, political and cultural context. She further argues that indigenous writers of fiction have managed to find their own voice and create a new literature, while indigenous scholars are still struggling because language and the citing of texts are based on the traditions of Western academia – thereby reinforcing the validity of this tradition. Smith argues that the existing academic disciplines also frame the approaches available to indigenous scholars, thereby making it difficult to take indigenous perspectives into full account because of the differences in language and epistemology. This does not mean that Smith wants us to reject all knowledge production of so-called Western origin; rather she wants us to pay attention to the fact that research is not neutral and therefore we should pay attention to the practices that determine who counts as legitimate researchers and what counts as legitimate knowledge (production).

In line with this critique of academia and the discussions of the effects that Western epistemologies have on indigenous populations, there has been a call for Africanisation of the curriculum. As explained in Chapter 1, the Africanisation debate has been most pronounced in South Africa where it became part of the academic discourse in the 1990s. Its prominence in South Africa was a result of Africanisation being used as a vehicle for African identity in the period following democratic elections in 1994, where it was linked to frameworks such as the African Renaissance and Ubuntu (Crossman, 2004). In relation to higher education, the Ghanaian born, Canadian professor of social justice education, George Sefa Dei has written about indigenising curriculum (Dei, 2014). He argues that African universities are a colonial satellite of the Western academy and recommends the introduction of indigenous knowledge systems in the university curriculum which requires 'an interrogation of what constitutes Eurocentric understanding of history, modernity, and belonging' (Dei, 2014: 168). In his recommendation of a decolonialisation of education, he is in line with Chen, the author of *Asia as Method* (2010). Moreover, Dei's strong focus on different epistemologies is on par with Smith and Breidlid. Hence, one may argue that Dei's approach to the particular view is special to Africa. For instance, Dei calls for a strong focus on reflexivity through journal writing, creative group inquiry and mentorship. Africanisation of the curriculum can be seen as an African approach to the particular view. However, as Dei mentions, it is difficult to talk about one approach to such a large and multicultural continent as Africa.

Summing up, we can see that there are different approaches to the particular view. While all the authors mentioned here agree on taking the local context into account in regard to education and research, they do not agree on how this should be done. We will use these authors for analysing how Khanya College addressed the particular view. However, in order to understand the strategies employed at Khanya College, it is not enough to focus on the particular view. Another important aspect is 'powerful knowledge'. We use the concept of powerful knowledge that comes from Michael Young (2007, 2008), Johan Muller (2014) and Leesa Wheelahan (2007, 2012). In the discussions of powerful knowledge, Michael Young points to a key tension that, as we will see, Khanya College also faced. According to Young, there is a difference between what he terms 'powerful knowledge' and 'knowledge of the powerful'. Young explains that powerful knowledge gives access to better and more reliable explanations of the world as well as abstract ways of thinking, which then 'provides learners with a language for engaging in political, moral and other kinds of debates' (Young, 2008: 14). When Young refers to knowledge of the powerful he means to express how: 'Knowledge of the powerful is defined by who gets the knowledge in a society and has its roots in Marx's [...] well-known dictum that the ruling ideas at any time are the ideas of the ruling class' (Young, 2008: 14). Beck has noted that there is an important relationship between powerful knowledge and knowledge of the powerful: 'The powerful' promote and ratify selections of knowledge and types of discourses that thereby define what counts as powerful knowledge (Beck, 2013). Young himself asserts that while powerful knowledge and knowledge of the powerful are not the same, there is often significant overlap. In the analysis, we show how access to powerful knowledge plays an important role in the teaching philosophy at Khanya.

Before analysing how Khanya College used a particular view in order to enable black South Africans the possibility to perform within white universities and to negotiate what constituted legitimate and powerful knowledge in the racist university system, we need to situate Khanya College in the higher education landscape of South Africa under apartheid.

The higher education landscape of apartheid South Africa

This section aims to situate the case of Khanya in the contemporary climate of higher education in South Africa. South Africa's national system of racial segregation that began in 1948 had a significant impact on the education system. A complex legal and administrative system of separate and unequal education was put in place for the different racially designated groups (Baker, 1995) and the racist system was perpetuated and reproduced through the education system (Harber, 2001). Black students were forced to attend so-called Bantu Education institutions which were expected to ensure a supply of appropriately trained black workers to contribute to South Africa's post-war industrial economy, while attempting to influence students ideologically. The differences were particularly stark between the Bantu Education system and the educational system set up for those designated white: there were differences in the mechanism of funding between Bantu education and the other race groups, there were large disparities in government funding for each of the race groups, Bantu primary schools employed mother tongue instruction instead of English and the syllabus in Bantu education emphasised practical rather than academic subjects (Christie and Collins, 1986; Hlatshwayo, 2000). The consequences of such a system for black students were large classes, high pupil-teacher ratios, poor facilities, poorly trained teachers and a high dropout rate. All this was to have an effect on university admissions for black students (Baker, 1995).

The origins of the three types of universities, which contemporary commentators categorise as the historically white English-medium universities, the historically white Afrikaans-medium universities and the historically black universities, can be traced to South Africa's colonial history (Sehoole, 2006). The pre-apartheid era beginning in the early 1900s and ending in the late 1950s was characterised by semi-institutionalised discrimination by the settlers of British and Dutch (hereafter referred to as Afrikaners) origin against members of the indigenous African communities of the region, against people of mixed parentage and against the Indian and Malay immigrants imported as cheap labour. The British and Dutch settlers conceived of themselves as belonging to a 'white' race while all the other inhabitants of South Africa were conceived of as belonging to a 'non-white' or 'black' race (Hlatshwayo, 2000).

The four universities that were set up by members of the British community (English medium universities) were the Universities of Cape Town (UCT), Witwatersrand (Wits), Rhodes and Natal. In spite of a liberal philosophy and classifying themselves as 'open', the English-medium universities at this time followed an ambiguous but nevertheless racially discriminatory path as far as the admission of black students was concerned and racial discrimination in student selection was practised in some form or another. The universities set up by the Afrikaner community (Afrikaans-medium universities) were the Universities of Stellenbosch, Pretoria, Orange Free State and Potchefstroom, and they developed within the context of a resurgence of Afrikaner nationalism. Students were admitted largely on the basis of being white and speakers of the Afrikaans language. Black students were seen as not merely as a separate 'nation', but also as a subordinate one, and were thus excluded from these universities on political rather than academic criteria. The South African Native College that opened in 1916 in the Eastern Cape was the first institution of higher education that was set up primarily for black students (black universities). The College began as a private institution that was established as a joint enterprise by missionaries, especially the missionaries of the Church of Scotland. In 1952, the South African Native College was renamed the University College of Fort Hare and it later became the home of a number of high profile political activists (Baker, 1995; Bunting, 2006).

By the 1950s, universities were racially and culturally segregated and were already establishing the principles by which they would relate to each other, to the field of politics and to the intellectual field. The mode of state regulation on university education changed substantially after the coming to power of the Afrikaner Nationalist Party in the elections of 1948. Whereas racial segregation, labour repression and white minority political rule had characterised South African society under British rule, the laws now aimed at racial segregation were systematically elaborated and extended and control was centralised under the state (Price, 1991). After 1948, the new government's domestic policy was directed at enforcing the separation of the racially designated groups in every conceivable sphere, which included interpersonal relationships, residential rights, social and economic organisation and the political organisation of the government. Prime Minister Verwoerd's plan to divide South Africa into 'independent' African states (homelands) and white South Africa was of particular importance to the development of the university sector. This plan was developed in the context of mass black resistance activities organised by the African National Congress (ANC) and the Pan African Congress (PAC), and it functioned partially as a response to the international outcry against apartheid (Bunting, 2006; Christie and Collins, 1986).

Through the Extension of University Education Act (Act 45 of 1959), the university system was statutorily divided into four racial categories: 'White', 'coloured', 'Indian' and 'African'. Using admissions as a pivotal mode of state control, the Extension of University Education Act stipulated that students could only enrol at universities designated specifically for their race groups. The Act thus extended the access of black students to university education, at the same time as prohibiting the entry of black students to white universities. Black and white institutions were subjected to differing degrees of management and control by the state. While they were formally restricted in admitting black students, universities designated as white retained a high degree of autonomy in all of their internal activities. In contrast, the black universities were governed by 'state-control' (Behr, 1978).

Universities under apartheid could be divided into four main categories: historically white universities in the Republic of South Africa which were either Afrikaans-medium or English-medium, historically black universities in the Republic of South Africa and historically black universities in Transkei, Bophuthatswana, Venda, and Ciskei (the so-called TBVC States)[2] (Bunting, 2006). These four different types of universities had quite different intellectual agendas. While the white Afrikaans-medium universities were marked by the perception that they had a duty to preserve the apartheid status quo, the white English-medium universities had the perception that they were international institutions with the same type of knowledge production as universities in, for example, Britain or the USA. Likewise, the Afrikaans-medium universities had a predominantly local South African research focus, involving policy work for the government and government agencies, and technological work undertaken on contract for defence-related industries. Research at the English-medium universities was not limited to such instrumental knowledge, but despite the anti-apartheid stance adopted by the historically white, English-medium universities, these were not major agents for social and political change in South Africa, at least not in the early years. The six historically black universities had a strong training focus and often used material taught in previous years at historically white Afrikaans-medium universities – they had quite instrumentalist notions of knowledge and gave little emphasis on the production of new knowledge. Finally, historically black universities in the TBVC countries mostly enrolled African students, many of whom came from the urban areas of the Republic of South Africa. These universities were primarily regarded as the training grounds for the civil servants and teachers (Bunting, 2006). The University of Fort Hare was an exception as it was one of the most important higher education institutions for black Africans from its foundation by Christian missionaries in 1916 until the takeover by the National Party government in 1959. Despite its Eurocentric type of education, its traditions of non-racism, critical debate and high academic quality attracted students from across sub-Saharan Africa, forming the black African elite that was critical towards oppression. Many independence movements and governments of newly independent African countries have had Fort Hare alumni among their key members. During apartheid, the government exerted strong control over Fort Hare and in spite of widespread opposition the Extension of University Education Act transformed the university-college into an ethnic university for Xhosa speakers while placing the institution directly under the control of the Department of Bantu Education. Nevertheless, Fort Hare was home to constant student protests and it became a stronghold of black consciousness aligned organisations, ANC and similar organisations, which were quickly and brutally suppressed by the regime. After 1990, the apartheid-era administration was expelled and many opted to work at the university of Fort Hare due to its strong tradition of for critical thinking, tolerance and academic quality (Morrow and Gxabalashe, 2000; UFH, n.d.).

Situating Khanya College in the higher education landscape

Khanya College has been labelled one of South Africa's greatest academic success stories (Piurek, 2013). It was founded in 1986 by the South African Committee of Higher Education (hereafter, referred to as SACHED) in order to address the limitations of the apartheid educational system by providing those black students who had shown academic potential (but who were disadvantaged by the apartheid educational system) with a one year programme where they could thrive within a university (Baker, 1995). As previously mentioned, there were two campuses at Khanya – namely Johannesburg and Cape Town – and both operated under SACHED although they had separate administrative and management structures.

Khanya College was conceived and opened at a time in history when resistance to apartheid in South Africa was at its peak and it was born out of the ideas of constructing concrete alternatives to apartheid education in order to transform society (Pape, 1997). Neville Alexander was an important influence on the origin and vision for Khanya College. In 1981, Alexander became Western Cape director of SACHED and he turned it into an important centre for alternative anti-apartheid education. Through SACHED, he established Khanya College, the National Language Project (1985) and the Project for the Study of Alternative Education in South Africa (Praesa) in the 1990s (Dollie et al., 2012). The central idea behind SACHED was 'education for liberation', as it not only questioned the existing hegemonies, but it also looked at the alternative social forms that could be promoted (Magnien, n.d.). Alexander wrote a book entitled *Education and the Struggle for National Liberation in South Africa*, in which he reiterated that the resources put into education would lead to the liberation of South Africa, not the other way round. He said: 'The beginnings of trouble in any modern society usually make themselves felt in the schools before they become evident in other institutions precisely because it is so difficult in a modern state to control this process completely' (Alexander, 1990: 21).

Alexander asserted that it would be useful for education to enable students to know exactly what is true, what is half-true, what is simply false, what has been

202 Naidoo, Adriansen and Madsen

omitted, and why: 'That they, in one word, reflect upon what is been taught to them' (quoted in Magnien, n.d.). Upon his death, the Director of Khanya College said in tribute:

> It was visionary of him to be one of Khanya College's founders in the midst of the apartheid education system. The organisation continues to be committed to justice and education and to work with community organisations. It is a tribute to the work he did.
>
> (Oupa Lehulere, director of Khanya College, quoted in Vally et al., 2012)

From 1986, Indiana University in the USA became involved in Khanya, joining forces with SACHED to provide discussion and accreditation for the preparatory first-year university courses (Piurek, 2013). Khanya brought together a core group of experienced and young staff classified as white, coloured, Indian and African under apartheid laws. In terms of course content, Khanya College wanted to break away from apartheid education's emphasis on apartheid South African history and the sole study of Europe as world history. Instead, the emphasis was primarily South African and broadly African. Faculty from Khanya graded the South African students' major assignments and final exams and moderation were conducted by faculty from Indiana. Students who managed to successfully complete their courses received a transcript from Indiana University that enabled them to gain admission to two of the top universities in South Africa: the University of Cape Town and the University of Witwatersrand in Johannesburg. During 1986–1989, more than 400 students completed the Khanya course of study (Piurek, 2013).

In his Freirean analysis of Khanya College, Pape (2006) sees Khanya College as having two somewhat conflicting goals: first, to assist black students in gaining entrance to one of two historical white universities; and secondly, to provide an alternative to apartheid education at the university level. The latter primarily focused in three areas: course content, teaching methodology and institutional governance. We will return to this later.

From its conception to the present day, Khanya College has been committed to Paulo Freire's ideas about education as a means for liberation for the oppressed. With the end of apartheid, however, the mission of Khanya College changed. In the mid-1990s, Khanya stopped its bridging programme for black university students, Indiana University considered their work finished and South African staff took over all of Khanya's activities (Piurek, 2013). In their own words, the mission of Khanya College today is to:

> provide education which is relevant to the needs of historically oppressed communities, to contribute to the strengthening of community based organisations, trade unions and non-governmental organisations, to contribute to a process of social change and development, and to operate democratically, accountably and efficiently.
>
> (Khanya College, 2014a)

Khanya College – contesting existing knowledge

The empirical material analysed in this section is constructed through a number of qualitative, time-line interviews (Adriansen, 2012) conducted with Naidoo by the other two authors in 2014. Quotes without reference are from the interviews. The three authors (of whom Adriansen and Madsen had no prior involvement in South African higher education) have made the analysis collaboratively. Thus, the analysis presents both an insider and an outsider perspective on the case. Naidoo was part of the core faculty that set up Khanya College's Cape Town campus and she worked there for six years (until 1991) and her story about Khanya College can be seen as a reflective narrative (Webster and Mertova, 2007).

Khanya College was established at a time of unrest in apartheid South Africa and the philosophy of Khanya was to act as a model for the transformation of higher education in South Africa. In those days, what they wanted to do at Khanya was quite radical. Naidoo explains that setting up Khanya College was a challenge for the involved staff and students in a number of different ways. First, because it was illegal to establish an independent or private university institution, Khanya College was founded as a campus linked to the American Indiana University, which provided the legal grounds as well as accreditation for the courses. Secondly, it was a challenge because of the daily struggle in creating and acting in a learning environment that was located within a draconian police state. The security police raided the campus and arrested students with no need for a warrant or a trial. There were also various interventions by political groups in society. Moreover, Khanya College worked to challenge the existing university system in apartheid South Africa and thereby also to transform society. Hence, the following analysis is divided into four sections; the first three are based on the means for assisting black students' access to universities and the latter relates to societal transformation:

- finding alternative ways of assessing the students' competencies
- increasing the students' self-efficacy through teaching an African curriculum
- providing the students with academic capital through teaching them critical thinking and debating skills
- transforming universities and society.

These four issues are outlined and then analysed with reference to how the particular view was addressed at Khanya, but we also draw on other concepts and debates within higher education in this analysis, e.g. powerful knowledge and the cultural production of the educated person and engaged pedagogies.

Finding alternative ways of assessing competencies

Khanya College had an annual acceptance of approximately 90 students, the majority of whom would not have been admitted to the existing universities.

They were political activists who had been compelled to attend inferior, poorly resourced and racially segregated schools. Naidoo explains that in order to address this, Khanya College used alternative criteria for assessing students. This assessment was based on personal interviews that focused on students' potential and engagement with writing and thinking. This was unlike traditional university assessment criteria in South Africa at the time, which was based on school grades.

At the time, the apartheid government was threatened by the possibility of a social upheaval and began to reform some elements of the apartheid system, including the segregation of universities. From 1986, universities in South Africa were legally desegregated and for the first time since the Nationalist government came to power in 1948, universities were allowed to recruit students of different 'racial' groups. The white, English-medium universities argued that they would like to admit more black students but it was not possible because the majority of black students did not have the academic qualifications needed and admitting them would lower academic standards. Hence, the official view of English-medium universities was that they really wanted to change but they did not want the university to be compromised by lowering its standards. At the same time South African universities were also feeling the effect of the international academic boycott and there were major pressures to transform higher education. One of the initiatives that was introduced was academic support programmes which were sub-degree bridging programmes and they functioned by preparing (black) students for mainstream university courses. Hence, in the view of the white universities, black students who were the majority population should change to fit the university system rather than the other way around. At Khanya College, however, the philosophy was that in an unequal and segregated society where black students were disadvantaged and in the majority, it was the university system rather than the students that should change. Based on this philosophy, Khanya College did not perceive it as a compromise to admit students without the appropriate grades; on the contrary, it was seen as a necessity in an unequal and racist country, which had entry criteria that only allowed access to advantaged white students and provided these students with the quality of education needed for university admission.

Further, in order for universities to change society, they needed to include a broad range of students who were representative of society. At Khanya, this was done by establishing a campus with transcripts accredited by the University of Indiana and having the students subsequently admitted to the University of Cape Town. The agreement between the University of Cape Town and Khanya College in Cape Town was one where Khanya took in students that had potential, worked with them for one year and, if the students passed the Khanya courses, students would gain guaranteed admission to the University of Cape Town. This agreement was possible because of the pressures of the international academic boycott alluded to earlier, but it was also made possible by a number of powerful and influential academics and administrators within the University of Cape Town who worked with Khanya to transform the University of Cape Town.

Admitting black students from Khanya College would thus contribute to challenging the ways in which the higher education system in South Africa reproduced race and class inequalities.

Using Levinson and Holland's (1996) notion of the cultural production of the educated person as a means of inspiration, the admission procedures at Khanya College can be seen as a means to challenge the existing notions of 'an educated person' and a way to question who had the legitimate right of access to higher education. By enrolling political activists and acknowledging their competencies as valid for entering higher education, Khanya College extended the existing view of the educated person from someone who had received schooling to a potential intellectual activist with 'real life' experiences. This was done by showing how experiences gained from political activism, including writing political pamphlets, public speaking and organising political and community groups, could be translated into academic skills, e.g. writing a pamphlet provided the student with skills for writing scholarly papers. Khanya College therefore also challenged social reproduction, which, according to Levinson and Holland (1996), often takes place in education systems. This debate about admitting black students resembles the discussions following the change in higher education from elite to mass systems in the Global North. As Sue Clegg recently pointed out, the argument about massification inevitably leading to an overall lowering of academic standards is often a code for defending the elite parts of the system (Clegg, 2014). Following this line of thought, Khanya College could be seen as challenging existing notions about quality, notions which equated quality with those areas of higher education dominated by the white elite.

Increasing self-efficacy through teaching an African curriculum

The students at Khanya College were offered six courses (mathematics, physics, sociology, economics, African history and African literature) and seminars in practical philosophy. The students needed to take two of the six courses and the majority of the students also attended the practical philosophy course.

The teaching philosophy at Khanya was twofold: first, to give the students confidence and empower them by strengthening their identity of where they came from based in part on their African history, language, traditions as well as factors based on social class; secondly, to give students access to powerful knowledge, to teach the students to act and adapt within a 'white', elite, English educational system and to teach them to recognise the implicit rules and how to challenge the rules. Hence, the students were introduced to the hegemonic discourses and practices within elite universities. They were taught to understand these as hegemonic but were supported in finding the tools to challenge these and develop alternative ways of seeing the world, including ways which not only took their own experiences into account, but also ways which critiqued their own knowledge and experiences.

To address the first part the teachers devised a curriculum that was quite different from the one taught at the University of Cape Town and other South

African universities at the time – for example, the students studied oral African literature and African history. However, the students were also reading 'Western' literature such as Lenin and Freire as well as more academic texts from within their political organisations and in Khanya College and they were putting what they read into practice. Students were also creating pamphlets to raise popular awareness about apartheid and were developing strategies towards alternative higher education systems.

Another aspect of creating an academic identity was to address the identity of inferiority that the system of apartheid tried to impose on students. At Khanya they addressed this by acknowledging and respecting the identity and struggles of students, their parents and communities. The lecturers therefore needed to address how different racial groups were represented in hierarchy and the implicit and explicit ways in which this was transmitted and reproduced in society. Hence, the task was to provide an environment in which students acknowledged and were proud of their own identity and an environment that would support them in understanding how to navigate their way through a dominant culture. Teaching methods were recognised as important in this aspect. The teachers facilitated classes so that students interacted cognitively and critically with the material, they created space for emotions to come into the classroom and acknowledged the students' contributions in whatever form or content while creating space for constructive criticism and dissent. In practice, this meant facilitated group and individual work, the practical application of ideas and highly reflective and reflexive teachers.

An example of enhancing self-efficacy through teaching an African curriculum was the African literature course. This course, developed by faculty at Khanya and University of Cape Town who wished to challenge the Anglo-Saxon nature of the literature course at their home university, linked historical materialist criticism with more formal literary analyses. Khanya wanted the student to understand how literature was produced in a social, political and economic context as well as to understand the different genres and internal structure of literature. As Naidoo explains, there were arguments on how to choose novels, whether the novels should always be political and/or useful to society or if these could also be chosen on the basis of their literary and aesthetic qualities. They agreed to have a canon of novels that were chosen not only because they allowed for a historical materialist reading, but also because of important literary genres. Most important was how to analyse a novel in a critical manner. Quite a broad range of texts from all over Africa were included in the course and students were also introduced to some standard English literature so that students could learn about these texts before they entered the University of Cape Town, where they would be expected to have such knowledge. Additionally, the students brought oral literature, literature from their community and organisations, and their own poetry into the classroom. At first this was not something the lecturers had planned on, but they decided to incorporate what the students brought in. In other words, the students were actively engaged in building the curriculum.

A number of researchers have addressed the issue of positioning disadvantaged people in the Global South and indigenous people as inferior, e.g. Smith (2012) and Chen (2010). As described in the beginning of this chapter, Smith has argued that reading can in fact be dangerous for indigenous people because they are represented in an inferior way. She further notes that: '[O]n the international scene it is extremely rare and unusual when indigenous accounts are accepted and acknowledged as valid interpretations of what have taken place' (Smith, 2012: 36). Hence, Khanya College's approach, where students engaged critically with dominant and alternative texts while being encouraged to take part in their own identity constructions, was quite unique – especially at that time in South African history.

Khanya College's approach can also be understood as not merely providing formal access but also providing epistemic access. The South African philosopher of education, Wally Morrow, explains that formal access is not enough, access to knowledge the so-called 'epistemic access' is also required (Morrow, 2009). Students, who were disadvantaged by the apartheid system, needed epistemic access. This was provided at Khanya College in different ways: the first was to acknowledge African history, literature and oral culture as important; the second was to provide access to dominant knowledge. This occurred in the period before Wally Morrow's work on knowledge was published and it was thus not discussed in this way. However, faculty at Khanya were primarily left-leaning, anti-apartheid activists who were themselves educated at elite universities in South Africa, and for many of these faculty members the combination of incorporating locally grounded knowledge with powerful, elite knowledge was perceived as essential, as we will argue below.

Providing academic capital through teaching critical thinking and debating skills

The second part of the teaching philosophy was to empower the students to succeed in elite white English institutions. This was done by facilitating students' understandings of the institutional culture that they were entering as well as by facilitating an understanding of both the explicit and implicit rules of this elite institution and how to challenge such rules. The questions that were raised included: what does it mean to be challenging? And what are the difference between being challenging and being aggressive? How far can you go without getting into trouble? The goal was to get the students to go as far as they wanted, but with full knowledge of the rules and the consequences. They also needed to adapt to the institutional culture and part of this was to be aware of powerful knowledge.

Naidoo refers to the philosophy of Khanya as encompassing the idea of 'knowledge for liberation'. She explains that at Khanya this was perceived as 'knowledge that empowers people with a sense of their own multi-faceted identity, the ability to understand the relationship between knowledge and power and the tools to critique and transform society'. For example, Khanya

College knew that teaching African literature as a core part of the curriculum would mean that the powerful English department at the University of Cape Town would not recognise the student's qualifications. Hence, the students would be restricted to continuing their studies on a specialised African literature course and prevented from entry to the high status English literature course. However, the faculty at Khanya felt that African literature was an important aspect of building an African identity and it contributed to transformation in the higher education sector and in society. At the same time, students were introduced to some aspects of the dominant English literary canon because it was felt that students needed insights into this canon when they went to the University of Cape Town. Khanya staff were also involved in petitioning the English Literature Department with support from some members of the University of Cape Town faculty to accept students who showed a high level of achievement in the Khanya College African literature course.

As mentioned in the previous quote from Neville Alexander, the knowledge that dominated in South African universities was also challenged by critical thinking. Therefore, students' own critical insights developed in the context of their political work were linked to more formal modes of critical analysis. For example, in the African literature course, students were taught formal text analysis, the social, economic and political conditions of production of the text and its real world implications, including insights for their own organisation and community group. Khanya also developed a series of workshops on practical philosophy. This was not marked or assessed but was conducted in reading and discussion groups. The course was part of Khanya's goal of wanting to give the students wider access to various forms of critical thinking.

Khanya's knowledge for liberation concept has many synergies with the concept of powerful knowledge mentioned previously (Muller 2014; Wheelahan 2007, 2012; Young 2007, 2008; Young and Muller, 2013). In their discussions of powerful knowledge, Michael Young points to a key tension that Khanya also faced, as we have seen in the discussion above. The knowledge for liberation strategy of Khanya College can be understood as an attempt to facilitate students' access to powerful knowledge held by dominant groups in society, while at the same time equipping students with the dispositions to develop strong alternative identities and the critical skills to challenge the 'knowledge of the powerful' from which they were gaining access. Khanya believed that these negotiations around the constitution of powerful knowledge and the challenge of the knowledge of the powerful were essential for societal change. In this respect, the approach applied at Khanya College was different from the Africanisation of curriculum approaches mentioned above (e.g. Dei, 2014), which do not include the powerful knowledge dimension.

Transforming universities and society

The philosophy of the college was to act as a model for the transformation of all universities in South Africa. In the days of apartheid South Africa, the entry criteria, pedagogy, curriculum and assessment implemented by Khanya College were truly alternative. The only other university taking such a radical stance in admissions policy during this period was the University of Western Cape. Disadvantaged students classified as black by apartheid legislation and who would never have been able to enter the high status universities (which in turn gave access to advantaged positions in society) were recruited and selected by Khanya on alternative selection criteria. While academic faculty at the college read Paulo Freire and other transformative educationalists and applied some of these principles, the pedagogy also evolved through a close relationship between the academic faculty and the students, where staff began to understand the students' aspirations, insecurities, identities and the knowledge that they possessed as well as the knowledge that they lacked. This insight and understanding was incorporated into the pedagogy. The pedagogy was in this sense a living pedagogy that evolved with a greater understanding of the students and the many ways in which they learned and learned how to succeed. Formal lecturers were interspersed with group discussion and critique and application of the concepts learned. The assessment was highly formative and students were given the chance to learn and progress by weighing the proportion of grades given in the second half of the year more than those given in the first half of the year. The selection criteria, the curriculum and assessment were all premised on the understanding that an alternative system of higher education was required in South Africa. There was criticism of the fact that the elite universities were located in a country where the vast majority of the population was classified as 'black' and yet the vast majority of the students at these universities were classified as 'white'. The response of the elite universities was to develop academic support programmes, which enabled a small number of mainly black students to enter the university at sub-degree level. The faculty at Khanya College, like that at the University of the Western Cape, believed that rather than the majority of students being forced to adapt to the university, the university should recognise its location and adapt in order to offer the majority of South Africans a high quality and empowering education. Moreover, students were expected to act as change agents in the universities that they entered after their time at Khanya College. Naidoo recalls that when talking to the students afterwards they would describe their experience in the University of Cape Town lecture hall as follows: 'Nobody in the big lecture room would ask questions and suddenly the Khanya students were asking questions and then other students would start asking questions.' Khanya students, particularly in the Humanities and Social Science subjects, had the confidence to raise their voices in white, elite universities where they were in the minority.

While the faculty actively discussed the Freirean pedagogies, they were also influenced by different forms of neo-Marxism and other critical theories and believed education to be a political act that could not be divorced from pedagogy. The principle of education for liberation also meant that in transforming universities, Khanya would contribute to the transformation of society. The majority of staff and students were members of political organisations and a link was drawn between Khanya's aim to transform the higher education sector and the transition to a democratic and equal society. Students were required to undertake community support activities, which culminated in a group community project that would be assessed. There were also political discussions and debates on how to challenge apartheid and whether socialism, social democracy or nationalism would lead to a more equitable society.

In their pedagogies, Khanya College can be seen as developing what Brooks and Waters (2011) refer to as 'engaged pedagogy'. This pedagogy is developed in reference to the dilemmas of teaching about global inequalities in an international classroom. For example, Brooks and Waters note: 'Academics are struggling with the contradictions of lecturing about neo-imperialism and global inequalities whilst at the same time being themselves directly involved in the recruitment of international students' (Brooks and Waters, 2011: 125). To address these dilemmas, Brooks and Waters call for an engaged pedagogy that includes actively attempting to contest 'the centre', engaging in genuine dialogue with students, and practising care and responsibility beyond the classroom. Even though Brooks and Waters write with a different student group in mind, their arguments can be translated into Khanya's case within apartheid South Africa. Despite being developed at a later point in time and in a different context, Khanya College did employ 'engaged pedagogy' as they were active in contesting the hegemonic discourses within society in general and within academia in particular. Also, the whole way that Khanya College was organised and the form that teaching took was based on a very close dialogue with the students. Finally, practising care and responsibility beyond the classroom was very important to the faculty, as we described earlier. The pedagogical approaches employed at Khanya can also be seen as similar to Dei's (2014) call for reflexivity as part of the Africanisation of curriculum approach. However, we do not see these approaches as particularly African, rather we understand them as critical pedagogies also seen in many universities in the Global North and similar to Freire's critical approach.

Discussion and concluding remarks

This chapter began with Freire's call for addressing the particular view of the world held by the people in any educational or political action programme. We wanted to see if and how a particular view can be explored in African higher education. In different ways, other authors have addressed the particular view by focusing on Africanisation as a means to counter the role of Western hegemonic knowledge production (Dei, 2014), the need to situate research in its historical, political and cultural context (Smith, 2012) and the significance of different epistemologies for primary education (Breidlid, 2013).

Based on these ideas, we have used Khanya College as a case for analysing how the particular view can be addressed. The analysis shows that the particular view not only concerns the content of the educational programme but also concerns access to the programme. At Khanya College, the particular view in regard to admission requirements meant that Khanya acknowledged skills other than grades – namely skills derived through e.g. political organisation and activism and life experiences in general, which were seen and equally valuable for signalling academic potential. Regarding the particular view in relation to the content of the curriculum at Khanya College, this had two dimensions: first, to include African history and African literature in the respective courses and to use texts, oral histories from the student's communities, and their own poetry. Secondly, it was to give the students confidence and empower them by strengthening their identity of where they came from based on both their African history and their social class. As Pape has argued: '[T]hus, while universities were still defining knowledge in abstract academic terms, Khanya courses were attempting to reconstruct that knowledge to include the experience of the oppressed majority' (Pape, 1997: 303). Some of the recent literature on education and development in the Global South focuses on the hegemonic role of Western epistemology (e.g. Breidlid, 2013; Dei 2014; Smith 2012). Within this literature, 'the particular view' is seen as indigenous knowledge and it is recommended to indigenise the curriculum based on non-Western epistemologies. Educational development consequently becomes a struggle between epistemologies. At Khanya College they did not discuss the curriculum in terms of competing epistemologies and did not argue in terms of Africanisation. They had a central focus on oral African literature and oral history but in other areas they were much more global and mostly constructivists, in that they incorporated what the students brought with them. Naidoo explains that she is not sure whether they had a coherent alternative epistemology: 'I think we had pockets of it [Freirean and other critical pedagogies] that then linked up to dominant views of seeing the world and I think we merged the two.' In reflection, this merging was linked to powerful knowledge: Khanya college worked by focusing on the local context without disconnecting from the 'Western' context. The academic faculty had a modernist world-view in the sense that they believed that there was a better world that they wanted to fight for, which included ending apartheid. They constructed the curriculum in dialogue with the students and showed them how different things were valued differently across different cultures. They tried to 'walk in two places', connecting local, African knowledge with Western knowledge to provide the students with the capacity they needed to transform society. Khanya College wanted to challenge apartheid by empowering their students through pride in their African culture and by providing them with access to powerful knowledge.

Even though the particular view employed at Khanya College can be seen as part of an Africanisation of curriculum approach, we are not convinced that this is the right label. The discourse employed at Khanya was not one of Africanisation and there was critical debate about the different epistemologies. Instead following Wally Morrow and Sue Clegg, we find the notion of epistemic access a more appropriate way of describing how Khanya College integrated a particular view. As already shown, Khanya College provided epistemic access both through their admission criteria and through their curriculum. Moreover, it is important to notice that Khanya College employed a dual strategy that combined epistemic access with access to powerful knowledge. Without the access to powerful knowledge, the students would not be able to enter into debate and participate on par with the designated white students in university and in society in general.

We wish to conclude by discussing what may be learned from the Khanya case. While Khanya College and South Africa may seem like a special case because apartheid in South Africa rendered the divisions based on race and disadvantage so visible, we would suggest that apartheid South Africa was an extreme case of the social fault lines that divide many societies today, both in the Global North and in the Global South. Hence, the insights from South Africa and Khanya may also be useful in other contexts where elite universities contribute to the reproduction of inequality in society, rather than the transformation of such inequality. Thus the Khanya case is also useful beyond the African continent as it offers insights into issues related to massification of higher education systems, widening participation and the subsequent increased diversity of students (Clegg, 2014).

Concerning the future of Khanya College, its winter school in Johannesburg 2014 is called *Liberation: Struggle and Quest for Knowledge* (Khanya College, 2014b). The theme is 'Reading the word and the world: the role of study groups in working class education' and it is described as a return to the roots of Khanya by focusing on education for liberation and on educating young activists to exercise their social agency. Based on a Marxist discourse, it critiques capitalism in general and the neo-liberal education system in particular, and Khanya wants to enhance the theoretical, analytical and conceptual capacity of the youth. Hence, while there has been a change from focusing on inequalities in terms of race and colour to focusing on class, Khanya's work in empowering youth is still continuing.

Notes

1 Frantz Fanon was an Afro-French psychiatrist, philosopher, and revolutionary who inspired anti-colonial and resistance movements all over the world including in South Africa.
2 The so-called TBVC States were Bantustans or black homelands, i.e. territories set aside for black inhabitants of South Africa as part of the policy of apartheid. The four mentioned South African Bantustans – Transkei, Bophuthatswana, Venda and Ciskei – were declared independent, although this was not officially recognised outside of South Africa.

References

Adriansen, H.K. (2012) 'Timeline interviews: a tool for conducting life history research', *Qualitative Studies*, 3 (1), 40–55.
Adriansen, H.K. and Madsen, L.M. (2009) 'Implications of doing insider interviews: studying geography and geographers', *Norwegian Journal of Geography*, 93 (3), 145–153.
Adriansen, H.K. and Madsen, L.M. (2013a) 'Facilitation: a novel way to improve students' well-being', *Innovative Higher Education*, 38 (4), 295–308.

Adriansen, H.K. and Madsen, L.M. (2013b) 'Quality assurance or neo-imperialism: developing universities in the third world'. Paper presented at SRHE Annual Research Conference: *Experiencing Higher Education: Global Trends and Transformations*, 2013.

Adriansen, H.K. and Madsen, L.M. (2014) 'Using student interviews for becoming a reflective geographer', *Journal of Geography in Higher Education*, 38 (4), 595–605.

Agar, D. (1992) 'Evaluating academic support programmes: what have we learned in the last six years?' *South African Journal of Education*, 12 (2), 93–100.

Alexander, N. (1990) *Education and the Struggle for National Liberation in South Africa*. Braamfontein: Skotaville Publishers.

Baker, M. (1995) *Khanya College: A Historical Case Study: 1981–1994*. PhD dissertation, The Pennsylvania State University, 431.

Beck, J. (2013) 'Powerful knowledge, esoteric knowledge, curriculum knowledge', *Cambridge Journal of Education*, 43 (2), 177–193

Behr, A.L. (1978) *New Perspectives in South African Education*. Durban: Durban Butterworths.

Breidlid, A. (2013) *Education, Indigenous Knowledges, and Development in the Global South: Contesting Knowledges for a Sustainable Future*. New York: Routledge.

Brooks, R. and Waters, J. (2011) *Student Mobilities, Migration and the Internationalization of Higher Education*. Hampshire: Palgrave Macmillan.

Bunting, I. (2006) 'The higher education landscape under apartheid'. In Cloete, N. et al. (eds) *Transformation in Higher Education*, Dordrecht: Springer, pp. 35–52.

Chen, K.H. (2010) *Asia as Method: Toward Deimperialization*. Durham: Duke University Press.

Christie, P. and Collins, C. (1986) 'Bantu education: apartheid ideology and labour reproduction'. In Kallaway, P. (ed.) *Apartheid and Education: The Education of Black South Africans*. Cape Town: Ravan Press, pp. 160–183.

Clegg, S. (2014) 'System diversity, inequality, curriculum and (possibly) hope'. Keynote speech at Society for Research into Higher Education Annual Conference 2014. Available at: www.srhe.ac.uk/conference2014/downloads/SRHE_Conf_2014_System_diversity_and_inequality.pdf (accessed 18 December 2014).

Cornell, C. and Witz, L. (1994) '"It is my right to participate in the subject": contesting histories in the first year lecture room', *Social Dynamics*, 20 (1), 49–74.

Crossman, P. (2004) 'Perceptions of "Africanisation" or "endogenisation" at African universities: issues and recommendations'. In Zeleza, P.T. and Olukoshi, A. (eds) *African Universities in the Twenty-first Century*, Vol. 2, South Africa: CODESRIA, pp. 319–340.

Dei, G.J.S. (2014) 'Indigenizing the school curriculum'. In Emeagwali, G. and Dei, G.J.S. (eds) *African Indigenous Knowledge and the Disciplines*. Rotterdam: Sense Publishers, pp. 165–180.

Dollie, N., Mahate, H., Marsh, J., Motala, E., Pease, J., Samuels J., Solomon, M., Vally, S. and C. Soudien (2012) 'Tribute to Neville Alexander'. Available at: www.sahistory.org.za/archive/tribute-neville-alexander (accessed 18 December 2014).

Fanon, F. ([1961] 1968) *The Wretched of the Earth*. New York: Grove Press.

Freire, P. ([1970] 2000) *Pedagogy of the Oppressed*. 30th anniversary edition. New York: Continuum.

Freire, P. (1973) *Education for Critical Consciousness*. New York: Seabury. Freire, P. (1985) *The Politics of Education, Culture, Power and Liberation*. USA: Macmillian.

Freire, P. and Macedo, D. (1987) *Literacy, Reading the Word & the World*. London: Routledge and Kegan Paul.

Giroux, H.A. (1985) 'Introduction'. In Freire, P. *The Politics of Education, Culture, Power and Liberation.* USA: Macmillian, pp. xi–xxv.

Harber, C. (2001) *State of Transition: Post-Apartheid Educational Reform in South Africa.* Monographs in International Education. Oxford: Symposium Books.

Hlatshwayo, S.A. (2000) *Education and Independence: Education in South Africa, 1658–1988.* Westport: Greenwood Press.

Khanya College (2014a) 'About Khanya College'. Available at: http://khanyacollege.org. za/programme/education-liberation (accessed 25 September 2014).

Khanya College (2014b) 'Khanya annual winter school'. Available at: http://khanya college.org.za/programme/khanya-annual-winter-school (accessed 25 September 2014).

Levinson, B.A. and Holland, D. (1996) 'The cultural production of the educated person: an introduction'. In Levinson, B.A. Foley, D.E. and Holland, D.C. (eds) *The Cultural Production of the Educated Person: Critical Ethnographies of Schooling and Local Practice.* Albany: SUNY Press, pp. 1–54.

Madsen, L.M. and Adriansen, H.K. (2006) 'Knowledge constructions in research communities: the example of agri-rural researchers in Denmark', *Journal of Rural Studies,* 22 (4), 456–468.

Magnien, N. (n.d.). *Dr Neville Edward Alexander.* Part of project South African History Online: Towards a people's history. Available at: www.sahistory.org.za/people/ dr-neville-edward-alexander (accessed 18 December 2014).

Morrow, W. (2009) *Bounds of Democracy: Epistemological Access in Higher Education.* Pretoria: HSRC Press.

Morrow, S. and Gxabalashe, K. (2000) 'The records of the University of Fort Hare', *History in Africa,* 27, 481–497.

Muller, J. (2014) 'Every picture tells a story: epistemological access and knowledge', *Education as Change,* 18 (2), 255–269.

Naidoo, R. (2000) *Admission Policies and the Politics of Access: A Case Study of Two South African Universities* (1985–1990). Unpublished PhD dissertation, University of Cambridge.

Naidoo, R. (2004) 'Fields and institutional strategy: Bourdieu on the relationship between higher education, inequality and society', *British Journal of Sociology of Education,* 25 (4), 457–471.

Naidoo. R. (2010) 'Global learning in a neo-liberal age'. In Unterhalter, E. and Carpentier, V. (eds) *Whose Interests Are We Serving? Global Inequalities and Higher Education.* Hampshire: Palgrave/Macmillan, pp. 66–90.

Naidoo, R. (2011) 'The new imperialism in higher education: implications for development'. In King, R. et al. (eds) *A Handbook on Globalization and Higher Education.* Cheltenham: Edward Elgar, pp. 40–58.

Pape, J. (1997) 'Khanya College Johannesburg: ten years of 'education for liberation': an assessment', *International Journal of Lifelong Education,* 16 (4), 290–307.

Piurek, R. (2013) *IU's South African Connections Run Deep.* Indiana University homepage. Available at: http://global.iu.edu/blog/africa/2013/08/28/ius-south-african-connections-run-deep/ (accessed 09 May 2015).

Price, R.M. (1991) *The Apartheid State in Crisis: Political Transformation in South Africa 1975–1990.* Oxford: Oxford University Press.

Rassool, C. and Witz, L. (1990) 'Creators and shapers of the past: some reflections on the experiences of the Khanya College Oral History Projects', *Perspectives in Education,* 12 (1), 96–101.

Sehoole, C. (2006) 'Internationalisation of higher education in South Africa: a historical review', *Perspectives in Education*, 24 (4), 1–13.

Smith, L.T. ([1999] 2012) *Decolonizing Methodologies: Research and Indigenous Peoples*. Croydon: Zed books.

UFH (n.d.) 'University of Fort Hare, history'. Available at: http://www.ufh.ac.za/history (accessed 23 April 2015).

Vally, S., Ramadiro, B. and Duncan, J. (2012). 'Neville Alexander: revolutionary who changed many lives'. *Mail & Guardian*, 30 August, 2012.

Webster, L. and Mertova, P. (2007) *Using Narrative Inquiry as a Research Method, an Introduction to using Critical Event Narrative Analysis in Research on Learning and Teaching*. London: Routledge.

Wheelahan, L. (2007) 'How competency-based training locks the working class out of powerful knowledge: a modified Bernsteinian analysis', *British Journal of Sociology of Education*, 28 (5), 637–651.

Wheelahan, L. (2012) *Why Knowledge Matters in Curriculum*. Abingdon: Routledge.

Young, M. (2007) *Bringing Knowledge Back in from Social Constructivism to Social Realism in the Sociology of Education*. Abingdon: Routledge.

Young, M. (2008) 'From constructivism to realism in the sociology of the curriculum', *Review of Research in Education*, 32 (1), 1–28.

Young, M. and Muller, J. (2013) 'On the powers of powerful knowledge', *Review of Education* 1 (3): 229–250.

11 African universities and rights in African polities and communities

Africanising universal knowledge?

Fergus Kerrigan

Introduction

The field of human rights poses particular challenges to academic cooperation between African and Northern researchers and institutions. Scholars and activists have long debated whether human rights are a vehicle for the Global North to present its values as universal, and human rights are often criticised for their Eurocentric origins, frameworks and power structures (Ghai, 2007). The purpose of this chapter is to analyse how African universities can equip law graduates to provide African societies with legal tools suited to their needs and contexts, and to discuss how they can navigate the demands of international human rights standards on their own terms.

Rather than building on a single case study, this chapter attempts a 'tour d'horizon' drawing on my experience of cooperating with individuals and organisations to analyse and improve access to justice in African countries. My perspective is primarily informed by encounters with African legal professionals, and (mostly) indirectly with legal education in Africa. I refer particularly to Zambia, where I worked with a national team to produce a comprehensive study of access to justice on behalf of the Ministry for Justice. Following this, I co-developed programmes to improve cooperation among statutory and customary justice actors. Prior to working in Zambia, I worked with post-genocide justice in Rwanda, focusing on legal aid and support to the faculty of law at Rwanda's National University.

Initially focusing on legal professionals, my work gradually widened to include traditional leaders and village based paralegals. This move was motivated by a growing sense of the inadequacy of some standardised conceptual frameworks and the methodological baggage usually available. I am by no means alone in this 'turn towards the local' (see e.g. Mac Ginty and Richmond, 2013). In recent years, development partners and the UN have signalled openness to so-called 'informal' justice mechanisms as part of the 'rule of law' (UN, 2012). Because of its strong outset in state obligations and the often centralised state justice systems, the human rights system faces challenges in addressing informal justice mechanisms. These challenges inform the chapter.

International human rights treaties set out human rights standards and goals, but leave flexibility as to the means to achieve them. The choice of Northern-type legal and institutional frameworks is neither demanded nor necessarily optimal in human rights terms. For example, Article 2(3) (b) of the UN Covenant on Civil and Political Rights requires states to provide remedies to those whose human rights are violated. While judicial remedies seem to be preferred, the Article mentions remedies by 'any other competent authority provided for by the legal system of the State'. This leaves room for a plurality of institutional structures and approaches. Nevertheless, recourse to formal state structures is often the 'default' way of thinking for bilateral and multilateral justice assistance programmes.

While African law schools, like their counterparts elsewhere in the world, must do their best to equip graduates and societies to function and thrive in today's globalised world, this chapter discusses how they can be enabled to do so on their own terms. African academic and legal communities, despite their many constraints, do contribute their own distinctive concepts of human rights, legal doctrines and methods. This chapter will attempt to provide at least partial answers to questions of how African philosophies, identities, concepts and solutions to social and legal challenges can be expressed in African legal education.

The challenge of universality in human rights facts and values

It is trite but tempting to begin with universities and the idea of the universal. In Europe, the university is indebted to the idea of 'the whole' (*universitas* – see Chapter 2 of this book for a more detailed exploration). This assumes the possibility of knowledge that is independent of the individual knower and capable of being communicated and discussed by a critical community of scholars. While universality is conventionally discussed in relation to both facts and values, distinguishing the two is a complex challenge (Putnam, 2004). The discipline of law is by its nature an attempt to assert values in the world of facts.

For a chapter addressing legal knowledge, it is of interest to recall the importance of law studies in the origins of the oldest of modern universities. Law featured prominently among the subjects studied at the Al Azhar 'madrasa' in Cairo, where this knowledge was increasingly necessary with the expansion of the Fatimid Caliphate (Halm, 1997). In Europe, the University of Bologna was founded upon the study of tracts of Roman law (the *corpus juris civilis*, meaning 'body of civil law'). The study of these legal doctrines assisted what the EU might today call a project of harmonisation while paradoxically also providing a basis for separatist claims. Students who flocked to Bologna from across Europe employed the common language of Latin, but used the *corpus* to buttress claims of autonomy by the developing European city states against the centralising power of Pope and Emperor. Also studied in Bologna was the *ius gentium*, or law of peoples, which was considered to be based on natural reason and thus common to all peoples (Coquillette, 1988). Universality and particularity were two sides of the same coin. A common language and framework of legal principles paradoxically served as an instrument for the assertion and legitimation of distinct and particular identities (see generally, Berman, 1983).

In a much cited article, the Kenyan legal scholar Makau Mutua (Mutua, 2001) criticised Northern human rights activists for their simple characterisations of and their reflexive impulse to intervene in countries of the South, confident of their ability to stop bullies and protect victims in distant parts of the world. Is this simply a problem of well-meaning and mostly good engagement that occasionally slips into arrogance, clumsiness and quixotic interference? Or does the problem go deeper, requiring an examination of the conditions under which African rights holders and societies can exercise agency?

Quite aside from the question of the universality of human rights values, it is necessary to examine the institutions that are assumed to uphold them, asking whether these are also universal. Leading scholars of politics and development in Africa doubt the universality of many notions common in discourses on law, political science and international development. They question whether notions of the 'modern' bureaucratic state, the rule of law, civil society (Chabal and Daloz, 1999) and the public sphere are 'globalized localisms', projections onto locations of the Global South of 'the epistemology of the North' (De Sousa Santos, 2012). If so, there is a risk that these concepts distort African realities and misdirect capacity building efforts.

Nevertheless, the triumph of relativism is not a given. Many authors point out that the great resemblances among state and government systems across the world today (see for example the Constitute Project) give human rights political legitimacy (An Na'im, 2000; Donnelly, 2007), and that human rights are sufficiently open to adapt to contexts of the Global South. Human rights have proved their worth in Southern contexts; indeed they have grown and developed through agonistic struggles of peoples and movements of the South (De Sousa Santos, 2002b). Nevertheless, in the interpretation, application and packaging of human rights, the disproportionate wealth and influence of Northerners may still induce them to project their own particular notions and social structures as universal in projects to 'improve' the conditions of those in the South (Murray Li, 2005). In this regard it may be useful to maintain a distinction between universality on one hand, and globalisation on the other (Baudrillard, 2002). While globalisation is a descriptive term for the increasing interlinkages of trade, investment and communication across national borders (see e.g. the *Stanford Encyclopedia of Philosophy* entry on the subject), human rights universality contains normative concepts valuing recognition, diversity, equal dignity and autonomy, both of individual and collective identities. While operating within a political and legal framework, the human rights project requires intercultural understanding (De Sousa Santos, 2002a).

Santos has called for a multicultural conception of human rights, achieved not through the imposition from above of global ideologies and institutional formations from particular (Northern) local settings, but through a cosmopolitan, multicultural process that recognises that all cultures have notions of human dignity, not necessarily expressed in the language of individual rights. Such a process would consist of looking for isomorphic concerns and a constant need to translate back and forth between cultures.

African scholars must therefore navigate a discourse of human rights that is occasionally hegemonic, and occasionally empowering. In a context of extreme imbalance of financial, technical and intellectual resources, cultural power and rapidly changing societies, the question is how African legal scholars can critically examine concepts, so that autonomous production and co-production replace the one-way traffic of export from the North. This chapter will look at some examples of how African jurists have worked to develop a version of universality that reflects notions of dignity nurtured in African culture, and to valorise African notions of law.

International human rights and human rights law in Africa

The notion of universal human rights and the movement to promote them has legal, philosophical and political aspects (Donnelly, 2007). The Universal Declaration of Human Rights (UDHR) is a political document that makes foundational assertions about human values, well-being and human society. It asserts that human rights are inherent in the human person, and as such not necessarily dependent on law for their validity. While the UDHR emphasises the rule of law in protecting human rights, the Declaration's authority is generally moral and political rather than legal. These rights were later adopted as law in international conventions binding sovereign states in their mutual relations and towards individuals subject to their jurisdiction. The UDHR and the conventions are the foundation for institutional arrangements permitting an ever widening discussion of human rights issues, as well as political, legal and even military actions to promote human rights.

The American legal scholar Howard Berman remarked that 'universality remains an inspirational goal rather than an immediate reality' (Berman, 1984: 60). The human rights codification work of the United Nations that began in 1948 should, like the evolving law of nations of which it is a part, be seen as a global conversation among cultures and value systems as well as states. NGOs, faith-based organisations and scholars from all regions contribute in multiple ways to the evolving corpus of international human rights law.

It is beyond dispute that the international law of human rights was formulated with scant participation from the colonised peoples of the African continent prior to decolonisation. Although the constitutions of Ethiopia and Liberia, like those of other UN member states, were taken into account in the drafting of the UDHR, no African was present in the central group of drafters who conceived the document. South Africa, though present at the drafting and abstaining rather than voting against, opposed the notion of a universally applicable framework of rights because of the government's wish to uphold apartheid (Morsink, 1999; Schabas, 2013).

Nevertheless, African states engaged actively with the development of later human rights law in the UN system, and are some of its keenest supporters at the international level (Viljoen, 2007). The Danish historian Steven Jensen has documented the particular acumen of diplomatic representatives of Jamaica, Ghana and the Philippines in developing the international system of human rights in the 1960s. Thus the first major achievement of international human rights law-making in the UN framework was not, as Northern powers might have wished, the transformation of the civil and political rights provisions of the UDHR into binding law, but the 1964 UN Convention on the Elimination of Racial Discrimination (CERD). The success of these newly independent states in cajoling and embarrassing the powerful North (particularly the USA) into the drafting and signing of this instrument was pivotal in the international struggle against apartheid, and even contributed to the fight against racism in the United States, as well as bringing the then Soviet Union and Warsaw Pact countries into the system of legally binding human rights obligations (Jensen, 2015). Successes like these are all too little known and understood among African lawyers and universities.

African states also developed their own collective instruments and human rights protection system. The African Charter on Human and People's Rights (the Banjul Charter of 1981, hereinafter, 'the Charter'), repeats the assertion that human rights 'stem from the attributes of human beings'. There is a rigorous and growing African legal scholarship focused on the practice and jurisprudence of the African Commission on Human and People's Rights, (hereinafter the African Commission) established under the Charter. Similarly, the jurisprudence of regional bodies such as the East African Court of Justice, the Economic Community of West African States (ECOWAS) Court of Justice and the Southern African Development Community (SADC) Court and its (ill-fated) attempt to bring the Government of Zimbabwe to account on issues of human rights connected to the seizure of white-owned farms[1] are the subject of scholarly examination. This legal scholarship has been greatly helped by regional or continental academic human rights programmes such as the Master's level programmes in Human Rights at the University of Pretoria, the *Diplôme d'études approfondies* (Diploma in Advanced Studies, or DEA) Programme on Human Rights and Democracy offered by the UNESCO Chair at the Université d'Abomey-Calavi in Cotonou, Benin, as well as many similar programmes at national level. These programmes enable researchers to explore the exchange of legal ideas and concepts between national legal systems in African and the concepts and guarantees of the Charter.

African social structures, African values and the protection of human rights

Universality of human rights is most often discussed in regard to ensuring that the group of persons covered is comprehensive and inclusive. Less often evoked is the understanding of universality mentioned above, that relates to 'the whole' of what it is to be human. The most frequent area of contention between AU and UN approaches to human rights relates to the notion and importance of community. African scholars have explored the Charter's articulation of a human rights conception that esteems communal identity, protection and responsibility, values considered closer to African thinking and social life. The Ghanaian scholar Dr Josiah Cobbah explored these aspects during the 1980s debate on cultural relativism and human rights. Cobbah did not deny the usefulness of human rights, but doubted that they succeeded in being truly cross-cultural. He also argued that the African view provided a firmer basis for protection of economic, social and cultural rights (Cobbah, 1987). Cobbah evoked scholarship showing how the growth of industrial production in the Global North, aided by liberal theories, eroded and even obliterated the authority of intermediate social structures. Cobbah's critique that the Global North concept of human rights 'fundamentally denies culture' is important in the African context, where non-state structures founded in 'culture' and society are among the most important sources of protection of human beings. Other African scholars point out the need to distinguish between culture and its political mobilisation, asking whether African states in their national practice take communitarian values seriously, or simply use them as a shield against outside criticism (El-Obaid and Appiagyei-Atua, 1996).

Cherished community values may owe as much to economic modes of production and social structure than to any African 'cultural essence'. In urban settings and cash-based economies, loyalty to clan and extended family may gradually give way to smaller family units. Nevertheless, although services such as care for children, the aged and the sick are increasingly purchased on the market or in some cases provided by the state, family networks remain overwhelmingly important in Africa. They often involve fixed gender and social roles. For international human rights to retain their relevance, they may need to adapt conceptual frameworks to less statist frameworks. My argument is that this adaptation would benefit the international human rights system and African societies, and that African scholars of legal and social science are best placed to assist it.

Many African scholars have written about pre-colonial social orders and their relation to state-based ideas of law. In human rights literature, this often consists of reflections on the extent to which notions of rights, or human rights existed in these orders. Writers such as El Obaid and Appiagyei-Atua (1996) take issue with what they see as an over-emphasis on the primacy of communalism in Cobbah's work of that period (e.g. Cobbah, 1987). In their view, communal and individual rights are not mutually negating, and scholarship should look at the persons who enjoyed rights and the nature of the entities that ensure(d) them. Likewise, Zeleza and McConnaughay criticise Eurocentric notions of a 'traditional' Africa where rights did not exist, and where Africans at best had notions of human dignity. For them, the view of human rights to mean 'primarily the institutional enforcement of individual claims against the state' (Zeleza and McConnaughay, 2004: 12) and with a main focus on negative freedom is overly narrow. These authors call for transcendence of the narrowness of the universalism/cultural relativism debate (as well as facile oppositions between community and the individual, tradition and modernity) criticising both for an idealism that abstracts human rights from social history.

The continuing importance of non-state structures leads the emphasis away from a focus solely on the ratification of international treaties and incorporation or transformation of international guarantees into national law. It demands a search for principles of African custom and law that embody legal protection of human rights, as well as towards the systems and mechanisms that tend to succeed in protecting them. As the Danish scholar Sten Schaumburg-Muller (2003) wrote:

> In large parts of the world the problem is not an omnipotent state power, but weak and failed states. How do we make similar human rights propositions that can pose an answer to the problems of human rights violations relating to failed states?
>
> (Schaumburg-Muller, 2003: 153)

At one level, the question is about foundations. In countries of the Global North, legal systems have to some extent become 'naturalised', and the doctrine of legal positivism (see below) may even consider positive law to be the true foundation of human rights. In countries with weak legal systems lacking historical and social legitimacy, this proposition may become deeply problematic. Thus the core of human rights doctrine, unlike international human rights law, allows us to put human rights first, and proceed to ask which structures would best fit the purpose of ensuring their enjoyment. This is the truer and larger challenge of human rights in Africa. Once the scales of legal formalism fall away, many human rights concepts can retain their relevance in the light of African society and culture. Freedoms of association, speech and assembly and the right to participation in government can be contextualised to apply to local and customary forms of organisation and participation.

While consideration of African social traditions and structures is essential to this effort, it remains incomplete without consideration of how African concepts may be adapted within state frameworks. The Dutch Africanist scholar Wim Van Binsbergen sees possibilities as well as limits in the 'Ubuntu' concept. He advocates for a creative expansion and revision of the concept, suited to the contemporary world. He is mindful of the limitations of 'Ubuntu' where the level of aggregation is too wide to be serviceable for the problem at hand (Van Binsbergen, 2001). The challenge for African jurists is not to invent or discover African essences, but rather to use and adapt social forms of family, clan and community on the one hand, and state and market on the other, in solving problems and finding solutions. State and customary law should be conceived and used in crafting solutions that achieve a legally and socially legitimate balance between individual and collective interests.

The late Kenyan legal scholar H.W.O. Okoth-Ogendo described the structure of traditional African society in terms of an inverted pyramid, where the family was at the tip, the clan in the middle and the community at the base (Okoth-Ogendo, 2002). State law can recognise structures of this kind, subject to constitutional principles of liberty, equality and accountability. The challenge for African jurists is to devise models whereby the state valorises and protects, as well as monitors and controls, those forums where people's rights and interests are contested and determined. The legal principle of proportionality can guide the relative weight of individual and collective interests, while the principle of subsidiarity should inform the discussion of the levels at which collective action and individual protection is most appropriate.

The protection of social security as a human right under Article 9 of the (UN) International Covenant on Economic, Social and Cultural Rights (ICESCR) illustrates some of these issues. The Covenant refers specifically to social insurance, an instrument found in industrialised societies where wage-earning is the norm. Anyone familiar with African societies knows that the family is the most important guarantee of social security, especially in rural areas where extended family and communal structures remain strong. At the time the ICESCR was written and adopted, the prevailing view was that European style state social welfare systems would inevitably replace intermediate structures in Africa. In fact, many state welfare and social security systems in Africa do less today than they did two or three decades ago, partly because of internationally imposed Structural Adjustment Programmes (see Easterly, 2000). Meanwhile, a number of researchers, initially mostly in the Netherlands, began to conduct research on the subject of social security in contexts of the Global South in the 1980s and 1990s (Von Benda-Beckmann and Kirsch, 1999). Human rights scholars need to translate the concept of social security in settings where a more feasible duty of the state might be to protect and facilitate extended families in providing social security to their members (see Tostesen, 2008).

Dominant concepts of law in African state legal systems

Fifty or more years after the gaining of independence by African states, the challenge of legal systems that are poorly adapted to social realities persists. Howard Berman, writing about the imposition of alien state systems on indigenous peoples, observed that:

> Like an animal abstracted from its natural and balanced environment and transplanted to another ecosystem without natural defences to it, the State system was extended to the Third World. Panikkar is correct to say that institutions are not easily transplanted from one culture to another. Nevertheless, history teaches that they can be imposed.
>
> (Berman, 1984: 58)

By suppressing alternative meanings and distorting existing ones, colonial state law attempted to create a new social reality. The new, written law was not to be interpreted or adapted to fit local reality, but to be applied by rote, like a mathematical formula, all the more absolute, 'global' and unquestionable because it was written far away, in the language of the coloniser, and sanctioned by an all-powerful empire. Looking at the Zambian statute book today, it is remarkable how much of the inherited colonial law remains unchanged. Apart from minor adjustments to penalties, the Penal Code, the Criminal Procedure Code and the Juveniles Act remain largely as they were fifty or more years ago. Statutory civil law may be important to (predominantly urban and middle-class) owners of state (i.e. not customary) land, public employees and in issues such as road traffic accidents. For most poor Zambians though, statutory civil law is of little relevance to their lives (Kerrigan et al., 2012). The Intestate Succession Act, an ambitious, reform oriented piece of legislation from the late 1980s, has seen only limited implementation due to lack of familiarity with its provisions and lack of popular acceptance, especially in rural areas (Matakala, 2012).

What has remained unchanged from colonial times is perhaps not only the text of particular laws, but ways of thinking about law. The late American scholar Robert Seidman decried the unthinking application of 'analytical positivism' in African law (Seidman, 1984). As Seidman describes it, this school of legal thought is based on a command theory of law and the premise that a law that is good in England or Switzerland is also good in Zambia or Nigeria, because what makes it good is its elegance and internal consistency as an instrument for trained lawyers rather than its social content. The focus is on what the law is, and not what it ought to be. Thus:

> 'Practical' lawyers in Africa today are dominated, usually without being aware of it, by the ghosts of positivism. When put to the task of drafting a new law for a particular purpose, they all but invariably copy the laws of some metropolitan country, not infrequently with sad or ludicrous results [...]
>
> (Seidman, 1984: 280)

The problem is not coherence or elegance as such, but the risk that this concern will overwhelm other concerns, especially that of social relevance. World market structures pressure African elites to adopt standardised legal frameworks on investment, trade, commerce, corporate regulation, mineral extraction and taxation. In regard to land tenure, the overwhelming regional tendency continues to be towards further expansion of individual freehold at the expense of traditional forms of ownership.

The problem of inappropriate Northern models exists not only in regard to inherited colonial-era legislation but also vis-à-vis new legislation initiatives. Two examples from Zambia illustrate the problems. A survey conducted for the Zambian Ministry of Justice revealed that less than 10 per cent of married persons surveyed had entered into civil marriages. Why so few Zambians organise their family lives according to state law is a complex question, but some of the answers are glaringly obvious. According to national legislation, any legal action regarding a civil marriage has to take place at the High Court. For most Zambians living outside urban areas, the High Court is extremely distant, expensive and alien. Similar considerations apply to written wills.[2] In short, statutory law frequently fails to provide legal and/or institutional frameworks that respond to people's legal needs, largely because it dates from the colonial period and was designed fora small foreign elite with access to urban institutions (Mamdani, 1996). In recent years, the Zambian Law Development Commission has undertaken research as a basis for national legislation to regulate customary marriage, as has been done in some other African countries,[3] but this has not yet resulted in legislation.

Import of legislation may save time and effort, but failure to contextualise it may often render it useless. This is seen in regard to the second example, which concerns criminal procedure. In 2010, at the strong urging of (no doubt well-meaning) American advisers, Zambia amended its law to allow plea agreements.[4] While the amendment adopted the sensible American safeguard that courts should not accept a plea agreement unless a defence lawyer had been on hand to advise the defendant, the law has effectively remained a dead letter, because only a tiny proportion of criminal defendants benefit from representation by a lawyer. As Seidman wistfully noted: '[T]he notion that new law might be adapted specifically to the needs of the national community is not considered' (Seidman, 1984: 280).

Although each country has its particularities, this picture may sadly not be unrepresentative of much of Sub-Saharan Africa. There is little doubt that there has been much direct export of legislation in many areas of law in recent years, especially in areas that are of concern to foreign partners, including laws on investment, public procurement, commercial transactions, drug trafficking and terrorism and human rights. Even when legislation is not imported directly, the overall paradigms within which justice system reform is planned and executed may reproduce the same pathologies.

How can African universities help make good laws for African societies?

Many Sub-Saharan African universities trace their origins to colonial times (see Chapter 2). Under colonial governments, legal education was frequently neglected, as law was seen as a training ground for politics. This meant that many African countries, including Zambia, faced a dearth of lawyers in the immediate post-independence period (Ndulo, 2002). Even for those universities and law schools established after independence, attempts to meet local needs and conditions took place within an overall drive towards modernisation (whether in its socialist or capitalist versions) that dominated the thinking of governing elites. Many law professors from the USA and European countries engaged in teaching in African universities in the post-independence period, and some of these partnerships continue today.

Universities, and especially lawyers and law students, generally come from the urbanised, elite segment of society that is fluent in the official, European language, often closely linked to state agendas and discourses linked to international human rights. In working with human rights in Africa it is not unusual to hear human rights advocates (both African and foreign) complain that the main problem is that 'people do not know their rights'. While statements of this kind are superficially true, they may confirm a bias towards top-down programmes to get rural, illiterate and marginalised populations to conform to the model of the urban minority, rather than to craft legislation and institutions that respond to the needs of the former. There may be implicit and highly problematic assumptions about who in society – the 'human rights activists' or the supposed rights holders – properly exercises agency (Englund, 2006).

What alternatives are there for African universities and legal communities to the blind application of a legal positivist paradigm criticised by Seidman? My assertion is that there are two distinct though complementary approaches to developing grounded, appropriate sets of legal rules. The first, Seidman's own focus, is a law-making methodology grounded in pragmatic problem solving. The second, outlined below, is engagement with so-called 'living customary law'. Both approaches require scholarship that bridges the gap between the received (i.e. originally European) systems of law and African social realities. While not every model is transferable, the experiences of other countries are relevant. The Nordic countries, as well as Canada, the USA and Australia, have extensive experience in trying to correct the errors and abuses of previous times with regard to indigenous land rights, for example.

Instead of beginning with a diffuse and vaguely described end result to be achieved, and then searching for the means to achieve it, Seidman proposed starting with a detailed empirical study of the social behaviours that constitute a particular social problem. Then, rational choice is exercised to design laws that are considered likely to induce behaviour that would solve the problem (Seidman et al., 2001). This involves a painstaking effort to examine national social, economic and cultural contexts before debating policy options. The legislative choices will naturally take place within a framework of values drawn from a number of sources, including those set out in the national constitution. It goes without saying that crafting legislation specific to the needs of African societies is no easy task, either legally or politically. Even painstakingly prepared legislation often requires adjustment when unforeseen problems arise. Legislation may disturb relations of patronage upon which the national and local political economy is effectively based. At a micro-level, existing gender and family relations are also likely to be affected by some legislation. Any change introduced will take time and political resources, and may not succeed without significant effort. Seidman's approach to legislation calls for these factors to be explicitly considered when devising legislation. While assessments of the legislation differ, an example of the kind of analysis and consultation that Seidman calls for may be seen in the process that led to Tanzania's Village Land Act of 1999 (Shivji, 1998).

For present purposes, a central question is how African legal academies can provide the research and expertise that can contribute to better processes and outcomes. This requires an approach to legal education that is grounded in national and local contexts, where socio-legal studies are of prime importance. Legal education needs to foster pragmatic, creative thinking that aims at finding solutions to social and economic problems from an ethical base, where good law enables successful governance to promote the common good. While law is not an empirical science, empirical enquiry is needed to assess the success of law in achieving its aims. While not descriptive of social reality, law also needs to succeed in hermeneutic terms – to create or represent normative meaning for the people it aims to serve.

For practitioners, quality legal work is a matter of 'knowledge' and 'craft'. 'Knowledge' in this context means a correct understanding of substantive and procedural law that enables predictable outcomes. Thorough legal research is necessary to achieve this knowledge. The *craft* of law is about making well-written laws, regulations, contracts, legal strategies, arguments and judgments. A correct knowledge of legal foundations and the application of legal craftsmanship ensure that a legal text – whether a law, a regulation, a brief or a judgment – stands up to legal scrutiny.

For a select and often rather limited number of individuals in countries of the Global South, legal craftsmanship can lead to a well-paid job in legal practice, business and finance as well as influence in the world of politics. For others, it yields more moderately rewarded, but still comparatively attractive positions in public service or civil society. Most law schools, in Africa and elsewhere, know that they will be assessed according to their success in equipping practitioners (in the widest sense) with legal knowledge and craftsmanship.

At the same time, societies and justice systems require that universities also provide them with knowledge of a wider scope and a different order. Unlike some fortunate countries of the North, where legal systems developed in tandem with politics and moral philosophy, African countries contend with a deep historical disjunction between society on the one hand, and the state and the power of global forces on the other. Developing legal and constitutional responses to social challenges requires analysis at a deep level, involving the very architecture of the state (see Fombad, 2014). Legal education and legal philosophy that is anchored only in analytical positivism is not up to this task.

Thus, there is a need for African law schools to teach and study philosophy of law, and the historical and current political context in which the legal system operates. There is also a need for anthropological and sociological studies of how people in all kinds of positions understand, use, shape and respond to law, as well as for wider sociological samples to illuminate larger patterns over time and place. All of this is necessary to gain some knowledge of whether a legal system is meeting the needs and expectations of society and the rights of individuals. A 'truly African' university would examine these questions as they apply to African justice systems, including the vast domain of customary systems. The task of Africanising legal education (Fombad, 2014) thus requires a sensitivity to location, a place-based approach (as discussed in Chapter 2 of this book) that counterbalances discourses of universality and globalisation.

Legal pluralism – from a liability to an asset – living customary law

The second approach outlined earlier is, using a legally pluralist frame of reference, to ensure that state actors understand and valorise the legal frameworks that have been developed by African communities. This requires an approach to law that goes beyond formal legislative texts. Most African states neither effectively possess nor claim a monopoly on law-making and adjudication (Cuskelly, 2011).[5] Article 23 of Zambia's constitution recognises custom, so that the people, constituted in traditional communities, are a source of law. Recognising and applying this kind of law requires an understanding of the nature of customary law.

While some traditional African systems of government undoubtedly produced positive law through legislative acts (Alabi, 2006), most did not make a strict separation between domains of ethics, religion, politics and law (Idowu, 2009). In this regard, pre-modern Africa resembled other parts of the world (Rohl, 2005). Neither in Africa nor in most countries is 'law' limited to legislation. The distinction between customary law and legislation in Africa is similar to the two kinds of law referred to by Roman jurists as *leges* and *mores* – statutes and customs. Moreover, law requires general principles as well as detailed texts. Even prominent representatives of today's Anglo-American legal thought reject the possibility of a full separation between the domains of law, ethics and politics (Altman, 2001).

Ironically, while development institutions have begun to devote more attention to legal pluralism, the African legal academy shows signs of moving in the opposite direction.[6] In Anglophone Africa, with some exceptions, customary law appears to be losing ground in legal education (Manteaw, 2007, see also Shivji, 2000).

Neither legal centralism nor legal pluralism are inherently good goals. As De Sousa Santos says: '[T]here is nothing inherently good, progressive or emancipatory about legal pluralism' (De Sousa Santos, 2002b: 89). Similarly, the French legal scholar Rene David, who developed a European-inspired civil code for Ethiopia, acknowledged the harm that could be done by legal centralism when he wrote that:

> By wishing to install prematurely the rule of law, such as it is understood in the West, we have upset the old order of societies which were not ready to receive western legal ideas. African civilisation was founded on certain values: a sense of community [...] Unconsciously, perhaps, we have thus contributed to the breaking-up of the ties of family and clan, and we have been incapable of replacing them with a sense of solidarity extending to African society as a whole.
>
> (David and Brierly, 1978: 520)

International human rights bodies may not always have a full understanding of this context. They sometimes appear to exhibit a bias against customary law.

Thus, the UN Committee on Economic, Social and Cultural Rights, in its concluding observations of 2004 on Zambia, echoed the Government of Zambia's own proposed course of action, and recommended that Zambia codify customary law (UN CESCR, 2005). Most scholars agree that codification as an approach to the challenge of legal pluralism is fraught with difficulties (Bennett and Vermeulen, 1980). Zambia later abandoned its ambition to comprehensively codify customary law, adopting a more modest aim of producing legislation on customary marriage (UN CCRP Zambia, 2009).

African constitutional frameworks and canons of judicial interpretation may allow considerable leeway for interpretation that allows a more nuanced application of the law, taking account of societal needs and realities. Legislation, both old and new, can be interpreted in the light of constitutional human rights and other imperatives. Denials of the 'legal' character of non-state law may give support to the one hundred year old denial of rights based in customary law, including the appropriation of the property of great numbers of Africans. Indigenous concepts of governance and property ownership – in particular, the corporate character of African communities – were either rejected outright or distorted by colonialist legal thinking, including the facile use of a common law concept (of a trust) as an analogue for an indigenous concept (Okoth-Ogendo, 2002).

In an effort to ensure against future wrongs of this kind, the legal restructuring of post-apartheid South Africa included a full recognition of customary law as a source of law under the constitution. Its implications have been explored by the South African courts in far reaching judicial decisions that call for a deep understanding of the bases of indigenous African law (Pienaar, 2012). One challenge of this reconfiguration is to ensure harmony between different levels and systems, and between state unity and decentralisation of power.

Devolving authority to community structures also raises the question of how to guard against abuse of power that might arise within those structures. Revitalisation of traditional communities as instruments of self-government, including rule making and adjudication, must take account of today's realities and of constitutional guarantees of gender equality and accountability for the exercise of public authority (James, 2007).

Recognising the distortions of custom that have taken place over a long period of political oppression that made written and often judicial versions of customary law unreliable, the South African judicial and academic community has explored the notion of 'living customary law' to insist on customary law as a democratic and community based phenomenon that requires particular techniques of discovery and interpretation (Himonga, 2011). Academic research needs to explore whether 'living customary law' might – with the right support – actually be a good method of finding appropriate legal solutions to local problems. In some contexts, African law schools have gone beyond research in order to engage directly with communities, as seen with the engagement of the University of Namibia with so-called self-statement processes (Hinz, 2012).

Only African universities are positioned to systematically influence legal thinking so that constitutional recognition of customary law is translated into the crafting of legal solutions by legislators, judges or lawyers that balance custom and local understandings with constitutional principles. While space does not permit discussion of the political aspect of recognition of customary authority here, it is an equally vital focus of scholarship, especially in view of concerns about separatist or irredentist claims that may arise. Also needed is capacity on the part of researchers to make realistic assessments of what state structures can actually deliver in terms of support, supervision and appellate frameworks, and what customary systems are capable of in terms of access, participation and accountability. Thus, the importance of interdisciplinary research is primordial to the task of developing appropriate legal structures.

Deep legal pluralism and the call for 'cognitive justice'

Any granting of state authority to customary adjudicators in African societies must grapple with the reality that local, non-state systems of justice may embed views of the world based in spiritual beliefs and non-materialist epistemologies. In some communities, ancestors, spirits and mediums may be called upon to provide answers in adjudication processes, and supernatural agency may be accepted as causal. This is evidently deeply problematic for state legal systems, which rely on materialist causality for criminal and civil liability. A clash of epistemologies of this kind is revealed in a most interesting way in the review of 'Kupilikula' Harry West's much admired work on 'uwavi' spiritual beliefs among the Makonde people of northern Mozambique (West, 2005). While West calls for a balance between such beliefs and modern scientific governance, an African reviewer of the work disagreed with his suggestion that political leaders should cultivate a language of power that interprets 'modern' political and social phenomena in cultural terms such as those of 'uwavi', seeing these traditional beliefs as a source of disempowerment (Mtyingizana, 2006).

How should African legal systems that recognise legal pluralism balance respect for culture with the materialist premises and value claims of state legal systems? While science has often served ideas that are not only morally repugnant, but false according to evidence now in our possession, the law cannot fully embrace postmodernist scepticism or radical value pluralism. How should these considerations be reconciled with calls for 'cognitive justice' (De Sousa Santos, 2014) where respect is demanded for the religious or spiritual beliefs of traditional/ indigenous communities?

The solution of human rights law to conundrums of this kind in the Global North is generally to confine spiritual beliefs to the private sphere. This contrasts to some extent with countries such as Kenya, which recognise Islamic Kadhi Courts and religious beliefs as a source of law. In facing these challenges, African jurists can draw some inspiration from recent constitutional developments in other parts of the Global South, where Latin American countries have given greater space to indigenous cultural communities to find their own justice solutions. Although these remain subject to ultimate constitutional control, this is of a less interventionist nature than previously, carried out through a mechanism of collateral review rather than a simple overruling (Pimentel, 2010).

In practice, the problem needs to be seen in the light of the inaccessibility of state services, whether of education, health or justice. 'Development' brought by these services may bring about a shift in cultural values that is voluntary and gradual. A cultural meeting between the 'modern' in the form of the state and the 'traditional' in the form of local communities and beliefs can, to a large degree, take place in conditions of curiosity and respect, where culture is not seen as an unchangeable essence, but as a fluid and dynamic social phenomenon. Here again, there is a great need for socio-legal and anthropological studies by African universities. Very interesting in this regard are the studies on gender and sexuality in African society and culture by a number of African academics. The work of scholars at Makerere University in Uganda stands out in this regard, not only for its academic interest, but for its ability to challenge imported puritanical discourses on sexuality and religion (see for example Tamale, 2011). Within human rights law, the field of cultural rights remains ripe for development and could be a fruitful field for researchers.

Concluding remarks

Unfortunately, African law faculties face severe challenges on many fronts. It goes almost without saying that all too often in practice, the challenges faced by African law faculties are likely to be of the mundane and depressing, rather than the intellectually uplifting kind. Lecturers' schedules may be overburdened, students have difficulty in accessing materials of any kind, let alone those based on national jurisprudence, which is often difficult to avail of. This is not even to speak of electrical power cuts, strikes, transport and logistical difficulties, or students insufficiently prepared by secondary schooling for the challenge of university education. A large number of African academics contend heroically with these challenges, but the constraints placed on their efforts are often close to overwhelming. After graduation from university, opportunities for continuing legal education are often very limited, and any that do exist are likely to be found only in urban centres, making it difficult for governments to convince professionals to locate in more remote towns.

Too little of the jurisprudence crafted in African courts is even available to African students and scholars. As Ndulo suggests, the lack of local legal materials (especially case reports from superior courts and academic treatises by African scholars) has consequences for the kind of teaching that is possible. He noted the exclusion of more reflective subjects from the law curriculum, and an emphasis on formalism and a heavy focus on learning of rules rather than on developing of skills of legal reasoning. He found this troubling for the development of the law in Africa (Ndulo, 2002). Some African legal research programmes have gone far in the attempt to engage critically with concepts in this way. 'Grounded theory' is used by research programmes such as the Southern and Eastern African Regional Centre for Women's Law at the University of Zimbabwe, where data and theory constantly engage with each other in an iterative process, contributing to a gradual development of concepts and methods that challenge legal and theoretical frameworks with practical realities and the lived imaginaries of community members and justice actors (Weis Bentzon et al., 1998). This programme relied on an extraordinary degree of international commitment and financial support provided mainly by NORAD. In many contexts, university legal aid clinics succeed in bringing law students and faculties into the challenge of meeting the legal needs of ordinary people.

Returning to the theme of this book as a whole, a response to the question of whether an African legal university 'exists', would be positive, though with some reservations. Positive because of the great efforts that have been made by African scholars to ask necessary questions and formulate interesting theses, but tentative because the obstacles remain great, much of the scholarship remains fragmentary and much of the potential seems to remain latent. Too few African universities have the resources to foster a scholarly milieu that can bring many of the most knowledgeable and questioning minds together in an interdisciplinary enquiry. Many creative and knowledgeable scholars plough valuable furrows, but this scholarship too often takes place outside the African continent. Likewise, opportunities for scholars and academic communities to bring the various threads together into a larger narrative remain too few.

There is no immediate prospect of African universities being able to provide research environments that permit African legal scholars to fully realise their transformative potential. At the same time, Northern institutions are hampered by their distance, as well as by the legitimacy of their claims to knowledge concerning Africa. Thus, relations of co-production of knowledge remain vital. Meanwhile, the aid community, particularly at the field level, benefits far too little from the available knowledge, and the full range of the empirical data gathered through aid efforts is seldom made fully available to scholars.

A programme for improvement would thus address the issues of continuing and strengthening scholarly links between North and South, including emphasis on multi-disciplinarity, as well as deeper issues of legal philosophy. It would aim to improve conditions of teaching and learning at African universities (possibly linked to bonding schemes whereby graduates are bound to serve their own societies for a period), and sharing of knowledge between scholarly and development fields.

Notes

1 See the case of Mike Campbell (Pvt) Limited and Others v Zimbabwe (2008) AHRLR 199.
2 Laws of Zambia, Wills and Administration of Testate Estates Act, Cap 60, section 66.
3 Notably, Sierra Leone. See: Sierra Leone, Registration of Customary Marriage and Divorce Act 2007, Sierra Leone Gazette Vol. CXL, No. 5, 22nd January, 2009.
4 Laws of Zambia, Plea Negotiations and Agreements Act, No. 20 of 2010, section 7.

5 Even in regard to the 'monopoly of violence', most African states demonstrate legal and factual divergence from an idealised Weberian model (Baker, 2010). In Zambia, the Chiefs Act gives chiefs and their retainers (known as *kapasus*) coercive powers of arrest and detention. See: Laws of Zambia Cap. 287, Chiefs Act, section 11.
6 A 2012 meeting of Deans of African law faculties observed that most Southern African law schools teach customary law as a standalone topic, but that this was not the case in East or West Africa (African Law Dean's Forum, 2012).

References

African Law Dean's Forum (2012) *African Law Dean's Report*, Johannesburg, South Africa 15–17 August 2012. Available at: www.ialsnet.org/wordpress/wp-content/uploads/2012/09/AFRICAN-DEANS-FORUM-FINAL-REPORT-AUGUST-2012.pdf (accessed 18 May 2015).

Alabi, M.O.A. (2006) 'Law making in pre-colonial Yorubaland'. In Falola, T. and Genova, A. (eds) *The Yoruba in Transition: History, Values and Modernity*. Durham, USA: Carolina Academic Press, 111–124.

Altman, A. (2001) *Arguing about Law: An Introduction to Legal Philosophy*, 2nd edition (revised), Wadsworth: Thomson.

An Na'im, A. (2000) 'Islam and human rights: beyond the universality debate: religion and the universality of human rights', *ASIL* 94 Proceedings 214.

Baker, B. (2010) *Security in Post-Conflict Africa*. Boca Raton: CRC Press.

Baudrillard, J. (2002) 'La Violence du Mondial'. In Baudrillard, J. *Power Inferno*, Paris: Galilée, pp. 63–83.

Bennett, T.W. and Vermuelen, T. (1980) 'Codification of customary law', *Journal of African Law*, 24 (2), 206–219.

Berman, H.J. (1983) *Law and Revolution: The Formation of The Western Legal Tradition*. Cambridge MA.: Harvard University Press.

Berman, H. (1984) 'Are human rights universal?' *Interculture*, XVII (1–2), 82–83.

Chabal, P. and Daloz, J.P. (1999) *Africa Works: Disorder as Political Instrument*. Oxford: James Currey.

Cobbah, J.A.M. (1987) 'African values and the human rights debate: an African perspective', *Human Rights Quarterly*, 9 (3), 309–331.

Coquillette, D.R. (1988) *The Civilian Writers of Doctors' Commons, London: Three Centuries of Juristic Innovation in Comparative, Commercial and International Law*. Berlin: Dunker & Humbolt.

Cuskelly, K. (2011) *Customs and Constitutions: State Recognition of Customary Law around the World*. Bangkok: IUCN.

David, R. and Brierly, J.E.C. (1978) *Major Legal Systems in the World Today: An Introduction to the Comparative Study of Law* (2nd edn). London: Steven & Sons.

De Sousa Santos, B. (2002a) 'Towards a multicultural conception of human rights'. In Hernandez-Truyol, B. (ed.) *Moral Imperialism – A Critical Anthology*. New York: New York University Press.

De Sousa Santos, B. (2002b) *Toward a New Legal Common Sense: Law, Globalization, and Emancipation*. London: Butterworths.

De Sousa Santos, B. (2012) 'Public sphere and epistemologies of the South', *Africa Development*, XXXVII (1), 43–67.

De Sousa Santos, B. (2014) *Epistemologies of the South: Justice against Epistemicide*. Boulder: Paradigm Publishers.

Donnelly, J. (2007) 'The relative universality of human rights', *Human Rights Quarterly*, 29 (2), 281–306.

Easterly, W. (2000) 'The effect of IMF and World Bank programs on poverty'. Available at: www.imf.org/external/pubs/ft/staffp/2000/00-00/e.pdf (accessed 20 February 2015).

El-Obaid, A. and Appiagyei-Atua, K. (1996) 'Human rights in Africa – a new perspective on linking the past to the present', *McGill Law Journal*, 41 (4), 819–854.

Englund, H. (2006) *Prisoners of Freedom*. Berkeley: University of California Press.

Fombad, C.M. (2014) 'Africanisation of legal education programmes: the need for comparative African legal studies', *Journal of Asian and African Studies*, 49 (4), 383–398.

Ghai, Y. (2007) 'Globalization, multiculturalism and law'. In De Sousa Santos, B. (ed.) *Another Knowledge is Possible: Beyond Northern Epistemologies*. London: Verso, pp. 383–416.

Halm, H. (1997) *The Fatimids and Their Tradition of Learning*. London: I.B. Tauris.

Himonga, C. (2011) 'The future of living customary law in African legal systems in the twenty-first century and beyond, with special reference to South Africa'. In Fenrich, J. et al. (eds) *The Future of African Customary Law*. Cambridge: Cambridge University Press, pp. 31–57.

Hinz, M.O. (2012) 'The ascertainment of customary law: what is ascertainment of customary law and what is it for? The Experience of the Customary Law Ascertainment Project in Namibia', *Oñati Socio-legal Series*, 2 (7), 85–105.

Idowu, W. (2009) 'Eurocentrism and the separability-inseparability debate: challenges from African cultural jurisprudence', *Journal of Pan African Studies*, 2 (9), 123–150.

James, D. (2007) *South African Land Reform*. Abingdon: Routledge Cavendish.

Jensen, S. (2015) 'The Jamaican broker: UN diplomacy and the transformation of international human rights, 1962–1968'. In Andersen, E. and Lassen, E. (eds) *Europe and the Americas. Transatlantic Approaches to Human Rights*. Leiden: Brill, pp. 91–129.

Kerrigan, F., Matakala, L., Mwenya, W., Dinda, C. and Møller, M. (2012) *Access to Justice Situation Analysis*. Lusaka: Ministry of Justice of the Republic of Zambia.

Mac Ginty, R. and Richmond, O. (2013) 'The local turn in peacebuilding: a critical agenda for peace', *Third World Quarterly*, 34 (5), 763–783.

Mamdani, M. (1996) *Citizen and Subject: Contemporary Africa and the Legacy of Late Colonialism*. Princeton: Princeton University Press.

Manteaw, S. (2007) 'Legal education in Africa: what type of lawyer does Africa need?' *McGeorge Law Review*, 39 (4), 903–976.

Matakala, L. (2012) *Inheritance and Disinheritance of Widows and Orphans*. Saarbrucken: LAP Lambert Academic Publishing.

Morsink J. (1999) *The Universal Declaration of Human Rights: Origins, Drafting, and Intent*. Philadelphia: University of Pennsylvania Press.

Mtyingizana, B. (2006) 'Review of West's Kupilikula', *African Sociological Review*, 10 (1), 244–252.

Mutua, M.W. (2001) 'Savages, victims, and saviors: the metaphor of human rights', *Harvard International Law Journal*, 42 (1), 201–245.

Murray Li, T. (2005) 'Beyond "the state" and failed schemes', *American Anthropologist* 107 (3), 383–394.

Ndulo, M. (2002) 'Legal education in Africa in the era of globalization and structural adjustment', *Cornell Law Faculty Publications*, Paper 54, 487–503.

Okoth-Ogendo, H.W.O. (2002) 'The tragic African commons: a century of expropriation, suppression and subversion', *Occasional Paper no. 24, Land Reform and Agrarian Change in Southern Africa*. Cape Town: University of the Western Cape, 2–7.

Pienaar, G. (2012) 'The methodology used to interpret customary land tenure', *Potchefstroom Electronic Law Journal* (15) 3, 153–183.

Pimentel, D. (2010) 'Rule of law reform without cultural imperialism? Reinforcing customary justice through collateral review in Southern Sudan', *Hague Journal on the Rule of Law*, 2 (1), 1–28.

Putnam, H. (2004) *The Collapse of the Fact/Value Dichotomy and Other Essays*. Cambridge, MA: Harvard University Press.

Rohl, W. (2005) 'Generalities'. In Rohl, W. (ed.) *The History of Law in Japan Since 1868*. Leiden: Brill, pp. 1–23.

Schabas, W.A. (2013) *The Universal Declaration of Human Rights: The Travaux Préparatoires*. Cambridge: Cambridge University Press.

Schaumburg-Muller, S. (2003) 'Truth, law and human rights'. In Bankowski, Z. (ed.) *Epistemology and Ontology: IVR-Symposium Lund*. Stuttgart: Franz Steiner Verlag, Bind 4, pp. 153–162.

Seidman, R. (1984) 'Law and stagnation in Africa'. In Ndulo, M. (ed.) *Law in Zambia*. Lusaka: East African Publishing House, pp. 271–295.

Seidman, A., Seidman R.B. and Abeysekere, N. (2001) *Legislative Drafting for Democratic Social Change: A Manual for Drafters*. London: Kluwer Law International.

Shivji, I. (1998) *Not Yet Democracy: Reforming Land Tenure in Tanzania*. Dar es Salaam: IIED/HAKIARDHI/ Faculty of Law, University of Dar es Salaam, pp. 2–30.

Shivji, I. (2000) 'Contradictory perspectives on rights and justice in the context of land tenure reform in Tanzania'. In Mamdani, M. (ed.) *Beyond Rights Talk and Culture Talk*. New York: St. Martin's Press, pp. 37–60.

Tamale, S. (2011) *African Sexualities, a Reader*. Cape Town: Pambazuka Press.

Tostesen, A. (2008) 'Feasible social security systems in Africa', *Development Issues*, 10 (2), 4–7.

UN (2012) UN document A/RES/67/1, Declaration of the High-level Meeting of the General Assembly on the Rule of Law at the National and International Levels, see paragraph 15, October 2012.

UN CCRP Zambia (2009) 11 December 2009, Consideration of Reports Submitted by States Parties, under Article 40 of the Covenant, Information Received from Zambia on the Implementation of the Concluding Observations of the Human Rights Committee, CCPR/C/ZMB/CO/3/Add.1.

UN CESCR Zambia (2005) Consideration of Reports Submitted by States Parties, under Articles 16 and 17 of the Covenant, Concluding Observations of the Committee on Economic, Social and Cultural Rights, ZAMBIA E/C.12/1/Add.106.

Van Binsbergen, W. (2001) 'Ubuntu and the globalization of Southern African thought and society', *Quest*, XV (1–2), 53–89.

Viljoen, F. (2007) *International Human Rights Law in Africa*. Oxford: Oxford University Press.

Von Benda-Beckmann, F. and Kirsch, R. (1999) 'Informal security systems in Southern Africa and approaches to strengthen them through policy measures', *Journal of Social Development in Africa*, 14 (2), 21–38.

Weis Bentzon, A., Hellum, A. and Stewart, J.E. (1998) *Pursuing Grounded Theory in Law: South–North Experiences in Developing Women's Law*. Oslo: Mond Books.

West, H. (2005) *Kupilikula: Governance and the Invisible Realm in Mozambique*. Chicago: University of Chicago Press.

Zeleza, P.T. and McConnaughay, P.J. (Eds) (2004) *Human Rights, the Rule of Law and Development in Africa*. Philadelphia: University of Pennsylvania Press.

Conclusion

Conclusion

12 Dilemmas and paradoxes of capacity building in African higher education

Concluding remarks

Lene Møller Madsen, Stig Jensen and
Hanne Kirstine Adriansen

Introduction

The chapters in this book have explored higher education and capacity building in different African contexts. In innovative manners they have contributed to our understanding by applying a geographical view on knowledge. As Meusburger explains:

> The geography of knowledge studies spatial variations in the generation, dissemination, and application of various categories of knowledge. Scholars in this area are interested in the places and spaces of knowledge generation and the impact of local milieus (environments) and spatial relations on the generation and diffusion of knowledge. They analyse the reasons for spatial disparities of knowledge and their consequences for society and economy.
>
> (Meusburger, 2015: 91)

By using this approach, the chapters in this book offer readers a rich resource for exploring and understanding the complexity of knowledge production and capacity building in African higher education, and how these issues are intertwined. The chapters provide diverse illustrations of the geography and power of knowledge production under changing environmental, social and political conditions. As several of the authors argue, knowledge production has spatial dimensions and is embedded in global power relations. A number of chapters draw attention to how sciences conceived of in the Global North are transferred as universal to the rest of the world. Hence, the collection confirms the importance of using a geographical approach for understanding how capacity building influences and affects African academics, institutions and degree programmes. As mentioned in the introduction, the chapters attempt to decolonise research by having a focus on reflexivity and positionality. While the geography of knowledge tradition emphasises how knowledge is spatially situated

(Livingstone, 2003), the reflexive turn highlights that research is made by people, for instance by drawing attention to positionality:

> These notions [of reflexivity] are informed by an acknowledgement that our knowledge of the world is always mediated and interpreted from a particular stance and an available language, and that we should own up to this in explicit ways. The self is not some kind of virus which contaminates research.
> (Cousin, 2010: 10)

We find that the reflexive approach with an emphasis on positionality has been pertinent for our endeavour.

Findings of the chapters

In the following, we provide a brief summary of the main findings of the case-based chapters organised under the headlines of the three parts of the book. This constitutes the background for the subsequent outline of three dilemmas and paradoxes of capacity building in African higher education.

Capacity building of African universities – asymmetrical power relations?

Today, some 50 years after many of the African countries gained their independence, it is relevant to ask how independent African higher education has become and how capacity building affects education and research at African universities. Has a certain type of 'African' university emerged? To what extent are old power relations still reproduced in partnerships between African and European researchers? How do new partners affect the power relations? These were some of the questions we wanted to address in this part of the book.

While African universities share many structural and financial problems, they are also products of specific social, political and economic contexts. They have distinct histories and their lecturers and researchers have different social experiences. Appreciating these differences is crucial, not least when designing donor driven collaboration. In Chapter 3, *Dilemmas of knowledge production in Ugandan universities*, Whyte and Whyte elaborate on their scepticism about the 'African' university as a concept, drawing on 25 years of experience with Danish-Ugandan university level collaboration, by illustrating how two Ugandan universities (Makerere and Gulu) experience their societal role very differently due to different historical, political and geographical locations. The authors argue that development agencies that finance capacity-building projects have a notion of the university as a development project. This notion requires objectives and milestones to be set, and a framework that determines what activities, expenditures and procedures can and should be undertaken. Whyte and Whyte argue that such a perception and framing is ill suited for universities and their knowledge production. Instead, they propose more spatially grounded and participatory approaches to university development in Africa, based on specific university histories and contexts.

While Whyte and Whyte emphasise the importance of context, there is a call for long-term partnerships in Chapter 4, *Collaborative education across continents: lessons from a partnership on sustainable resource management education,* by Sithole, Birch-Thomsen, Mertz, Hill, Bruun and Thenya. The authors analyse and reflect upon the nature of their collaborative education of Danish and African students established between Danish universities and universities in Southern Africa and Kenya on the Sustainable Land Use (SLUSE) model of teaching natural resource management with a focus on the delivery of a joint field course. The authors stress that collaboration and participation developed on the basis of strong personal relationships, mutual trust and in informal arenas where synergies at a personal level were valued as much if not more than those at an organisational level. SLUSE represents a type of collaborative education that is becoming less common due to increased internationalisation and commodification of higher education in Africa when new players enter the arena.

One of the new players is China, which has increased its engagement in the internationalisation of higher education in Africa through the establishment of Confucius Institutes. Chapter 5, *The Confucius Institute at the University of Zambia: a new direction in the internationalisation of African higher education?* by Kragelund and Hampwaye, is a case study of the newly established Confucius Institute at University of Zambia. The authors explore the extent to which Confucius Institutes is a type of South–South collaboration in higher education, or rather should be seen like soft power initiatives of Africa's Northern partners. Kragelund and Hampwaye argue that the establishment of Confucius Institutes resembles soft power more than South–South collaboration, and that an aim of establishing Confucius Institutes is to make China more appealing to the Zambian public. Hence, the authors conclude that despite the Chinese 'equal partners' rhetoric, the Confucius Institute is as donor driven as the other partnerships in which the University of Zambia has engaged historically.

Together, the three chapters reveal some of the challenges inherent in capacity building in African higher education, arguing that capacity building should be based on long-term partnerships and close consideration of the geographical and historical context. They illustrate how asymmetrical power relations can be seen in different types of cooperation.

Researching and teaching climate change in Africa – whose reality counts?

In Chapter 2, which sets the scene for the case-based chapters, we pointed to the hegemony of Western thought in education and knowledge production in Africa. Hence, when studying African higher education, it is relevant to ask whose knowledge counts. How has the colonial heritage in African school systems influenced scholars in their learning journeys? What is the role of Western thought in present day higher education? Where and how do negotiations of legitimate scientific knowledge take place? These are some of the questions the chapters in this part of the book analyse by using climate change and climate change research as a lens.

Global events such as climate change are often portrayed as creating crisis in knowledge in local communities because contextualised knowledge modes struggle to respond to changing conditions. In Chapter 6, *Power of knowledge under changing conditions: lessons from a Sahelian village under climate change*, the authors Nielsen, Gravesen and Jensen question this through a study of how people in a village in Burkina Faso have adapted their need for knowledge in order to negotiate recent climate variability and socio-economic change. Changing rainfall patters have caused a decline in agricultural production which is no longer sufficient to feed the village. Turning towards alternative livelihood strategies, non-agriculturally related knowledge becomes important in the village. Tracing which knowledge is deemed valuable and who possess it, a major point of the case is that knowledge must be understood as locally negotiated, but that global events often open up for such negotiations. The authors show that climate change, declining agricultural production and the presence of development projects in the village lead to changes in local power relationships through interpretation and negotiation of legitimate knowledge. This is the only chapter in the book that does not address higher education; instead, it shows how changing conditions mean that Western schooling becomes important, with power relationships moving from the elderly with 'local knowledge' towards a younger man with 'Western competences'.

The colonial heritage in schooling is also illustrated in Chapter 7, *Producing scientific knowledge in Africa today: auto-ethnographic insights from a climate change researcher*, where the authors Adriansen, Mehmood-Ul-Hassan and Mbow analyse conditions for scientific knowledge production in Africa based on a qualitative life history interview with an African climate change researcher, Mbow. The authors show how the post-colonial school system in Senegal was modelled over the French system and thus how difficult it was for Mbow to become independent of the colonial heritage. Through a capacity-building programme, Mbow gained the competences necessary to question the transfer of theories and methods from the Global North and become an African emancipated researcher producing knowledge of relevance for Africa. While Mbow appreciated a system where freedom of thought was highly valued, it was a challenge to learn how to question colleagues and professors. In reflecting over how to make climate change research of relevance for African societies, Mbow argues that it is necessary to take local experience-based knowledge into account in climate change research; therefore, researchers need to problematise climatic knowledge, particularise climatic experience and pluralise climatic meaning by integrating local experience-based knowledge.

Climate change research and capacity building is also the focus of Chapter 8, *Negotiating scientific knowledge about climate change: enhancing research capacity through PhD students* by Madsen and Nielsen; the perspective here, however, is that of the partners from the Global North. Based on a case study of a Danish programme aimed at supporting the education of West-African doctoral students within climate change research, the negotiations of legitimate research knowledge between the involved partners are explored. Using desertification and bush fires as examples, the authors address how these topics are inscribed in different research and political discourses and hence constitute contested research knowledge, and consider how the topics play a role in the research relationship between Global North and Global South. Madsen and Nielsen unfold the negotiations of the scientific knowledge production between the partners and thereby the authors show what is perceived as legitimate scientific knowledge. On the one hand, these negotiations are situated within what could be termed a Western methodological hegemony; on the other hand, the very access to this methodological hegemony can be interpreted as an opportunity for African partners to obtain access to powerful knowledge and technical skills – an access that can enable them to engage in the scientific and political debate of land degradation and bush fires, or, in other words, empower them. The methodological hegemony made it difficult, however, for the African researchers to pluralise climatic meaning by integrating local experience-based knowledge – despite all good intentions.

Together, the chapters demonstrate that colonial heritage can still be identified at various levels of African educational systems. All three chapters concern the negotiation of what constitutes legitimate and useful knowledge. While Chapter 6 illustrates how local experience-based knowledge becomes contested under changing conditions, Chapter 7 argues that local experience-based knowledge is crucial for making climate change research of relevance for local communities. The chapters also exemplify how capacity building can be both emancipatory and maintain the exogenous mode of African knowledge production.

Creating and using academic knowledge in Africa – decolonising research?

Following the discussion in the first two sections of the role of capacity building, pointing to the influences of Western thought in African educational systems, the third section addresses ownership to knowledge and asks how to decolonise research. How are African scholars embedded in uneven geographies of knowledge production? Who has the power and right to speak on behalf of Africa? How can a curriculum be Africanised? To what extent should human rights be Africanised? These are some of the questions the chapters in this part of the book analyse by focusing on universality and particularity of knowledge.

The issue of ownership over knowledge, imagined boundaries between education systems in the Global North and the Global South, and the tensions between scientific and indigenous knowledge, are pertinent issues in an era of global knowledge production. In Chapter 9, *My knowledge, your knowledge, whose knowledge is it? Reflections from a researcher's journey through universities in North and South*, Sithole presents a personal perspective on academia and ownership to knowledge. The narrative is written from the perspective of a black scholar moving around in the diaspora; it gives face to a higher education experience that may be different from that of the majority of scholars in the Global South. By using episodes and encounters, Sithole shows how tensions and ambiguities are part of how her persona as a scholar is constructed. Her gender, race and historical experience situate her interpretation of the life journey within a cultural political space where the discourse of domination and imperialism is never far away. Thus, the chapter shows how power and politics over knowledge challenge everyday conceptions of identity, scholarship and place.

Power and politics over knowledge is also the issue in Chapter 10, *Creating an African university: struggling for a transformational curriculum in apartheid South Africa*. Based on a case from South Africa during the years of political rupture and transition in 1985–1991, Naidoo, Adriansen and Madsen analyse negotiations over what constitutes legitimate knowledge, appropriate curriculum and who are seen as qualified students. A narrative life-history interview with Naidoo, who was actively involved in constructing Khanya College, reveals a hitherto untold story about the struggle for an alternative South African university education during the apartheid era. Khanya College was inspired by Paulo Freire's critical pedagogies and based on a range of political ideologies; Khanya College wanted to challenge apartheid by empowering students designated as 'black' through pride in their African culture and by providing them with access to powerful knowledge. In the chapter, the authors show the different ways in which Khanya College worked with providing epistemic access for black students, e.g. by teaching an 'African' curriculum while paying attention to issues of powerful knowledge. In this way, the chapter provides new perspectives on the dynamic processes of empowerment and decolonisation.

How can North-based organisations cooperate with African academics and institutions to generate knowledge in a field based on a set of values that is supposedly universal, yet often contested as Eurocentric in its origins and power structures? This is addressed in Chapter 11, *African universities and rights in African polities and communities: Africanising universal knowledge?* by Kerrigan. The field of human rights poses particular challenges but also offers intriguing possibilities to equal partnerships in knowledge generation. Scholars and activists continuously debate whether human rights is a vehicle for the Global North to present its values as universal or a useful platform where Southern counter hegemonic discourses can be heard. Kerrigan finds that there is no immediate prospect of African universities being able to provide research environments that permit African legal scholars to fully realise their transformative potential. At the same time, Northern institutions are hampered by their distance, as well as by the legitimacy of their claims to knowledge concerning Africa. Thus, co-production of knowledge remains vital.

The chapters in this third part of the book demonstrate the difficulties related to Africanisation of curriculum and academic knowledge. This is embedded in questions of what is 'truly African' and who should be allowed to speak on behalf of Africans. By providing examples of power and politics over knowledge, the chapters illustrate that decolonialisation of knowledge (production) can be achieved by paying attention to the geographies of knowledge.

Dilemmas and paradoxes of capacity building in African higher education

The case studies in the book point to dilemmas and paradoxes inherent in capacity building of African higher education. In the following, we discuss these under three separate headlines, while acknowledging that they are interrelated. It should be noted that the dilemmas and paradoxes may not be the main argument of the individual chapters, but are issues we find pivotal in a wider discussion of the geography and power of knowledge.

Capacity-building projects and the power of knowledge

Capacity building of higher education in Africa is inevitably embedded in colonial history and the uneven economic relations of the present; therefore, capacity building can sometimes appear like neo-imperialism in disguise. While proponents argue that capacity building aims at assisting African universities to deliver high quality education, excellent research and thereby to become independent knowledge producers (e.g. Winkel, 2014), the critics argue that the standards for quality, excellence, etc. are set in the Global North and thereby Africa becomes dependent on what counts as good and relevant somewhere else, instead of setting its own terms (Dei, 2014a). An example of this is seen in Chapter 8 through an analysis of a capacity-building project that aims at empowering universities in West Africa to make their own analyses of satellite imagery and thereby their own theorising. This is exactly what authors such as Hountondji (1990, 1995) have called for. Furthermore, the project builds on the new ideas emphasising South–South cooperation. However, the authors conclude that the project is embedded in some of 'the usual' North–South power relations where the partners at the Danish university show flexible superior positionality through negotiations over the knowledge production.

In a more general perspective, Chapter 3 argues that capacity building in higher education is based on a perception of the university as a development target. This means that objectives and milestones are set, often based on a general template that does not contextualise where the capacity building takes place, thereby not allowing for other histories, societal needs or roles to play. Capacity building often focuses on 'catching up' with universities in the Global North, instead of focusing on how to enhance education and knowledge production that makes sense in the local or national contexts. Yet, if African universities want to be part of the global knowledge economy, they also need to produce knowledge of interest beyond the local and engage in intellectual debates beyond the continent. While this is currently happening, there is still a need for enhancing the capacity. The question remains how the Global North can assist in this without imposing a neo-imperialist agenda. The chapters in this book suggest that, in order to rethink capacity building, we need to address the negotiations of knowledge production, and the different historical, political and geographical contexts that specific capacity-building projects are situated within. As Dei has recently asked: 'How do we begin to think broadly about excellence in university education that addresses foremost the needs, aspirations, and knowledge systems of African peoples and, in particular, start from what African peoples and their communities know?' (Dei, 2014a: 165). This links to the dilemma of Africanisation of curriculum, which is discussed later.

The geography of knowledge and cultural production of academics

Due to the policies of the colonial powers, knowledge production in the African colonies was characterised by a theoretical vacuum; therefore, there was little capacity to develop critical, independent and African knowledge production when the colonies gained their freedom (Hountondji, 1990). This affected the conditions for the production of African scholars. This book has given voice to a number of personal narratives from African scholars who, in different settings, relate how their learning journeys are embedded in uneven geographies of knowledge production.

For Mbow, whose life history is the point of departure in Chapter 7, the Global North both represents the imposed curriculum through colonial heritage and the possibility to acquire the skills for becoming an emancipated academic capable of creating new knowledge. The chapter shows how methods and theories developed under and according to particular circumstances in the Global North have been transferred to Africa as if they were universal. However, Mbow's ability to question what is taken for granted, and especially his ability to criticise the blind transfer of methods from France to Senegal, is partly due to the competences he acquired through his involvement in a capacity-building project. Through this project, he was introduced to another cultural production of an academic closely related to issues of academic freedom and questioning of what is taken for granted even when it entailed questioning older professors. Paradoxically, through this way of being an academic, Mbow was able to question the way they worked with plant community assessment at his Senegalese university and come up with a new method adapted to the local context.

Chapter 9, based on Sithole's personal narrative, touches upon the dilemmas researchers from Africa face when they have been in the Global North whether as part of their educational training, through capacity-building programmes or employed at universities. She discusses the debate of who has the right to speak on behalf of Africa and how her 'Africaness' has been questioned by fellow researchers both in Africa and in the Global North. She relates how in the Global North she is at times the 'token' African scholar and at other times somebody whose knowledge needs validation and verification. These examples show how the cultural production of African scholars is situated and unfolded differently in different settings. Thus, a focus on the localness of knowledge, present in this book, and the questioning of universality, can also lead to essentialisation – what is the 'real' African scholar, African knowledge or African university? With this, different types of othering may follow, with researchers positioning themselves and others in fixed categories as e.g. an African researcher who has the right to speak about African issues.

Africanisation of curriculum and powerful knowledge

In relation to Africanisation of curriculum, we see a slightly different dilemma. There is no doubt that there is a need for a decolonisation of curriculum in African schools and a focus on knowledge related to the African context, whether we call this local or indigenous knowledge (see e.g. Shizha, 2011). Also at higher education level, decolonialisation of knowledge and methodology is necessary, which may be approached by paying attention to the apparent universality of knowledge. In the words of the Indian author and activist Vandana Shiva:

> The disappearance of local knowledge through its interaction with the dominant western knowledge takes place at many levels, through many steps. First, local knowledge is made to disappear by simply not seeing it, by negating its very existence. This is very easy in the distant gaze of the globalising dominant system. The western systems have been viewed as universal. However, the dominant system is also a local system, with its social basis in a particular culture, class and gender. It is not universal in an epistemological sense. It is merely the globalised version of a very local and parochial tradition. Emerging from a dominating and colonising culture, modern knowledge systems are themselves colonising.
>
> (Shiva, 2012: 9)

Africanising the curriculum is, however, not without problems, as it risks excluding people from the knowledge of the powerful. This is illustrated in Chapter 10, analysing the South African tertiary access programme, Khanya College, established under apartheid. The college faculty faced the dilemma that a curriculum embracing (South) African history, culture and language would not enable black students to participate on par in universities and society at large. Hence, at Khanya College, Africanisation of the curriculum was only one step in empowering students; the other step was to give them access to so-called powerful knowledge, the knowledge of the powerful (white, Euro-centric curriculum). Similar examples can be seen in relation to using English as the medium of instruction. Today, the use of local languages in African schools is in many ways a means of emancipating knowledge and curriculum from the dominating and colonising culture. However, local language instruction was used by colonial powers as a means of keeping people away from the knowledge and competences necessary for participating in society. Consequently, in many of the independent African states English (or other colonial languages) was seen as an essential language for empowerment and development (Breidlid, 2013; Woolman, 2001). This illustrates the dilemma that Africanisation and local language instruction cannot stand alone; access to powerful knowledge is also important for empowerment.

Africanisation of curriculum in itself is not liberating if it does not count as relevant, good and powerful knowledge. This can be seen in Chapter 6, which explores how local experience-based knowledge loses importance to the knowledge and competences derived through schooling when social and environmental conditions change. This might be interpreted as a new tendency that is in contrast to the wide-held notion that schooling has failed to improve life for many rural Africans (Woolman, 2001). In the words of Ali Mazrui:

> Western education in African conditions was a process of de-ruralisation. The educated Africans became [...] a misfit in his own village [...] when he graduated [...] his parents did not expect him to continue living with them, tending the cattle or cultivating the land.
>
> (Mazrui, 1978: 16)

In the Burkinabe case from Chapter 6, changing climatic conditions mean that the local knowledge of the elderly is no longer highly valued. Moreover, an increased number of development projects in the area calls for 'Western education' to interact with the development workers. Consequently, what constitutes useful, relevant and powerful knowledge is changing.

The future of capacity building in African higher education

What can we learn from the chapters in this book about future capacity building in African higher education and research of capacity building? The collection confirms the importance of using geography of knowledge as an approach for understanding how capacity building influences and affects African academics, institutions and degree programmes. They also illustrate how reflexivity and positionality can be important tools for highlighting the power relations inherent in capacity building.

The most important outcomes in relation to future capacity-building programmes are related to how to counter the neo-imperial effects of internationalisation. African higher education is facing an increasing demand for internationalisation as well as an increasing marketisation and subsequent privatisation (Teferra, 2008). While this is not unique to Africa, there is a risk that African universities will not escape their image of what Dei calls 'colonial satellite of Western academy' (Dei, 2014a: 169). Moreover, there is also a call for an increasing focus on local knowledge in higher education in order to make African universities better at responding to societal needs (Dei, 2014b). This, in turn, calls for an Africanisation of curriculum and consequently, African universities are struggling to balance the demands for internationalisation with demands for Africanisation of knowledge and curriculum. Hence, these opposing trends can be difficult for African universities to navigate:

> Neoliberal globalisation has been imposed on African educational philosophies to determine curriculum developments and implementation,

especially in science and technology. Neoliberal globalisation and indigenous knowledges are in a state of contestation.

(Shizha, 2011: 15)

The focus on indigenous or local knowledge and on Africanisation of curriculum is important for African universities. However, it is also important that Africanisation does not lead to essentialisation of what African knowledge is and can be, and who can possess this knowledge, because: 'Unless notions of Africanisation operate in a dynamic manner they cannot take on an emancipatory character' (Suttner, 2010: 519).

Based on an understanding of geography of knowledge, we argue that capacity-building programmes can be a means to assist African universities to 'find their own feet' if they are based on long-term partnerships, a close understanding of historical, political and geographical context, and not least a common exploration of knowledge diversity. This may help us avoid what Shiva calls monocultures of the mind: 'Monocultures of the mind make diversity disappear from perception, and consequently from the world. The disappearance of diversity is also a disappearance of alternatives – and give rise to the TINA (there is no alternative) syndrome' (Shiva, 2012: 5). This exploration of knowledge diversity is important, both for the future of African higher education and higher education in the Global North.

References

Breidlid, A. (2013) *Education, Indigenous Knowledges, and Development in the Global South: Contesting Knowledges for a Sustainable Future*. Sabon: Routledge.

Cousin, G. (2010) 'Positioning positionality'. In Savin-Baden, M. and Major, C.H. (eds) *New Approaches to Qualitative Research: Wisdom and Uncertainty*. Derby: Routledge, pp. 9–18.

Dei, G.J.S. (2014a) 'Indigenizing the school curriculum'. In Emeagwali, G. and Dei, G.J.S. (eds) *African Indigenous Knowledge and the Disciplines*. Rotterdam: SensePublishers, pp. 165–180.

Dei, G.S. (2014b) 'Reflections on African development – situating indigeneity and indigenous epistemologies'. In Shizha, E. and Abdi, A.A. (eds) *Indigenous Discourses on Knowledge and Development in Africa*. Sabon: Routledge, pp. 15–30.

Hountondji, P.J. (1990) 'Scientific dependence in Africa today', *Research in African Literatures*, 21 (3), 5–15.

Hountondji, P.J. (1995) 'Producing knowledge in Africa today. The Second Bashorun M.K.O. Abiola Distinguished Lecture', *African Studies Review*, 38 (3), 1–10.

Livingstone, D. (2003) *Putting Science in its Place: Geographies of Scientific Knowledge*. USA: University of Chicago Press.

Mazrui, A.A. (1978) *Political Values and the Educated Class in Africa*. Berkeley: University of California Press.

Meusburger, P. (2015) 'Knowledge, geography of'. In Wright, J.D. (ed.) *International Encyclopedia of the Social & Behavioral Sciences*, 2nd edition, Vol. 13. Oxford: Elsevier, pp. 91–97.

Shiva, V. (2012) *Monocultures of the Mind – Perspectives on Biodiversity and Biotechnology.* Penang: Third World Network.

Shizha, E. (2011) 'Neoliberal globalisation, science education and African indigenous knowledges'. In Kapoor, D. (ed.) *Critical Perspectives on Neoliberal Globalization, Development and Education in Africa and Asia.* Rotterdam: Sense Publishers, pp. 15–31.

Suttner, R. (2010) '"Africanisation", African identities and emancipation in contemporary South Africa', *Social Dynamics, 36* (3), 515–530.

Teferra, D. (2008) 'The international dimension of higher education in Africa: status, challenges and prospects'. In Teferra, D. and Knight, J. (eds) *Higher Education in Africa: The International Dimension.* USA: African Books Collective, pp. 44–79.

Winkel, K. (2014) *Udvikling: om Danmarks bistand.* Balto: Frydenlund.

Woolman, D.C. (2001) 'Educational reconstruction and post-colonial curriculum development: a comparative study of four African countries', *International Education Journal, 2* (5), 27–46.

Index

For Product Safety Concerns and Information please contact our EU representative GPSR@taylorandfrancis.com Taylor & Francis Verlag GmbH, Kaufingerstraße 24, 80331 München, Germany